OTHER BOOKS BY HAROLD F. BLAISDELL

Tricks That Take Fish (1952)
The Philosophical Fisherman (1969)
Trout Fishing in New England (1973)

The Art of Fishing with Worms

HAROLD F. BLAISDELL

The Art of Fishing with Worms

AND OTHER LIVE BAIT

With photographs by Mark Mitchell

Alfred A. Knopf New York 1977

This is a Borzoi Book
Published by Alfred A. Knopf, Inc.

Published in the United States by Alfred A. Knopf, Inc., New York, and simultaneously in Canada by Random House of Canada Limited, Toronto. Distributed by Random House, Inc., New York.
Library of Congress Cataloging in Publication Data
Blaisdell, Harold F.
The art of fishing with worms and other live bait.
Includes index.
1. Bait fishing. I. Title.
SH455.4.B56 799.1'2 77-890
ISBN 0-394-40039-9
Manufactured in the United States of America
First Edition

CONTENTS

INTRODUCTION

THIS BOOK IS DEDICATED to the proposition that the fisherman's main objective is to catch fish. Its purpose is to help him succeed.

It is true that many pleasant spinoffs accrue to fishing: the chance to observe nature, rapport with the outdoors, and many more. Yet when all in this vein has been said, as it has many times over, none of the fringe benefits can compensate for the lack of success.

Books intended to aid and guide fishermen have been written by the thousands, yet most seem to embrace the conviction that the country's fishing millions are intent on catching only the most glamorous species by only the most sophisticated methods. This has resulted in a wealth of fly-fishing literature concerned with the taking of trout and salmon, and very little intended to enlighten the bait fisherman.

The writer believes the foregoing premise to be grossly in error. Compulsive fishermen, those of us who *must* fish to satisfy powerful inner urges, cannot adopt this narrow viewpoint for the simple reason that there are not enough trout and salmon to go around. In order to achieve fulfillment these instinctive anglers must adjust their goals and methods along lines calculated to make full utilization of all fishing possibilities. They must disregard traditional prejudices and learn to fish with deep enjoyment for all available species, exalted and lowly, and by whatever methods are needed to bring success.

It is also the writer's belief that this omnivorous outlook comes naturally to all who are fishermen in the true and full sense of the word. He is more comfortable in their presence than in that of those who draw the line at some point in the scale of methodology, or who insist that only a few glorified species are worthy of attention.

The writer is also uncomfortable while employing an editorial third person, for it seems to "him" to be a pointless affectation. Commencing immediately, the first person will prevail, I hope without conveying an unbecoming lack of humility.

I have been inexorably drawn to fishing since early childhood, and the urge to fish has never diminished. In order to satisfy this urge I must fish the year round, depending on all that is available to sustain me. To substantiate this statement I submit the following list of freshwater species which I have fished for (and have caught with varying degrees of success) over the past twelve months: brook trout, brown trout, rainbow trout, lake trout, and landlocked salmon; brown bullheads and blue catfish; smallmouth bass and largemouth bass; bowfins, sheepsheads and eels; walleyes, saugers and yellow perch; sunfish, calicoes and rock bass; smelt and whitefish; northern pike and chain pickerel. Needless to say, I addressed this wide variety with everything from dry flies to nightcrawlers.

I'm sure that there are those who will critically arrange the foregoing species and methods in a descending order of acceptability. To me this is an exercise in the pointlessness implicit in the old toper's reply when asked to name a good brand of whiskey. "Hell!" he snorted. "They're *all* good!"

Damned right! It would be exaggerating to pretend that a day spent worming a pailful of bullheads for smoking was as exciting as one spent on a Maine lake when landlocked salmon walloped my trolled streamer with jolts which came as bolts from the blue. Yet it is an honest truth that, in its own way, laying in that big catch of bullheads was fully as *satisfying.* More to the point, I didn't have any choice. The bullheads and I were in the same place at the same time; those salmon and I were separated by nearly five hundred miles.

A specialist is sometimes defined as one who learns more and more about less and less. Some fishermen fit this definition, but it has always seemed to me that by becoming "purists" they miss out on a lot of real fun and enjoyment. This book is not addressed to the puristic minority, but to that great majority who, like myself, are intent on deriving maximum enjoyment from any and all fishing opportunities that are open to them. Its aim is to help them achieve this goal to whatever degree my fishing knowhow will permit.

I feel bound to confess that the title is something of a come-on, for it was selected to connote the down-to-earth nature of the contents. Its only sin, which I hope will be forgiven, is that of implying too narrow coverage.

Worm fishing is indeed an art. Although my writings on dry-fly fishing have been accorded a modest measure of respect, I know that I shall be hard put to do justice to the many nuances and profundities of masterful worm fishing. However, the art of worm fishing cannot be regarded properly as standing alone. The techniques of using *all* natural baits are projections of the same art, and these techniques will also be covered as fully as my experience permits.

This experience covers more than a half-century of intensive fishing for all the freshwater species common to the Northeast. It might seem that this experience qualifies me to write of fishing with finality and authority, but the sad truth is that it doesn't. I still never spend a day on a lake or stream without learning something new or without wishing to hell that I were a better fisherman. Instead of establishing credentials, this circumstance testifies to the generous dimensions of my ignorance!

If I'm brash enough to pass out advice, it is only in the companionship of humility and self-confessed inadequacy. If such brashness is justified, it is only because the opportunity to fish as frequently as I have done for so many years is becoming increasingly rare.

The desire to fish is as strong as ever, as is evinced by the millions of fishing licenses which are sold annually. Yet as opportunities shrink, many deserving enthusiasts are compromised, and denied success, by the sheer lack of experience. Although I'm all too keenly aware of the limited advice I can offer, and particularly aware of my fallibility, it is my hope that I can proffer counsel of sufficient soundness and significance to compensate to some degree for an enforced lack of experience.

To be truly helpful it seems important to begin with the most elementary basics of worm fishing. It is this level of angling, all but neglected by the experts, that provides fun and relaxation for the greatest numbers of fishermen and fisherwomen.

Basic worm fishing may seem to be less challenging than fly fishing or bait casting, but only because its subtle profundities, which exist in abundance, are never dramatically apparent. In fact, although the truth is seldom realized, or if realized seldom openly owned, true angling insight and empathy have their roots in worm and bait fishing.

Despite the fact that basic bait fishing lays the groundwork for more sophisticated methods, it will be treated here as an entity sufficient unto itself. It will not be pictured as a stepping-stone to greater things, but as an important adjunct for fishermen who wish to savor all that sport fishing has to offer.

Many ardent fishermen have no aspirations beyond bait fishing. Lord love them, and all power to them. Others, like myself, turn to bait fishing without apology whenever the move broadens the scope of their fishing. All good things to them, too.

May the chapters which follow be of some small help to both factions. They couldn't be addressed to more deserving people!

The Art of Fishing with Worms

1

THE CHALLENGE

SEVERAL YEARS AGO I was fishing a stream in western Labrador on a day early in September, a month which brings freezing nights and the imminence of snow to the subarctic.

The big squaretails, flamboyant with fall colors, had already worked their way into small streams preparatory to spawning. My partner and I knew that we were among dream fish, but only a few small trout came to our rotated offerings of dry flies, wet flies, and streamers. We had flown nearly a thousand miles to reach the spot, and the threat of a skunking loomed as a bitter pill.

When another of a succession of ten-inch brookies hung itself on my streamer, I broke its neck and then sliced a thin strip of skin from its belly. I hung this on the streamer's hook as a come-on to the strong cannibalistic leanings which are typical of all salmonids of the far north.

On the very first retrieve, a four-pound squaretail zoomed up to take the doctored streamer, treating me to a dramatic display of vivid colors as it rose and then dove. Another slice of trout belly promptly turned things around for my partner. From the pool where our naked streamers had gone begging we took trout after trout of trophy size. Two were sacrificed in the interest of documentary photographs, now long treasured. The rest went back into the stream unharmed.

When we returned to camp that night we talked over the day

with our host, Norm Hathaway of Brewer, Maine. Norm is one of the most, if not *the* most, experienced and accomplished subarctic fisherman of all who have fished the Canadian northeast.

I was a bit apologetic, or at least uncertain, in confessing that we started taking trout only after we had added a bit of bait to our flies, but I had no need to be. Above all, Norm is a practical fisherman, and his viewpoint agreed with mine.

"The important thing," he said, "is that after you found fish *you knew how to catch 'em!*"

No fisherman, least of all this one, knows how to catch fish of all kinds under all conditions. Nevertheless, knowhow is the name of the game, and the extent to which it is possessed is a much greater determinant of success than mere luck. While this may not seem to hold true in simple worm fishing, it applies at this level as fully as it does at all others. That skill and savvy are involved may not be apparent at first, but their involvement becomes manifest with a little reflection.

Bait fishing centers around the use of natural items of fish food as bait: worms, minnows, grubs, nymphs, crayfish, etc. In order to survive, fish must either lie in wait for these items to appear or they must deliberately seek them out. In the normal course of events, all such items are hungrily snapped up whenever carried within reach by the current or whenever discovered by search.

That being the case, and if no skill were involved in bait fishing, every natural bait would be gobbled up as soon as it was presented where fish could see and reach it. Yet many empty-handed fisherman can attest to the fact that this does not always happen. In fact, it usually happens with much less frequency than even the most highly skilled anglers would prefer if they could have their druthers. It's a good thing for all that it *doesn't* happen, of course, for if it did there soon would be no fish left to fish for.

The big question is: How come? If a hungry fish will snap up a freely drifting worm without a moment's hesitation, why won't it pounce on an identical worm which has been impaled on a hook and lowered on a line?

Before pursuing this question, let me pause to point out that the vast majority of anglers who fish at the simplest level of bait fishing do not tend to be analytical or questioning. Although they dearly love to fish, and better yet to *catch* fish, they tend to regard the matter of success as one dependent on luck. Either the fish bite or they don't, and there is little that they, as fishermen, can do about it.

Before taking up some of the things which *can* be done to persuade fish to bite, let me admit that luck does enter the picture and very few fishermen would have it otherwise. There *are* those rare days when normally cautious and elusive fish appear intent on committing suicide and bite like crazy. Fisherman who find themselves on the scene at such times are lucky in every sense of the word.

There is also the opposite end of the scale: days when seemingly no power on earth can make fish bite, and fishermen who happen to pick those days, as so many of us often seem to do, are definitely unlucky.

Our concern is not with these extremes, but with those average conditions under which fish feed with normal regularity while retaining their normal senses of caution. It is in this context that they go about their business of gathering in food items which appear free of external influence, but tend to refuse the same items when they are placed on hooks and lowered by line and leader.

One of the tricks of taking fish is the ability to "think" like a fish, and this approach is useful in answering the question before the house. If we were a hungry fish we certainly would grab anything that appealed to our appetite *unless something unusual dissuaded us.* It seems almost indecent to state the key to fishing success so simply, but success derives from little more than identifying the negative influences which prompt refusal and then, easier said than done, *eliminating them.*

To continue in the role of a fish, what about a baited hook would be likely to turn us off? The bait is for real, and we are hungry. Why do we refuse?

If we were smarter, we could deduce the threat implicit in a hook's cruel construction, but we lack the necessary intelligence. If we had more brains, we would recognize the unhealthy implications of the hook's mechanical connection to line or leader, but this association lies quite beyond our limited mental powers. Yet there must be an explanation of our reluctance. Why don't we dart in and grab *that* particular worm exactly as we are in the habit of grabbing all other worms?

As fish we cannot identify the sensation which deters, but as humans we can indeed define it: *suspicion!* We may not know exactly what is wrong with the setup, but we sure as hell know that *something* is!

Although we don't have very many smarts, we must cope daily with a world fraught with danger. We can't think our way to survival, but we manage to survive by special instincts and incredibly keen sensitivities. We see, we hear, and we smell. Beyond this, we take additional readings of our small world through other senses which have no human counterparts. If we don't comprehend the nature of our surroundings we are, nevertheless, keenly aware of them and as keenly attuned to their normal appearance and behavior. We sense how things *should* be and we are instantly alerted by any deviation from the norm. It is not our nature, nor is it within our power, to assess each anomaly in terms of the exact danger which it implies. Instead, it *is* our nature, and oh *how* it is, to cover all bets by strictly avoiding anything and everything which is the least bit strange or unusual.

Now, a worm on a hook which, in turn, is tied to a line is likely to violate normality in several ways. We know, for one thing, that a worm should sink. Yet the worm on the hook does not. Neither does it float. It just dangles. This, by itself, is grave reason for suspicion. We know what a worm looks like in its natural state, and we know that worms squirm. If the worm in question no longer looks like a worm, and if it fails to exhibit its natural tendency to squirm, add two more deterrents. We have a keen sense of smell, and still more doubt is aroused if the worm gives off a foreign odor.

In the presence of one or more of the foregoing anomalies we are likely to resist any temptation to grab the dangled worm, not because we know specifically that some fisherman is hoping to capture us, but because it is fish nature to avoid all things strange and different as an inborn matter of principle.

Should we be a trout, a bass, or some other species of game fish, our threshold of tolerance is likely to be very low indeed. Many generations of fishermen have fished for even more generations of our ancestors, resorting to ever finer shadings of guile with the passage of time. We have managed to survive only because our instincts and sensitivities have kept pace with an ever growing threat of extinction. We can be fooled, yes, but never easily. If we fall for an angler's pitch it is going to be one from which cause for suspicion has been carefully minimized or actually eliminated.

If we are a perch, a bluegill, or some other species of panfish, we are inherently several degrees less cautious. Nevertheless, the instinct of self-preservation is by no means completely lacking. We are likely to accept a bait in which a trout would see grave cause for alarm, but we, too, draw the line when deviations from the norm are flagrant.

It is because of this powerful instinctive aversion to all that is not strictly kosher that the use of bait does not place fish at a disadvantage so frequently alleged to be unfair. To conclude that the use of bait is virtually a guarantee of "limiting out" is an assumption which usually springs from lack of experience and angling insight.

A few weeks ago a fly-fishing aspirant sought my help in overcoming the troubles he was having in learning to cast a fly. Some beginners can pick up the knack quickly and easily, while others find it difficult to master the timing which, of course, is the key to the whole deal. The gentleman in question fell in the last category.

He had made it a point to look me up because of what I had written about fly casting in a book about trout fishing. During our back-lawn session he asked me when I was going to write another book. I told him that I was working on one, a book on worm fishing.

The guy did a double take, obviously to see if I was serious. When he saw that I was, there was no mistaking his sense of disillusion. Obviously, in his mind, I had sold out to the mercenaries.

"Worm fishing!" he declared incredulously. "That's like using a bulldozer to pick daisies."

Human nature, indeed, passeth all understanding. Here was a fellow desperately intent on learning to cast a few feet of fly line, and already programmed to scoff at all fishing methods but fly fishing! It would have been too embarrassing to us both had I pointed out that while I had long since learned to cast a respectable length of fly line, I was still trying to solve the many mysteries of bait fishing.

These mysteries do exist, and it is as important for the casual bait fisherman to be aware of them as it is for the more serious fisherman. Perhaps it is even more important.

Fishing is an important source of family fun and relaxation. But enjoyment is usually proportional to the numbers of fish caught, and to make good catches, even of panfish, usually requires a significant amount of angling savvy.

Unfortunately, many families fish in the almost complete absence of this necessary knowledge. As a result, they often go fishless when a few simple tricks would have put fish on the stringer. While a good catch is always gratifying to all hands, it is of special importance to youngsters. Many dads fail to interest their children in fishing simply because they can't set the stage for the fast action that's usually needed to stimulate enthusiasm.

As pointed out previously, the solution consists of understanding why fish *don't* bite, and then taking steps to eliminate the dissuading factors as completely as possible.

The ensuing chapters will deal with many of the variations of these problems, and as they apply to various species. Although I propose to begin with the more popular panfishes, do not make the common mistake of underrating the simple skills and techniques which are properly brought into play at this simplest level of angling.

Those whom I most envy and respect as expert fishermen have skipped none of the phases of sport fishing. Their genius invariably includes not only mastery of the most sophisticated techniques, but a deep empathy and understanding which could have been gained only by beginning at the very bottom.

It is impossible to become what I think of as a true fisherman by starting at any other point. A man may have caught trout, and even salmon, and lack a very vital something if he has never caught a bullhead or an eel on a nightcrawler or a chunk of cut bait.

Salmon and eels may be worlds apart in the eyes of many. Yet, to my way of thinking, each plays an important part in the evolution of a fisherman!

2

THE STARTING POINT

LONGER AGO than now seems possible, I spent a week of particularly fine smallmouth bass bugging in Maine's West Grand Lake Region, an area of many waters that is justly famed for its abundance of smallmouths. Val Moore, my guide, shared my enthusiasm for bass bugging and my sentiments concerning the near perfection of the days which had passed all too quickly. We were both glumly silent as the last minutes of fishing ticked into eternity.

"Well, I'll go back to bait fishing tomorrow," Val said finally, his tone reflecting little enthusiasm for the change. "Man and his wife; gonna have 'em for a week."

"What do you *do* to guide bait fishermen?" I asked with genuine curiosity. It seemed to me that that sort of guiding might consist of little more than anchoring over known bass grounds.

"Well, for one thing," Val said wryly, "I tell 'em when their lines hit bottom."

Val's remark reflected that sense of humor which enables guides to put up with all that they have to bear. It also brought into focus the importance in bait fishing of seemingly trivial details.

"You mean they can't tell when they're on bottom?" I asked.

"Hell, no!" Val replied. "They'd go on stripping line till the reel was empty if I'd let 'em."

This remark called attention to another fact of life: Many would-be fishermen not only fail to appreciate the importance of ostensibly simple ploys, but they are unable to execute them after their importance has been explained.

If Val Moore's comment carried mild overtones of contempt, it was because he had long since learned that depth has a whale of a lot to do with fishing success, that a nightcrawler fished close to the bottom is likely to draw a bite while one several feet above the bottom will go begging. It seemed incredible to him that people sufficiently affluent to pay for his guiding services could be ignorant of this elementary consideration. It struck him as even more incredible that they couldn't make the proper depth adjustments when the necessity had been explained to them.

I have made much of this small point because it supports my contention that knowhow and skill of execution enter into angling at every level. The required savvy may be extremely rudimentary, but its lack may forestall success. The small knacks of bait presentation may also seem ridiculously simple to the more experienced, yet the inability to execute them often accounts for failure.

The ability to "feel" bottom with a light sinker is merely one of dozens of small but vital knacks by which the fisherman usually sinks or swims. Also, of course, there must be an awareness of the need for each simple ploy, an awareness which takes into account the fish sensitivities the particular move seeks to satisfy.

In order to examine these basic "tricks" in the simplest context I shall try to point out how they apply to fishing for panfish. While dangling a worm for perch, bluegills, and the like may appear to be "simple," the term applies only relatively.

It has been my good fortune to fish for and catch almost every species of freshwater fish found in the northeastern United States and eastern Canada. There may be those who would lose interest in perch and bullheads after taking Atlantic salmon or arctic char, but I'm not among them. When I set out to fish for perch or other panfish it is not condescendingly, nor is it with any lack of enthusiasm. I'm usually fishing for the freezer or the smoker, hard-nosed and for the money.

Furthermore, don't think for a moment that I always have my way even with panfish. The hungrier I am for smoked perch or pan-fried calicoes, the more cussedly fussy they seem to become. As a result, I don't waste time trying to figure out how to outwit Atlantic salmon. I'm much too busy trying to deduce why the hell

I can't make perch bite whenever I want them to! The answer, of course, is that perch are often considerably smarter in their way than I am in mine!

Once I knuckle under to this hard-to-accept truth, the lowly perch becomes a fish of stature. To catch perch in significant quantities is a legitimate test of angling skill. By its survival alone, it shows that it is far from a complete dumbbell. It is admittedly more vulnerable than trout or bass, but its sensitivities still must be respected. When they are violated beyond the limits of its tolerance, the perch flatly refuses to bite. Although it has but little busted tackle to its credit, a big perch, a "yellowbelly" in Vermont terminology, puts up a lively battle on light gear. Finally, when properly cleaned and cooked, the yellow perch is one of the tastiest of all freshwater fish.

Since I've introduced the important matter of proper fishing depth, let's first resolve this issue with respect to perch fishing. Perch are primarily close-to-the-bottom feeders, so much so that they will pick a worm-baited hook from the bottom—if they happen to detect it. However, the chance that they will notice a bait that rests on the bottom is relatively slim. The same holds true for a worm that is held three feet above the bottom. The real pay zone for perch is a stratum that is a mere foot in depth or thickness, the layer which lies directly above the bottom.

Although the question may seem silly, how does one adjust his line so that the bait hangs in this narrow but productive zone? The trick is to drop the bait to the bottom and then raise it six or eight inches. Simple as hell. Yet as Val Moore clearly implied, inexperienced fishermen can't pull it off!

Detecting bottom with a sinker of one or two ounces would be easy; but the heavy sinker would do far more harm than good. The lighter the sinker, the more naturally the worm can be presented —another important consideration which we will get to presently.

Since one or two small split shot, or at the most a single buckshot, is appropriate to perch fishing, a considerable degree of perception is required to detect the precise moment when these light weights finally strike bottom. The tip-off comes when a slight kink of slack develops in the descending line, most evident in the short length of line between rod tip and the water. Even in a flat calm the clue is never markedly noticeable, and inexperienced fishermen can, and do, fail to detect it.

If the boat is swinging with the wind, even slowly, the slack doesn't develop at all; the boat's motion causes the line to continue to pay out unchecked, even after the sinker is resting on the bottom. It is under this condition, the one which usually prevails, that errors are doubly likely to occur; the fisherman believes that his bait is still sinking while it actually is resting smack on the bottom.

One solution is to wait for the boat to come to complete rest before attempting to determine the depth. Another answer, one requiring a bit more skill, is to "pan" with the rod to compensate for the boat's drift.

The knack of "feeling" bottom certainly involves no complex manipulations or physical skills, and it can be learned through practice. Yet, simple as it is, it *must* be learned if one is to be a successful bait fisherman.

Already, by a single example, we have laid bare the twin requirements which a fisherman must meet: 1. Acquire the awareness of those things which need doing. 2. Learn how to do them.

But we aren't quite finished with the critical matter of depth. After it has been determined, the distance of the sinker from the hook must be allowed for. Obviously, the sinker rests on the bottom along with whatever length of line it supports, usually around eight inches. If the line is raised merely six inches or so, the *sinker* will be at the fish-taking level, but the bait will *still* rest on the bottom where it is likely to go unnoticed. Thus, to achieve the proper depth of the bait, the line must be raised some fourteen or fifteen inches to bring the bait the desired six inches off the bottom. Too obvious to mention. Don't you believe it! Fishermen all too often go fishless because of just such trivial oversights.

Once the proper depth has been attained, what then? Some pages back we theorized on possible reasons why fish don't bite. One was the anomaly implicit in a worm which neither sinks nor floats. Perch are conditioned to regard such an oddity with the reservations humans would have with respect to a steak which hung in midair. Fortunately for the fisherman, there is a marked difference between the human reservations toward such a phenomenon and the suspicion it arouses in a perch. Let a steak act that wacky and the human reaction would be to have nothing to do with it from that time onward. The perch is more forgiving, or, more properly, more forgetful. It continues to be suspicious only as long as the worm continues to act strangely. If the worm adopts normal behavior, the perch then tends to regard it favorably.

The normal thing for a worm to do in water is to sink slowly. All that's needed to achieve this effect to the perch's satisfaction is to raise the tip of the rod a foot or so and then quickly lower it. The raised worm now settles back as it should, and although the illusion of normal behavior is only momentary, it is often enough to allay suspicion and prompt the watching perch to decide in favor of grabbing the sinking worm. Like all fishing tricks, this doesn't work every time on every fish. Nevertheless, if this simple jigging ruse is used steadily over a day of perch fishing, it can double the catch. This is particularly true on days when the fish are considerably less than ravenous and are inclined to be especially critical.

Another verse to the same tune: Know what needs doing. Do it!

Perch expect worms to sink, and they expect them to wriggle. Obviously, worms can't oblige in the last respect if they are compactly looped or wadded on a large hook. To con more fish, use small hooks and hook worms only lightly. A No. 8 is a good choice for perch, and hooking should consist merely of burying the small barb in the worm's midsection, leaving both ends to squirm enticingly.

Incidentally, the perch wormer has a choice between nightcrawlers and the smaller worms which are often called "garden hackle." I'm inclined to believe that the small worms are the better perch bait, but the difference is slight. I prefer nightcrawlers because of the greater attraction they have for smallmouths, walleyes, and other game fish. If you fish sensitively for perch with nightcrawlers you're likely to realize substantial fringe benefits: a three-pound smallmouth that comes cruising by and sees nothing suspicious in your carefully presented 'crawler, for example; maybe one or more big walleyes that come to the same conclusion.

If you are among yellow perch, and you steadily jig a squirming worm on a small hook, you usually find yourself in business. Yet, even though the perch may bite, there's still the matter of hooking them. Here again a simple knack is required. Some never learn it.

Bites are signaled by a downward tug against the tip of the rod. Competent fishermen are instantly alerted by the slightest twitch, while a bite fails to register with others until the rod is all but yanked from their hands.

In any event, the common mistake is that of reacting to the

downward pull by immediately yanking upward. While this may seem logical, it more often results in a missed fish and a lost worm.

The foiled fisherman usually writes off each such failure as a quirk of luck, but it is really due to yet one more lack of insight and understanding. Fish possess incredibly fast reflexes. The trout which rises to take a dry fly, for instance, detects its artificiality and rejects it almost instantly. The ability to veer off from the hint of danger is as pronounced and speedy as that of the fellow who picked up a hot horseshoe in a blacksmith shop.

"Kinda warm?" asked the blacksmith.

"Not particularly."

"Then why in tunket did you drop it so fast?"

"It just don't take me long to look over a horseshoe."

It doesn't take perch any longer to release a worm if they are warned of danger. The premature yank gives them just that warning. Here's what happens.

Perch usually begin with a tentative nibble. Next, if convinced that all is well, they take the worm in their mouths and move off. The inept hook-setter invariably tenses at the first nibble. Thus, when the fish moves away, the line draws taut against a firmly held rod. The tension warns the perch instantly that all is not on the up and up, and it drops the worm just as instantly. The fisherman *thinks* that the perch must have had the worm in its mouth when he yanks, but this isn't the case. It has dropped the bait in the split second it took for the fisherman to react, and the yank actually comes after the bait has been dropped.

Here's what should happen: At the first sign of a nibble, lower the tip of the rod to put slack in the line. Next, watch for the slack to straighten as the fish starts to swim away. Move the rod in the direction the fish is taking to create even more slack. The perch will feel no resistance and will retain the bait confidently. Set the hook the moment *before* the moving line comes tight against the rod. The fish will be hooked in almost every instance, mainly because cause for alarm has been eliminated by a very simple maneuver.

The matter of hook-setting carries over to bait fishing for all species. The knack is a subtle one, and for some it is difficult to learn if not impossible. A fisherman attuned to its importance can quickly detect its absence in fishing companions, and invariably shudders inwardly when they persist at yanking at what is obviously the wrong time while never dreaming that they are doing anything wrong.

It is perhaps a commentary on human vanity that fishermen can go on missing bite after bite without suspecting that the blame may rest on their own shortcomings. The fisherman cusses his "bad luck" but dismisses the possibility that he is being bested at his own game; a mere perch is too lowly to warrant entertainment of such an idea. Fishing won't make saints of sinners, but it will teach humility to all who are perceptive.

At the risk of belaboring a seemingly small point, I feel it important to emphasize that while the art of bait fishing centers around the matter of persuading fish to bite, no purpose is served if the deal can't be closed by setting the hook successfully. The moment of hook-setting is always the moment of truth, and the fisherman has much more control over his fate at this critical moment than is generally realized. Whether fishing with rod and reel, with handline, or with tilts in winter it is vital to control the line so that all is free and easy between you and the fish until the precise moment arrives for socking the hook home.

So far we've taken up the matter of catching perch while in their midst. There remains, among other things, the important matter of finding them in the first place.

Perch tend to move about in schools. This means that in sizable bodies of water there are many more places where they ain't than where they are. One way to find them is to drop anchor in various spots in the hope of hitting on a school eventually. This is tedious business which carries no guarantee of success.

Probably the surest and easiest way of locating concentrations of perch is by trolling a spinner-and-worm combination. The bait should travel close to the bottom, and trolling speed should be held to a crawl. (A future chapter will be devoted to trolling hardware, so the matter of rigging the trolling combination will be covered there.)

In spring and summer, perch are usually found in less than twenty feet of water, so troll accordingly. Bites may not come immediately, but they are almost certain to materialize eventually in any body of water in which perch abound. When you finally drag through a school you will feel perch pecking at the bait almost constantly.

Since perch are pesky to hook on a troll, and because taking

A spinner-and-worm trolling rig.

them on a weighted rig is dull business, the best move is to anchor wherever bites develop and worm fish as has been described. If you have happened on a large school, the fishing should be fast and furious.

Last spring, my son Mike and I spent an unproductive morning on nearby Lake Champlain. We were bumping bottom with worm and spinner, ostensibly for walleyes but with only two small fish to show for our morning's work. It was early spring and quite probably we had jumped the season by a week or so. Or perhaps the walleyes were there and we just weren't fishermen enough to catch them.

We didn't catch anything else either, for that matter. But along in the afternoon we ran into a bunch of perch which started stripping the nightcrawlers from our hook gangs as fast as we could replace them.

I started cussing the troublesome perch, but then I recalled a bit of advice passed on by an old outdoorsman, advice that I have come to respect more and more as time has passed.

"If you hit on something, no matter what, always make the most of it," he said, "even if it means giving up what you came for. Don't plan on coming back for it tomorrow, because tomorrow it ain't likely to be there."

I had the old-timer's words in mind when I suggested to Mike that we forget about walleyes and cash in on those perch. Mike needed no further persuading. We dropped anchor and immediately began catching jumbo perch almost as fast as we could rebait. I would rather have caught walleyes, and so would Mike. But we both had rather catch perch than *not* catch walleyes. Besides, I was mindful of the love I have for smoked perch.

Those of us who have knocked around a bit have usually learned that the time to watch out for trouble is when everything is going smoothly. This is as true in fishing as elsewhere. On a certain day, fish may go for a particular lure or bait like crazy. When you go back the next day, expecting to clean up with the proven offering, they're likely to ignore it.

Perch and other panfish are not as fickle in this respect as bass, for instance, or trout. Worms come close to being a specific for perch, but they don't quite make it. There are days when perch just don't seem to be worm-minded. On such days it is often possible to turn the tables by offering live minnows.

Large perch are quite capable of swallowing four-inch minnows, and sometimes they do. They greatly prefer the smaller sizes, however, from two-inchers down to "pinheads" so small that it is hard to keep them alive on the hook. Small, fine-wire hooks help greatly in presenting these little minnows naturally. Use No. 10 hooks for the "pinheads" and No. 8 for the two-inchers.

Last winter a veteran commercial fisherman watched critically as I rebaited after landing a hefty walleye on one of my tilt lines. When he saw me slide the hook under the skin of the minnow's back, just *ahead* of the dorsal fin, he commented favorably.

"I'm glad to see *somebody* hook bait the way it should be hooked," he declared. "More walleyes than you can count are missed each winter just because of hooking minnows too far *back!*"

It would be impossible to prove the old pro's contention, but I'm inclined to agree. Proper bait hooking is mighty important, and like most of fishing's "right ways" it seems largely a matter of common sense.

Most fish are cannibalistic, although to varying degrees, and many are caught with baitfish already in their gullets. It takes no great degree of perception to determine that all species, from perch to trout, invariably swallow forage fish head first. It is evident from this that the nearer the head of the bait the hook is placed, the more deeply it will enter the mouth of a biting fish and the more likely it is to engage when the fisherman makes his bid. Despite this obvious fact of life, many fishermen persist in hooking minnows behind the dorsal fin and thus overlook one of the small advantages that often combine to produce success.

Proper hook positioning is especially important when fishing for very light biters, walleyes and perch being outstanding examples. Perch, like their walleye cousins, are gentle, tentative, and deliberate in their manner of taking a minnow-baited hook, and the habit of placing the hook as far forward as possible will reduce the number of missed bites.

While line or leader diameter is not critical in worm fishing for perch, it takes on importance with the shift to minnows. Small minnows can swim about naturally, and thus advertise their presence to best advantage only when they are fished on a line of sufficient flexibility. Monofilament of four- or six-pound test is a good choice of spinning-line weight, or equally good when used as a leader on heavier line.

Minnows should be lowered to within a few inches of the bottom for the same reason that worms should be fished at that level. Perch do not expect minnows to sink, as they look for worms to do, but the same jigging technique often helps to draw bites. I suspect that it is for a different reason, however. Lifting and lowering a worm achieves a moment of natural behavior, but raising a minnow suggests the possibility of escape to a watching and undecided perch. If the perch has been torn between temptation and suspicion, the suggestion of flight may provoke a moment of rashness which will be its undoing.

Finally, there are days when perch show interest in neither worms nor live minnows. Nobody scores heavily on such days, but there are special steps that can be taken.

One which sometimes turns the tide for me is to clamp a small bobber to my spinning line as far above the hook as I can and still be able to cast. I remove whatever sinker I may have had on the line and rebait with a fresh and lively worm. Finally, I lob out the bobber and worm as far as I can cast handily.

I let the bobber rest, but only a little longer than it takes for the worm to sink as far as the line will permit. If the bobber doesn't dance and duck under, I reel rapidly for a few turns, then let the worm settle once more. The spurt of reeling draws the worm close to the surface, from whence it once more sinks slowly after the bobber again comes to rest. The distinction between this simple ruse and jigging is that the illusion of normality—a worm sinking

Drop anchor and fish with lightly weighted worms once a school has been found. Here, I'm cashing in on such a find.

slowly of its own weight—is greatly prolonged. This prolongation, combined with eye-catching action between pauses, is often what's needed to counteract the lethargy of what is essentially a poor fishing day.

Another trick for a dull day is to rig a live minnow behind a small spinner. Use a No. 8 hook with a ringed eye. (Hooks with turned-down eyes tend to cock at an angle when used with spinners.) Hook the minnow through both lips so that it will "swim" naturally behind the spinner.

As with the worm and bobber, lob out the minnow without using force that might snap the bait from the hook. Again, retrieve in alternate spurts and pauses, allowing time for the minnow to sink close to the bottom during each pause. The revolving spinner blade will come to the attention of any perch in the vicinity. They will be excited by the flash and turbulence. When the blade stops spinning their attention will shift to the live minnow. If things continue to work as they should, the aroused perch will then dart in and gobble the minnow.

Perch are year-round biters. (Ice fishermen often make catches of hundreds.) Rod-and-reel fishermen also make exceptional catches soon after they have spawned, usually in April. Perch spawn in the shoreline shallows of lakes and ponds as soon as the water has warmed sufficiently. They remain in the shallow water for a significant period of time after spawning and are invariably especially hungry. Those who make it a point to be on hand during this period need only cast a bobber-and-worm combination a short distance from shore. Catches run into the scores, and even hundreds. Fun is had by all, to be followed by much good eating.

I have dealt at length with perch fishing because the yellow perch happens to be the leading panfish in the waters of my home territory. In other areas, members of the sunfish family may predominate: sunnies, bluegills, crappies, and rock bass. While perch predominate in my home waters, members of the sunfish family are by no means rare. When I'm panfish-minded I welcome them one and all.

All that I have written about perch fishing carries over to fishing for the various sunfishes. Like perch, they are not as elusively sensitive as trout or bass, but their powers of discernment still must be honored. The only special requirement is an awareness of the rather sharp division between worm-feeding varieties and those which prefer minnows. Sunnies—the so-called "punkinseeds"—and bluegills love worms and grubs, but almost never will they take a minnow. Crappies are almost exclusively minnow-minded. Rock bass can be tempted with worms, but they seem to have an even greater taste for minnows.

This distinction points up the importance of carrying both worms and minnows on any panfish foray. Not only does the availability of both enhance the chance of making a big catch of perch, but it is only by having minnows handy that you can cash in on the happy discovery of a concentration of crappies.

In this vein, I remember a particular day when Mike and I were anchored off the mouth of a creek in Lake Champlain. We were trying to lay in a supply of perch, but our worms weren't producing.

"Maybe they're meat-hungry," I said finally. "Pass me the minnow bucket."

The water was clear, thanks to the creek's inpour, and this had enabled us to anchor over a sunken weedbed, for the tops of the weeds, some four or five feet down, were clearly visible. I put a small minnow on my hook and lowered it into the weeds. Nothing happened, so I raised the minnow with the rod tip, prepared to let it settle back. However, as it cleared the tops of the weeds I saw the flash of a taking fish. I provided slack and then set the hook in solid resistance when the line tightened. The fish turned out to be a black crappie (also called "calico" and "strawberry bass") the size of a luncheon plate.

I was delighted, for calicoes are both fun to catch and darned good eating. Better yet, it turned out that there were dozens under us.

I rebaited and Mike swapped his worm for a minnow. But as long as the minnows merely dangled amid the weeds in which the calicoes lurked they drew nary a bite. The trick was to lower the minnows where the calicoes could see them, then raise them above the weeds. As soon as the minnows cleared the weeds, those big black crappies would zoom up and gobble them.

Although my experience with calicoes is relatively limited, all that I have dealt with have displayed a similar liking for a moving bait. Consequently, when Mike and I hit on a school while fishing with minnows for perch, we immediately switch techniques. Instead of letting the minnows swim near bottom, we alternately raise and lower them. Quite often the fish will follow all the way to the top, finally taking with a lusty swirl that breaks the surface.

I cannot account for this tendency, for the minnow, hooked

through the back, rises in a most unnatural manner. Yet if my experience is a valid criterion, it is precisely this unorthodox presentation that will account for the most calicoes.

Mention should be made of a panfish that is especially popular wherever it occurs in the Northeast: the white perch. The term "perch" is incorrectly applied, however, for the fish is actually a member of the sea bass family.

Although I have caught white perch in Maine, it has been inadvertently, while fishing for landlocked salmon or smallmouth bass, except on one occasion. In that instance my guide suggested that we catch a few for lunch, a project into which I entered willingly. He anchored in what he declared to be a proven spot, and produced a can of worms from under the stern seat of the canoe. Bites came promptly, and in no time at all we had the half-dozen that would pave the way to broiled steaks. They were fun to catch, and like all freshly caught fish that have been fried on the scene they were absolutely scrumptious.

I have never been tempted to forsake the quest for salmon or bass to fish seriously for white perch, but Maine guides often speak of fall fishing trips during which they and their families fish for white perch to stow in the freezer, exactly as Mike and I fish for the freezer in Vermont. I envy them their fun and also the fine eating.

Because some fishermen hold panfish in contempt, panfish are often underrated, both as a source of fishing fun and as a source of food. I suspect that this is due largely to the human tendency to follow the leader and to conform. If one man cusses after catching a "pesky punkinseed" and disdainfully throws it back, others feel obliged to do the same lest they appear to be less discriminating and thus of lower status. In no time at all the practice has become the custom and all hands feel bound by it.

This is a crying shame, but one to which I don't fall victim, praises be! Whenever I get into a school of big sunfish I set my ego on automatic pilot and just let the good times roll. Those big enough to warrant cleaning go into the fish box. If others take a dim view of the eating quality of sunfish it is because they have never bothered to clean and cook them. Mike and I know how delectable they are, and we also know that we can stuff the freezer with them and other panfish with a perfectly clear conscience.

Finally, the quest for game fish grows more difficult each year

Mike holds a calico that came eagerly to a jigged minnow.

A single "hot spot" produced this catch of calicoes. All will go into the family freezer.

and in direct proportion to the relative desirability of each. On the other hand, perch, bluegills, crappies, and other panfish remain abundant and handily available. I, for one, am grateful for that circumstance, and fully as grateful for the fact that I'm not swayed by prejudice and therefore can truly enjoy fishing for panfish and eating them as well. They fill in very nicely those gaps between trips for trout and salmon, gaps which are becoming wider and wider for just about everybody.

3

IN BEHALF OF BULLHEADS

EARLY IN APRIL, soon after the ice goes out, an unpretentious but enthusiastic horde of fishermen flock to the shores of Lake Champlain and to the banks of the creeks and rivers which empty into this hundred-mile-long lake. Some carry rods, but many come equipped only with handlines and specially constructed line holders. The latter are little more than stakes which can be thrust into the bank, with spools attached to the sides and flexible shafts at the top, usually of spring steel, to which the handlines can be looped after they have been twirled and thrown out. The limber shafts signal bites by dipping and bobbing, but many fishermen attach small bells near the tips to make bite detection even more certain.

These fishermen are after what is probably the most underrated fish that swims—the common bullhead.

The bullhead could be classed among the panfish, but to the many who appreciate its special virtues this would rank as an injustice. Accordingly, the purpose of this chapter is to give credit where it is long overdue.

Admittedly, the bullhead has certain characteristics which do little to abet its popularity. First, it is easily the ugliest of all freshwater fishes, and its lines of construction are ungainly. Second, the spines of its pectoral and dorsal fins can inflict painful wounds which are invariably slow to heal. Next, it tends to swallow the bait very deeply, making hook removal especially difficult. Finally, for those who haven't mastered the knack, cleaning bullheads is a Herculean task.

Because its appearance suggests the charge, the bullhead is often called "sluggish" by those who pretend to know more about the critter than they actually do. Other equally uninformed critics attribute a "muddy" flavor to the bullhead's flesh, again on the strength of appearance and the fish's proclivity for waters with mud bottoms.

In defending the bullhead against the first charge I do not intend to imply that the bullhead is a fighter to be classed with the landlocked salmon and smallmouth bass. But sluggish? Not by a dang sight!

I remember a long-ago morning when a friend and I were fishing with live minnows for largemouth bass. I got the first bite, and when I set the hook, my rod bucked and bowed against bulldoggish resistance. The water was dark in color, and I was unable to catch even a flash of the fish, which continued to fight powerfully. The duration and intensity of the struggle gave me every reason to believe that I had hooked a dandy largemouth. When I finally brought the fish to within reach of the net I saw it was one of the biggest bullheads I had ever caught. My mistakes are legion, but never in this world would I mistake a sluggish fish for a largemouth bass.

As for the second complaint—a muddy flavor—my instant response is indignation. I like fried and smoked bullheads so much that I would go on fishing for them even if I detested the chore!

Quite to the contrary, I look on spring bullheading with affection, cherishing it as a fit ritual with which to celebrate the end of winter. I'm no less the fisherman when I go after bullheads, but I'm also an exuberant survivor of the winter past. I'm eager to catch fish, no matter the kind, from the first patch of water to open. Bullheads, bless them, are always there to enable me to satisfy this springtime urge.

I'm certainly not going to pretend that any special tricks are necessary to catch bullheads. My main purpose in writing this chapter is to try to broaden the scope of fishermen by calling attention to an angling resource which is often overlooked and often disdained.

Any who care to follow up can perhaps find helpful guidance in the following observations.

Bullheads bite ravenously almost immediately after the ice disappears from northern lakes and ponds. Wherever sluggish creeks empty into bullhead waters, large numbers of the fish will ascend these inlets and will often provide by-the-pailful fishing.

Probably the best terminal tackle consists of a bell sinker tied to the end of the line, with a couple of hooks spaced above on foot-long snells or droppers. This is the ideal rig for handlining, for it can be whirled and then flung for long yardage. It is equally well suited to spinning-rod use, for the bell sinker makes long casts possible.

Hooks should be sizable, for bullheads have large mouths and their table manners are anything but dainty. I like a No. 1, or even a No. 1/0. Some fishermen prefer hooks with long shanks, on the theory that they make unhooking easier. Although the claim seems logical, I doubt that much benefit derives from the extra shank length.

Nightcrawlers are the standard bait for bullheads, and as close to a specific as it's possible to come in fishing. I like to thread at least two on the hook to create a juicy, squirming blob. Bullheads are gluttonish, and are not inclined to bother with anything less than a substantial mouthful.

I have pointed out the major problems of bullhead fishing: sharp spines, cleaning, and the matter of hook removal. Pictures and directions for overcoming the first two obstacles will be found on pages 29–34. The problem of hook removal is not as easily resolved. It persists as an occupational nuisance for all bullhead fishermen, but there is a way to minimize it. But be warned in advance: Unhooking bullheads is not for the squeamish.

When a hook engages deep in a bullhead's gullet it simply cannot be removed by a direct pull. If the pull is on the line, it will usually break before the hook will tear free. Even if the hook is grasped with pliers, it is likely to break at the bend before letting go. The only possible way to retrieve the hook is to *back* it free from the tough tissue in which it is embedded. This means pushing it even farther down the bullhead's throat than it already is!

The above procedure is initiated by thrusting a forefinger down the bullhead's throat until the tip is cradled in the hook's bend.

The bullhead resents this treatment for reasons which can easily be understood, and retaliates by biting down as hard as it can on the intruding finger. In a bullhead of a pound or more, this amounts to a force which comes as something of a shock to the uninitiated. The solution? Pay it no mind! Although the bullhead is equipped with an abundance of teeth, they are short and fine, abrasive but not penetrating.

When your forefinger has found the bend of the hook, cram it down the bullhead's gullet until the barb of the hook pops free. Remove your finger from the bullhead's mouth and retrieve the hook by pulling on the line. Pull gently to make sure that the barb doesn't re-engage.

I reported as good news the fact that a bullhead's teeth are abrasive but not capable of penetration. This is all very fine when you are pushing with the grain, so to speak, but the bad news is that when you withdraw your finger the effect is something else again.

Like the teeth of all kinds of fish, the bullhead's are arranged to facilitate the intake of food and to oppose its loss or escape. Consequently, the emerging finger suffers minute lacerations. The effect is gradual, but in the course of filling a pail with bullheads the loss of skin becomes considerable and leads to a painful condition which usually lasts for days. My method of avoiding this annoyance is to wrap my forefinger with surgical tape. If the bullheads are coming fast, I sometimes have to do a second tape job before I'm finished.

Learning to catch, handle, and clean bullheads is worth every bit of the effort that goes into it, for the reward is what I believe to be the best eating obtainable among freshwater fish. The flesh of the bullhead is red, almost as red as raw beef, and I suppose that there are some who take a dim view of this oddity. Yet to yield to any such impulse is much like rejecting lobsters because of their odd appearance.

My favorite way of cooking bullheads is to roll them in salted cornmeal and fry in plenty of fat, bacon grease if it is available. Because bullheads are thick, large ones should be split down one side of the backbone to make thorough cooking easier. Even then the halves should be fried longer than most fish, for these fish are slow to cook and thorough cooking is a part of the secret of bringing out the best that is in them.

If you have a fish smoker, as every gourmet should, nothing you can process in it can beat a batch of bullheads smoked over corncobs or hickory sawdust. The fact that I'm out of smoked bullheads at the moment makes it torment for me even to write about them!

Although springtime bullheads bite during the day, they become mainly night-biters during the summer. And if you fish at night for bullheads you are almost certain to catch eels. The usual reaction is disgust, accompanied by fancy cussing, and I admit that my response conforms to the norm. Eels are slimy, repulsive critters, and any contact I have with them nowadays is never intentional on my part. But this has not always been so.

When I was younger, and less concerned with niceties, I fished for eels deliberately. My eel-fishing partner was a man twice my age and of Italian origin. To him, pickled eel was a delicacy to be broken out on special occasions as a dish of exquisite delectability. My enthusiasm for eel fishing was not similarly inspired. Rather, it owed its existence to the gallon jug of red wine which my partner brought along on each trip.

On one particular night we were accompanied by a mutual friend who evinced a sudden interest in eel fishing when he learned of our special method of fortifying ourselves for the task. What he neglected to tell us was that he looked on eels with the

SKINNING BULLHEADS

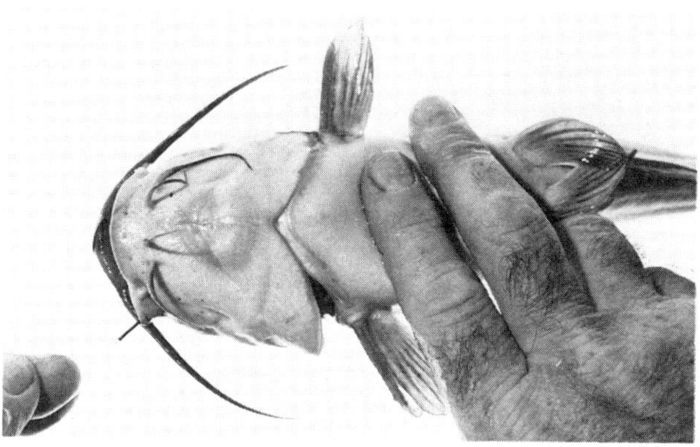

Do not attempt to grab a bullhead for unhooking while it is still flopping. Hold it by the line and steady it with first two fingers as shown. Fish will soon become quiet.

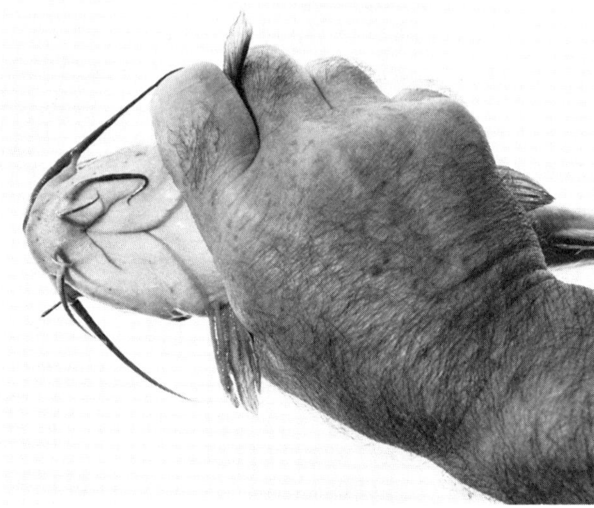

When fish comes to rest, grasp it quickly and firmly. Note that the spined pectoral fins project harmlessly.

Reverse view of unhooking grip. Spine located in dorsal fin is also avoided.

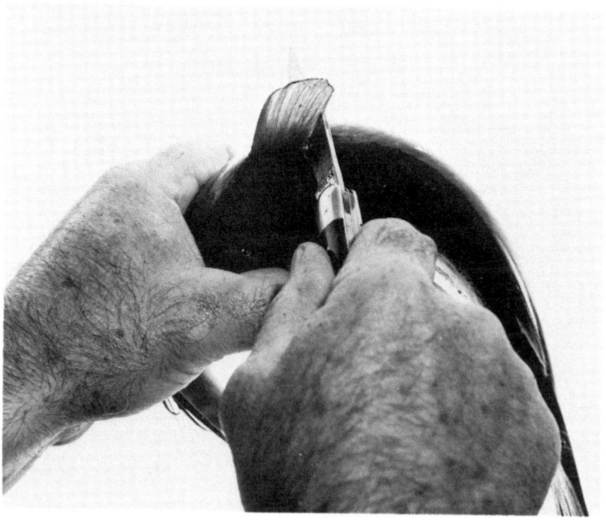

Hold bullhead in this manner preparatory to skinning. Thumb and forefinger are locked behind spines of pectoral fins. First cut starts at base of dorsal fin.

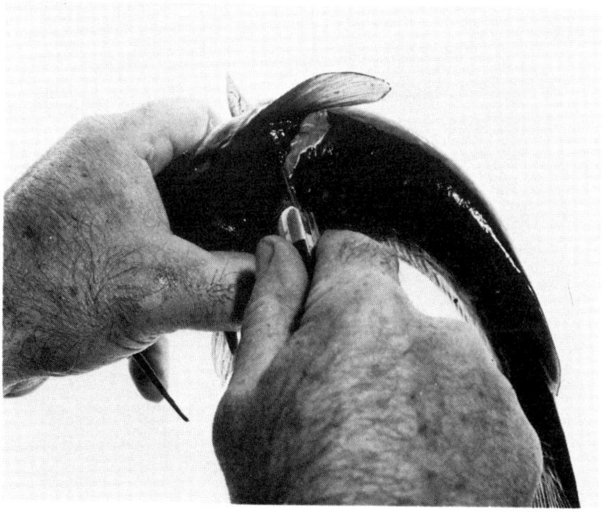

Cut forward on a long slant until knife strikes backbone. Do not cut through bone. Slanting cut is highly important.

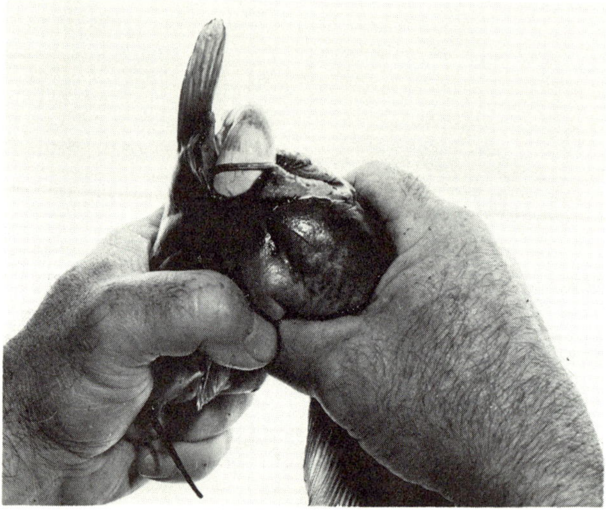

Break the backbone as though snapping a dry stick. Air bladder will pop up through break.

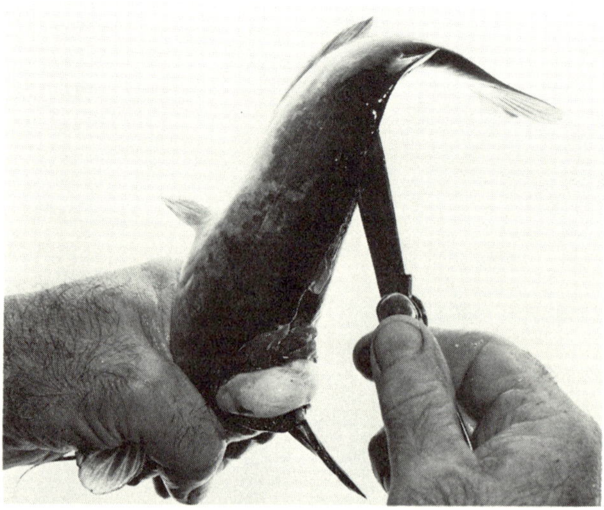

Turn fish over, shifting grip as shown in photo. Slit skin from apex of first cut to base of tail. Only the two cuts are required.

Return fish to original position and thrust right forefinger into break. Hook tip of forefinger under rib cage.

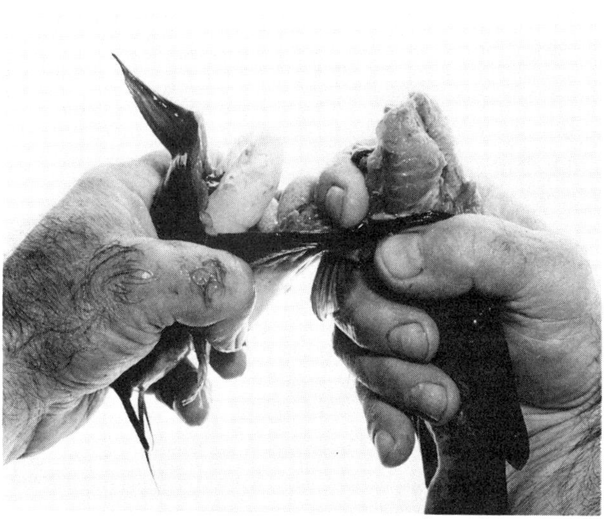

This is the most critical step: While head is pulled forward, crooked forefinger must serve as a blunt wedge to begin separation of skin and flesh. Essentially, finger forces flesh upward through slit made down skin of back. Considerable pressure must be employed.

Clear sailing from here on in. Continue to pull with the left hand; pull and *squeeze with the right. Skinned flesh is extruded while all waste slides under curled forefinger.*

All over but the cooking and eating! With practice, operation can be completed in as little as ten seconds!

instinctive horror that rattlesnakes inspire in most people. Apparently he was willing to risk exposure on the theory that if he drank enough wine, a precaution to which he looked forward with keen anticipation, his dread of eels would be blotted out.

Alas, things didn't work out that way. The guy was half-crocked by the time an eel took my chunk of cut bait, but still a long way from loving eels. Moreover, this first customer proved to be a giant of the species, thick as my forearm and nearly four feet long. When I finally boosted it aboard, loudly cheered by my Italian friend, the ugly devil began making rounds of the boat, slithering from bow to stern and back again like an ill-tempered boa constrictor.

In the course of each trip the monster made contact with each of us in turn. The moments of close intimacy which involved our guest served as a perfect test of the efficacy of wine, even in large doses, as a cure for eel-phobia. I can report from first-hand observation that it was an utter failure. Not only did my partner and I have to cope with the biggest eel we had ever seen, but also with a gibbering maniac who was more of a problem than a dozen eels.

By the time the ruckus finally ended, and the eel brought under control, the boat was a shambles. Lanterns had been tipped over, trails of slime led from bow to stern, one oar was broken after seeing service as a club, and our fear-stricken friend sat huddled in the bow, obviously on the verge of a nervous collapse.

But my partner counted the exceptional prize as well worth the cost. "We'll have that baby next Christmas," he exulted as he relit a lantern that had been tipped over and extinguished during the fray.

I no longer retain my early enthusiasm for eel fishing, but I can attest to the eel's superior quality as a food fish. I have found most alleged ethnic differences to be imaginary, but one exception seems to be the faculty of Italian people to fashion gourmet delights from sources that are either overlooked or scorned by the less perceptive. The utilization of eels is a good example. Contrary to the general belief, one based entirely on outward appearance, eels are delicious!

Therefore, although I don't solicit their business, I go prepared to cope with any eels caught by accident. It is almost impossible to handle eels with bare hands; they are slippery beyond belief and extremely powerful. Moreover, contact with the critters leaves a disgusting coating of slime that is very difficult to get rid of. The problem is largely solved if sections of dry newspaper are used as holders. These cut through the slime and make a firm grip possible without making actual contact. The trick is to get a good grasp near the head and then bat the devil into submission with a "priest." Oddly enough, wallops applied toward the tail end seem to be as quieting, or perhaps more so, then belts over the head.

An eel can be skinned and cleaned easily and quickly. Nail the head to a tree or post and cut through the skin just back of the head. Carry the cut completely around the body. Grasp the edge of the cut skin with pliers and pull downward until an inch or so has been turned inside out. Wrap a section of dry newspaper around the turned-back skin, grasp firmly, and strip the skin toward the tail. It will come off easily and slickly, leaving nothing more to be done than to remove the entrails and cut the body into chunks for frying.

Some claim that eels should be parboiled before frying, but I have never found this to be necessary. I simply roll the chunks in salted cornmeal and fry until the flesh flakes away from the backbone. The flesh is moist and the texture is unlike that of other fish, but the flavor is superb.

If there are those who choose to go after eels deliberately, they have both my blessing and my respect. While eels often bite during the daytime, they feed much more actively at night. They like nightcrawlers, but they like small chunks of fish even better. For best results, bait should be fished on the bottom.

All that has been written to this point has dealt with phases and levels of fishing which most contributors to angling literature pass over as unworthy of mention, let alone analysis. My preoccupation with this largely neglected area is genuine and sincere. No small part of my fishing fun derives from fishing for lowly species, and I'm convinced that it is in this area that the basics of angling must be learned.

Many regard the fish in this category as insufficient challenges, but in my case I haven't gained sufficient expertise to justify such a viewpoint. I find all fish hard to catch, particularly when I'm especially determined to catch them. The only difference among them is that some are harder to catch than others.

In the next chapter we'll start dealing with the one that's hardest to catch of all.

4

A PRELIMINARY LOOK AT TROUT

A COUPLE OF WEEKS AGO, Mike and I seined a bunch of minnows to renew the supply in our bait pond. The chosen site was a long, mud-bottom pool in a small brook. Each spring I worm-fish the brook for the season's first meal of brook trout. The past spring, the pool produced no trout but a horde of chubs swarmed to my bait. I was disappointed in one sense, yet pleased to have discovered a handy source of bait.

When we completed the first drag of the seine we were gratified to find it aflop with baitfish of various kinds and sizes: eight-inch suckers that would make prime bait for northerns, big largemouths, and bowfins; four- and five-inch chubs and redfin shiners for general-purpose use; a boodle of smaller minnows for perch and calicoes.

Yet we gave our haul of bait no more than momentary attention, for included in the catch were no less than five dandy squaretails. The two largest would have weighed a pound apiece, deep-bodied, beautifully colored brookies that would be real trophies in the public waters of this day and age.

I began worming small streams for brook trout before I reached my teens and I have kept my hand in for better than fifty years. I would be the last to claim that I know all there is to know about worm fishing for trout. Nevertheless, if the use of worms makes it *easy* to take trout, it seems logical to conclude that a guy with a half-century of experience should have been able to catch at least one of the trout in that pool. Moreover, you can be darned sure that there were others which managed to escape the net.

Now that I know such trout are there, I shall wait for the next heavy rain and then descend on that pool with rapacious intent and a box of worms. A sure thing? Not if I know anything at all about trout and trout fishing. In all probability I will get skunked, just as I was skunked on opening day—and for the same reasons.

The pool is thickly overhung with alders, making it all but impossible to get a hook into the water without setting up a prohibitive commotion. To make matters even more difficult, the surface is flat and glassy and the current almost imperceptible. No matter how cautious my approach, it is almost certain to alarm every trout in the pool.

While the state of being forewarned didn't enable five of the trout in the pool to escape our net, it is a sure bet to reduce my chances to a dismal low. If I catch a single trout I will be surprised, and if it turns out to be one of the one-pounders we netted and put back I will count myself extremely lucky.

I have used this incident to begin this chapter because it so eloquently refutes any belief that worm fishing for trout is simple or easy, that to fool a trout with an artificial fly requires a touch of genius while to catch a trout on a worm demands little more than threading the bait on a hook and lowering it into the water. Two facts of life oppose this notion: Trout are not that dumb and fishermen are not that smart.

In the preceding chapters I have stressed my conviction that all commonly sought fish, even the most lowly, are sufficiently cautious and elusive to test an angler's skill and insight. Perch and panfish were described as fish which, although less furtive than game fish, still recoil from any flagrantly unnatural presentation of bait. I also emphasized that it was to the advantage of all who fish for them to adopt an analytical attitude and approach, thereby gaining basic insights which carry over to all sport fishing.

In proceeding immediately to the art of worm fishing for trout we have jumped from one extreme to the other, from fish which are the easiest to catch to those which are the most difficult. The jump has been deliberate, for I believe that the basics of bait fishing which have been identified will be best appreciated if they are immediately applied seriously.

Angler inspects his hard-won prize. Note use of but a single small split shot despite heavy current.

If trout fishing isn't serious business it certainly isn't because trout fishermen don't take it seriously. Ever since men began fishing with hook and line, members of the trout family have been the most coveted prizes. Many generations of fishermen and fisherwomen have expended prodigious efforts in attempting the capture of trout. As long ago as the days of Izaak Walton, trout had become exotic in the thickly settled parts of the world, and the need for a high order of skill in their taking already was recognized.

During the centuries since *The Compleat Angler* first saw print, many factors have conspired to complicate further the problems to which its author addressed himself. Trout fishermen have increased in the same geometrical progression as the rest of the world's population. Human congestion and its by-products have greatly reduced the number of streams and lakes of sufficient purity to support trout. Technology has given birth to increasingly effective and efficient tackle, and human ingenuity has achieved ever greater refinement in trout-fishing methods.

In the areas of greatest population concentration, the effect has been the complete destruction of trout fishing. Yet elsewhere, even in regions of relatively heavy population and extreme fishing pressure, the result has been surprisingly different. With the help of sensible regulation and supplemental help from hatcheries, trout and trout fishing have managed to survive.

The Rutland *Herald* carries a weekly column entitled "A Hundred Years Ago Today" which I always read with keen interest. Reports of catches of trout made a century ago sometimes are mentioned, and the numbers of trout caught always arouse my envy.

Yet I was surprised to read recently of a complaint made a hundred years ago about "the disappearance of trout from our Vermont streams." Trout fishermen were described as up in arms over the alleged shortage of trout and were indignantly demanding that the state "do something about it."

The cry has a familiar ring, for it is often heard today. Yet, at least to date, the fears expressed have gone unrealized. Surely, if trout were on the verge of extinction a century ago, as then was claimed, trout fishing would now be a thing of the past.

Instead, trout fishing is very much a part of the local scene, a blessing which prompts me to give thanks frequently. Only one reason can account for this happy circumstance: Within the trout there have evolved the keener sensitivities and wariness that have been needed to ward off the ever-intensifying threat to their existence. In short, trout grow ever harder to catch, and fishermen must wise up accordingly in order to catch them.

Unfortunately, trout have no defense against pollution and high water temperatures, and they quickly pass from the scene wherever the human presence creates these prohibitive conditions. But where care is taken to preserve water quality, trout have been able to hold their own under proper management.

True, the only trout fishing possible in some areas is the put-and-take variety. Yet this is not because heavy fishing strips the waters of trout. Rather, it is because the water quality is so marginal that trout cannot survive the year round and thereby maintain a population by natural reproduction. Wherever the habitat is adequate, trout *are* self-sufficient to a far greater degree than is sometimes realized, often in the face of tremendous fishing pressure.

By surviving centuries of steadily increasing pressure, in which has been incorporated not only every angling ruse that can be contrived but also the unscrupulous wiles of the poacher, trout have clearly demonstrated that they are anything but dumbbells. It therefore does modern trout a grave injustice to insist that they can be seriously victimized by worm fishing. Not only that, the claim credits fishermen, whether they use worms or flies, with far greater skill and insight than they actually possess.

In this book, of course, I'm more especially concerned with the virtues and delights of worm fishing. But before dismissing my

Eloquent testimony that the worm rig is indeed deadly.

plea for worm-fishing respect as propaganda, please take into account the fact that I'm a fly fisherman by preference. I took my first fly-caught trout at age twelve (on a Silver Doctor wet), and from that moment on I have been a dedicated fly fisherman. My fly rods and fly reels are countable by the dozens, and my supply of fly-tying materials is so vast that it's a problem to find storage space for it. I find fascination in all the complexities of fly fishing, real and imaginary, and I relish the challenge of putting them all together in ways which lead to success. My preference for this form of fishing is so pronounced that I turn to worm fishing for trout only when and where fly fishing is out of the question.

But when I *do* make the switch to worms, it is with a clear conscience. In no way do I regard the move as condescending, for the use of worms does not reduce the task of taking trout to one of simplicity. I know from experience that I will meet my match, whether I try to con trout with the best dry flies I can tie, or whether I try to fool them with worms.

Wherever trout exist they are accorded top priority by the majority of anglers, and they will be given high priority in this text. In the chapters immediately following I will try to break down worm and bait fishing for trout into the categories which seem to me to be treated separately.

The temptation to digress may be too strong to resist at times, for it is difficult to write of trout fishing with unflagging objectivity. But for the most part, and to the best of my ability, I shall confine scrutiny to those periods when the bait is in the water and the question is what can be done to make a trout grab it.

5

DOWNSTREAM WORMING

AS THE PACE of life continues to accelerate, ritual plays a role of ever-diminishing importance. Although this is probably inevitable, it is nevertheless regrettable.

The emotional delights of any new and pleasant experience are indelibly stamped on human memory. If the experience is repeated, its immediate pleasures are enhanced by memories of the original joys. Ritual is established when repetition becomes an annual event to which one can look forward eagerly, and which contributes to an ever-growing backlog of fond recollections. Such backlogs are to be treasured, for they help a man to see life as something more than a rat race.

Many simple rituals help me to feel in harmony with the world, even if for no more than a day or perhaps a few hours. The sound of the peepers in early spring is sufficient to waft me into a past from which all unpleasantness is miraculously excluded. To set out bird hunting on the first day of the season is to relive a part of my life in which zest and *joie de vivre* seem to have been the sole ingredients.

In the same way, the opening day of trout fishing immunizes me against all irritants, leaving me free to bask in the memories of all the previous opening days that have led to the one at hand. However, to open the season just anywhere would be to break the ritual and rob it of much of its impact. For complete gratification I must fish as I did on opening days when I was a kid. It is the way which many Vermonters regard as the *only* way to fish for trout. It is a way quite unlike any other.

The way in question is that of fishing a brook which is too small and overhung to permit casting. Fly fishing is out of the question, and even the worm fisherman has no option but to fish downstream, depending on the current to carry his worm where he cannot possibly cast it. He has his work cut out for him, as we soon shall see.

Patience is the first requirement. Just getting a hook into the water is often a perplexing problem. Alders and other brush hamper every move, doing their darnedest to thwart attempts to drift a worm into the most likely spots. They get in more evil licks each time a trout is hooked, interfering, often disastrously, with efforts to bring it to hand or swing it ashore.

But patience is not the sole requirement. Also needed is a special brand of fishing skill. The deepest pools are seldom more than a yard in depth, and the majority of the trout will lie in water that is considerably shallower. Very little water separates fish from fisherman. Yet removing trout from that thin layer of water is fraught with many problems.

To appreciate those problems fully I ask that you recall the built-in defenses which I attributed to panfish. This defense goes far beyond a fear of obvious dangers: the shadow of an osprey, the splashing of a raccoon, or the pulsations of an otter's sinuous passage. It is an instinctive aversion to all that is abnormal. It acts independently of fright. A perch is not *frightened* by a worm which neither sinks nor floats, but is impelled by defensive instinct to *leave it alone!*

We have seen that this distrust of the abnormal is minimal in panfish. Usually, the perceptive fisherman can circumvent it by achieving an approximation of natural behavior in the bait he presents.

Conning the "educated" trout of this day and age is an altogether different proposition. While the sensitivities of trout and panfish are basically similar, those of the trout are enormously more acute and far-reaching.

Yet my premise that trout-fishing skills have their beginnings in worm fishing for lowly species still holds. In other words, the secret of taking trout is to do exactly what is necessary to catch panfish—but to do it somewhere around a thousand times better!

Thus, the nub of the problem is to achieve normal behavior in the proffered worm. To do this, it is first necessary to identify those qualities of normality which serve as the trout's criteria.

Just as the lowly perch expects a worm to look like a worm in its natural state, trout are immediately critical of a worm which has been threaded and looped on a hook until it looks like little more than a blob. If the hook is larger than necessary, this makes the worm's appearance and behavior even more anomalous. Therefore, to start off in the right direction, use small hooks. A No. 8 is a good choice under most conditions, but it is wise to drop down to a No. 10 or No. 12 when the water is low and clear or when using especially small baits.

There are many styles of hooks. One of the most popular is the "claw" type, which features a rolled-in point that is offset from the line of the shank. These have great eye appeal, for they look like sure hookers, but this style is not my favorite. After experimenting with most of the varying types, I have come to prefer the round bend of the so-called "Model Perfect," or the "Sproat," which is a slight modification of the round bend.

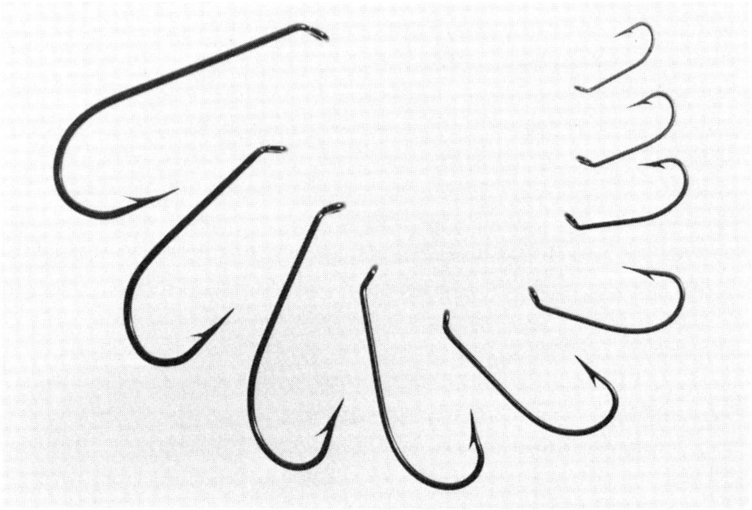

HOOK SIZES USED BY AUTHOR
Clockwise by hook number: 12, 10, 8, 6, 4, 2, 1, 1/0, 2/0.

Further personal preferences include hollow-ground points, turned-down eyes, and shanks of regular length. My choice for most bait fishing is the Mustad #3399, a style in which the foregoing features are incorporated. When using very small baits, larvae, nymphs, etc., I switch to hooks of extra-fine wire, usually the Mustad #94833. I buy my hooks in boxes of a hundred, and in such lots the cost of top-quality hooks is surprisingly slight—two cents apiece or less.

The importance of hook design and quality is often overlooked by beginners and casual fishermen, but it is never lost on experienced bait fishermen. Low-quality hooks cost a bit less money, but they also cost the fishermen in terms of lost fish. For those who would like to delve into the subject more deeply, I recommend the section devoted to hooks in the Herter manual *Professional Fly Tying and Tackle Making.**

In the past, before monofilament lines were available, snelled hooks were used by most bait fishermen. The theory behind the choice was that the short snell would serve as a bit of a leader to help conceal the hook's connection to the heavy and opaque line.

Because custom tends to endure, some fishermen still use snelled hooks, but they are neither necessary nor desirable. Whenever spinning rigs are used for bait fishing, the monofilament line serves as a continuous "leader" when unsnelled hooks are tied directly to it. When fabric lines are used they should be rigged with three- or four-foot leaders of the same level monofilament and the hooks tied to these. In either case, a much neater and more trustworthy connection results than when snelled hooks are used.

In the worming of small brooks, the leader should be no more than three feet long. Even then, the short leader will have to be drawn up into the guides frequently so that the bait can be poked through openings in the brush before lowering it into a likely spot. If leader is tied to line with a bulky knot, this will catch against the guides. This nuisance can be eliminated by attaching the leader to the line with a "nail knot," which makes a smooth connection that will slip through the guides easily. Directions for tying this knot and others will be given in a separate chapter.

Still on the subject of leaders, they should be a compromise between small diameter and the strength needed to free hooks

*Available from Herter's Inc., Waseca, Minnesota 56093.

from frequent snagging. I favor level monofilament of six- or eight-pound test.

As already indicated, the purpose of the small hook is to help retain the natural appearance of the worm. I suspect that most worm fishermen hook worms through their "collars," which lie near the head, but I prefer to hook them at the midpoint. When using small garden worms, the best for brook fishing, I merely bury the barb of the hook in the worm. When hooking nightcrawlers, I draw the barb free, mainly because the heavier and more vigorous crawlers tend to work themselves off the hook if the barb does not enter and then emerge.

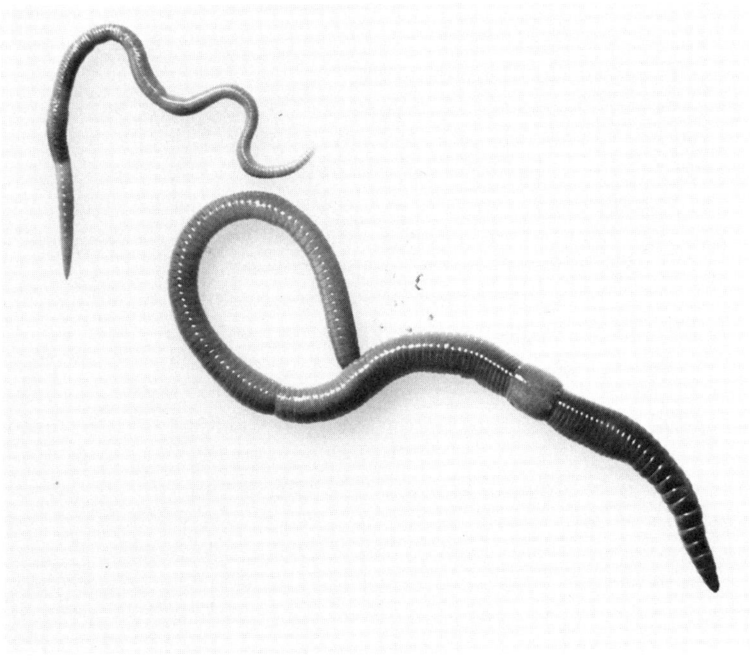

TYPES OF WORMS
Photo shows relative sizes of nightcrawlers and common garden worms. Small worms are best for trout and panfish. Use nightcrawlers for walleyes, largemouths, smallmouths, and bullheads. Notable exceptions: *Use nightcrawlers for big trout in high, roily water, and for deep trolling for trout in lakes and ponds.*

It would be hard to prove that I gain substantially by hooking worms in the middle, but I *think* that it helps to achieve better presentation. Also, hooking through the collar results in a long end which tends to hang downstream in strong currents. When biting trout grab this trailing end they usually steal the worm without getting hooked.

All stream trout are constantly affected by water currents throughout their lives. The current is alternately friend and enemy. Under normal conditions, trout depend on it to bring them their food. When feeding during periods of normal flow they take up positions either alongside or in a major current and gather in the items which this particular flow brings within reach. When sudden showers quickly raise the water level, trout gorge on the abundance of food which has been washed into the stream and comes tumbling along the bottom.

During spring floods, when streams overflow their banks and boulders are swept along the stream bed with grinding violence, the current becomes a dangerous adversary. Under these conditions, trout survival depends on the unique ability to locate safe positions in what, to human eyes, appears to be a churning maelstrom in which no fish could possibly survive.

The ability of trout to cope with strong currents is not strictly an inborn faculty. I learned this fact by chance while working up an article explaining how to distinguish boy trout from girl trout. A longtime friend, Ben Schley, was then superintendent of a nearby hatchery, and he volunteered to help by furnishing trout for photographing.

The chosen subjects came from a pool of "pet" rainbows, all whoppers, which lay close to the stream which bordered the hatchery grounds. In fact, the trout were fish that Ben had caught from the stream and transferred to the pool as a fun project. There, under his ministrations, they had grown to five- and six-pounders.

The first fish netted was a magnificent female. Ben started to hold her with a tail grip, but then hesitated.

"She may flop free," he said. "If she lands on her nose on the ground, it could kill her. I'll hold her over the water. If I drop her in the stream, she'll be there to give some fisherman a whale of a thrill."

Sure enough, before I could focus the camera, the heavy fish gave a powerful flop and her tail slid through Ben's hand despite all he could do to prevent it. The big rainbow landed safely in the stream as anticipated, and I expected that we had seen the last of her, at least for the time being, but I was wrong.

"Hey! Look there!" Ben exclaimed. "She's having trouble with the current."

He was right. Each time the big female righted herself the current, with which she had had no contact since early in her life, promptly rolled her over. Instead of barging off as expected, the fish was swept downstream at the whim of the current, belly up for fully as much of the time as she was belly down. Finally, drifting broadside, she lodged against a pair of boulders like a stick of pulpwood. Once pinned against the twin rocks by the rushing current, she was completely helpless and unable to escape. Ben waded to where she was trapped and cradled her in both arms.

The photos were finally taken, and the trout restored to the rearing pool. She cruised about majestically, apparently none the worse for the experience.

Needless to say, no trout which has spent its life in a stream is ever at such a disadvantage. The moving water, with its ever shifting patterns, is an ever present factor. Of necessity, trout must learn to cope with the threat to life which it sometimes poses, and also to take full advantage of its sustaining contributions of food.

Thus, the lives of stream trout are largely shaped by the moving water in which they live. In order to survive they must be able to weather inevitable periods of great violence. At the same time, in the interest of sustenance, they must be acutely aware of the effect which the current has on the floating, drifting, and tumbling food items upon which they depend.

To be more specific, picture a trout which has taken a feeding position on the downstream side of a rocky projection. The water behind the ledge is "easy," but a strong current sweeps past its outermost tip. The trout lies in the easy water, but its attention is focused on the fast current. It watches it expectantly for the items of food that it will bring within easy reach.

If an emerging mayfly rides jauntily past the ledge, the trout unhesitatingly moves from behind the rock to snatch it from the surface. If a sunken ant or other terrestrial insect appears, drifting beneath the surface, the trout darts out and gathers in that tidbit. It has eyes for the bottom as well as for the surface and middle level. If a washed-in worm or dislodged nymph comes tumbling along the stream bed, its fate is that of the mayfly and ant.

In each of the foregoing instances the item of natural food was free of all external influence and restraint. Consequently, it was instantly and completely responsive to every whim and nuance of the current which carried it. To the watching trout this subservience conveyed the assurance of normality, and it gathered in the morsels without hesitation.

Now, imagine a fisherman who approaches from upstream. He recognizes the cranny behind the projecting ledge as an extremely likely holding spot, and he lowers his worm-baited hook so that the current will sweep it by the tip of the projection. He has high hopes that his worm will be grabbed as it comes opposite the rock. It will—but only if the manner of its approach falls within the trout's very narrow limits of tolerance.

If we allow our imaginary fisherman to be successful, we can learn but little from his triumph. Therefore, let's suppose that his worm is spurned despite repeated drifts past the very nose of the critical trout. In the interest of insight, let's speculate on the reason for the trout's refusal to gather in the bait at a time when it is obviously on the feed.

The sinker? Perhaps our fisherman has pinched on a large buckshot or a clamp-on sinker, both unnecessarily and prohibitively heavy for the small stream he's fishing. If he has made this mistake, the result has been to slow the pace of the tumbling worm to a speed less than that of the current which carries it. This discrepancy is immediately noted by the trout, and the effect is to dissuade the fish from biting.

There are many verses to the same tune. Let's suppose that after introducing the bait to the selected current, our fisherman allowed the line to come taut against the rod. As a result, the bait slowed markedly, just as it reached the critical spot, and even planed toward the surface noticeably. If trout could be fooled by such flagrantly crude presentation, there soon would be none in the streams!

Obviously, a worm must respond to the current to be deemed acceptable by trout. But there is more. Trout know nothing of gravity, at least in Newtonian terms, nor are they specifically aware of the findings of Archimedes with respect to the buoyancy resulting from water displacement. But although they may be blankly ignorant of the scientific principles involved, they are keenly aware of how their various items of food are normally affected by the forces discovered by the two scientific geniuses. In other words, they know which objects should float and which should sink, and they immediately become suspicious when their expectations are violated.

The dry-fly fisherman honors these expectations by tying his flies with stiff hackles which will keep them afloat. The worm fisherman must pay his respects as well—if he intends to catch many trout. Trout expect worms to *sink.* Thus, to be properly convincing, a worm must not only travel at the same speed as the current, but *it must tumble along the bottom.*

It is obvious by now that our theoretical fisherman hasn't done his homework, so it comes as no surprise that he drops his worm only a short distance upstream from the trout's hiding place. We will charitably assume that he manages the proper speed of drift, but again the result is refusal.

Our reason must be a bit more penetrating if we are to deduce the reason. First, how do worms get into streams in the first place? They are never common, for they are not a form of aquatic life. Consequently, their entry is always by inadvertence; a section of undercut sod drops into the stream and any worms contained therein are washed downstream, or a sudden shower sluices a few worms into the drink and they go tumbling with the current. Thus, while worms are not foreign to trout, the fish seldom see them deposited in the stream. They encounter them as they come tumbling along the bottom, and it is here that they expect them to appear. A worm which is in the process of sinking, as though descended from directly overhead, is again a subtle anomaly and therefore a no-no!

I am sure that there are those who feel that I have exaggerated in depicting trout sensitivity, yet the truth, in my opinion, is that I have only scratched the surface. I can offer no proof, of course, but I proffer this warning: Trout-fishing success tends to be directly proportional to the degree to which the trout's sensitivities and powers of discrimination are respected by the fisherman. This is as true in worm fishing as in dry-fly fishing, and perhaps even truer. Allow me to digress in order to explain why this is so.

In dry-fly-fishing parlance, the failure of the floating fly to follow the true path of the current is called "drag." If, because of the restraining leader, the floating fly goes this-a-way while the current goes that-a-way, the result is almost always refusal. We have seen that much the same applies to worm fishing. Although "drag" is not generally recognized as a worm-fishing factor, it is a dragon which must be slain by fly fishermen and worm fishermen alike. The only difference is that drag is harder to conquer in worm fishing than in dry-fly fishing.

The forces exerted upon a floating fly by the current act only in a two-dimensional context, namely the surface. The sunken worm is influenced by forces which act not merely in a single plane, but in a three-dimensional continuum. With skill and good fortune the dry-fly fisherman may achieve a dragless float, or one which closely approaches perfection. The worm fisherman can virtually never effect the underwater counterpart, for his sunken bait is constantly subjected to impulses which come from all angles. You can be sure that any watching trout are instantly aware of the slightest lack of response, and that this lack, in excess of the most stringent standards, is regarded as anathema.

We have speculated as to possible reasons for our imaginary fisherman's lack of success, and have come up with what seem to be logical conclusions. By identifying possible reasons for refusal we are now in a position to try to circumvent them.

But before dealing with remedial steps, let me stress the fact that our chosen scene of operations, the small, overhung stream, is the ideal classroom and proving ground. In larger waters, open to all angling methods, the reasons for failure are obscured by a multitude of variables and are accordingly difficult to identify with any degree of certainty. In the small "worming" stream, the problem is so compressed and localized that analysis is necessarily confined to basic elements. The only option is to present a worm so naturally that a trout will grab it. Here it is much easier to pinpoint error, and then correct it, than where the opportunity for error spreads over a much greater area. Yet the advantage goes beyond ease of perception and identification. Small-stream analysis leads directly to fishing basics, the "rights" and "wrongs" which form the hard core of all trout fishing.

Finally, the fisherman who learns the lessons that a small stream can teach will be better able to distinguish angling truths from the superficialities which are often accorded unwarranted importance. He will realize, for instance, that to con a trout with a dry fly is primarily a matter of natural presentation, and that pattern selection is of only secondary importance. If this sounds a bit farfetched, take into account that the worm fisherman is using not a lifelike imitation, but *the real thing.* Even so, he must satisfy the trout's standards of acceptability to succeed. The dominating importance of presentation is thus inescapable.

Now, let's find basic answers for the various reasons for refusal about which we have speculated. First, the matter of proper sinker weight. Our fisherman pinched on too much. This slowed the bait to a speed less than that of the current, giving the trout grounds for suspicion.

The remedy is to use only enough sinker to draw the bait down close to the bottom. (It would be wonderful if all trout-fishing problems were as easily resolved.) The ideal approach is to use no sinker at all. This is both possible and rewarding wherever the water is especially shallow or the current especially weak. It should be noted that a baited hook would sink of its own accord in even the fastest flow if it could be relieved of the restraining influence of line and leader, for the density of hook and worm is greater than that of water. Much can be done to minimize this restraint, as we shall see presently, but it cannot be eliminated completely. Therefore, in all but exceptional instances, a bit of weight is required. In moderate currents a single split shot (BB) will suffice. In stronger currents a pair may be necessary. I pinch them to the leader about eight inches above the hook.

Before we tackle the next problem, let me say that in my opinion the fly rod is by far the best tool for downstream worm fishing. The spinning rod, with its continuous monofilament line, suggests itself, but the line lacks the weight and substance which we are about to see is needed. A G level line is a good choice. In my case, I reverse a forward-taper fly line whose heavy portion has seen better days. The small-diameter running section is usually still in mint condition and perfect for the job.

In providing the next example of what not to do, our fisherman allowed the drifting worm to come taut against leader and line at the critical time when it became visible to the trout. This caused the worm to halt, and then plane upward, a dead giveaway of its artificiality. The solution to this problem is more demanding.

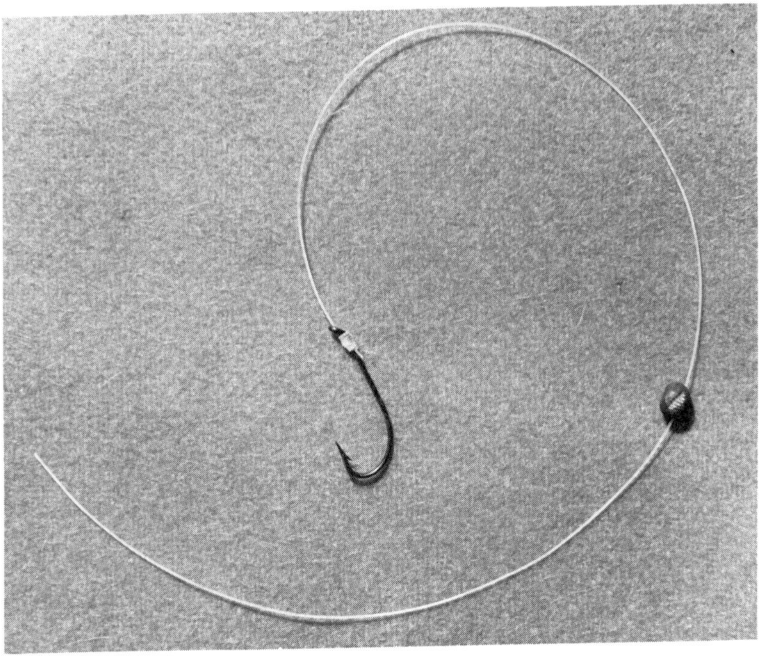

SINKER PLACEMENT
Photo shows hook with single buckshot pinched to line about eight inches above hook. I prefer this spacing for sinkers of all weights, from tiny split shot to heavy clamp-on sinkers.

Obviously, the need is to maintain a constant state of slackness between bait and rod tip to eliminate as far as possible the tension which otherwise develops. It might seem that merely stripping line from the reel would suffice, but it doesn't. It fails to achieve the desired effect because tension, slight but nevertheless excessive, is required to pull the stripped slack through the guides. The trick, one of the most important in downstream worming, is to effect a steady flow of line through the guides *without help from the current.*

The knack is typically paradoxical: simple, yet subtle; prosaic, but of determining importance. First, line must be stripped from the reel to provide a supply of slack between the reel and the stripping guide. Next, this slack must be fed through the guides in such a manner as *to have no effect on the portion of the line which is in the water.* It is clear that slack could be worked out handily by flexing the rod directly against the drifting line. Yet this would destroy the illusion of free drift, for each lift of the rod would act directly on the drifting worm and cause it to halt, or even move *against* the current momentarily. It would be easy and natural to dismiss this slight irregularity as inconsequential. I hope, however, that I have been sufficiently convincing in identifying the supersensitivities of trout to make clear the disappointing consequences which accrue to just such oversights and lack of empathy.

Interference with the worm's drift can be avoided only by tossing the rod tip so gently that it acts only on the inertia of the *short length of line which hangs from the rod tip.* This requires a fine sense of "feel," the ability to sense the slight difference between a direct pull against the extended line and one against only the short section that is free-hanging.

With each gentle toss of the rod, slack is allowed to flow freely through the guides in amounts commanded by the inertia of the short line section between rod tip and water. This payed-out line falls limply to the surface. The continuous process maintains a constant cushion of slackness between the tip of the rod and the length of line that is being carried downstream by the current. This, in turn, eliminates the tension which otherwise would develop between rod and extended line, and which would prevent the drifting worm from complying with the influence of the current.

Much ado about nothing? I'm sure that some will think so, convinced that I'm trying to aggrandize a humble pursuit by embellishing it with fine distinctions that are largely imaginary. Indeed, it is only hesitantly that I insist that such apparent trivia are the determinants of success, for I know that to do so is to invite skepticism if not ridicule.

In my defense I can only restate this book's purpose: to try to help people catch fish. If I am true to this cause, I must follow wherever my convictions lead. As should be clear by now, my strongest conviction concerning fishing, trout fishing in particular, is that success is mainly a matter of recognizing and honoring the importance of tiny details, distinctions which are so subtle that they are overlooked by many fishermen, if not by the majority.

So let's hold her steady as she goes. Let's return to our hypothetical fisherman and try to replace his bag of errors with a corrective bag of tricks.

In making his next mistake, let's concede that he contrived to have his drifting worm keep pace with the current by pinching on only the minimum sinker weight required and followed up by feeding slack line in the proper manner. Although he took these substantial strides toward acceptable presentation, he overlooked the important fact that free-drifting worms hug the bottom.

Heedless of this requirement, he lowered his worm only a short distance above the lie of the trout, causing the bait to come into the latter's view at the middle level. Again, my firm belief in the importance of small details impels me to submit that this departure from the norm was sufficient to induce refusal.

In this instance the solution is simple, of course. Whenever a promising spot is located, the worm should be introduced a sufficient distance upstream to allow it to reach bottom *before* it reaches the likely location. In small, twisting streams, it is often necessary to lower the bait at one's very feet if the worm is to be at the proper depth at the critical time.

If the downstream worm fisherman can achieve an unaffected drift of his worm at the bottom level, *I guarantee that he will take trout.* It is never easy, for all operative factors staunchly oppose this achievement. At the risk of redundancy, expertise consists of recognizing these opposing factors and then employing all possible means of circumventing them.

We have examined only a few of the many possible reasons for failure, but the list could go on indefinitely. It is not my intent to enumerate all, or even most. Instead, my purpose has been to identify what I believe to be the *basic* problems and to suggest methods of overcoming them.

The key to true expertise can be found in these basics. Their understanding can be parlayed to degrees of competence limited only by human differences in perception, differences in the ability to "think like a trout." Again, I know of no better way to acquire this ability than by worming a small stream—without condescension and with the utmost concentration and seriousness.

Compared to a sweeping river, with its deep and mysterious pools and its broad and inscrutable runs, a small worming stream appears to hold comparatively little challenge. Yet trout fishing is always the same game, regardless of where it is played. Common enigmas persist throughout, challenging the best efforts of all who address them seriously.

The only variable, in my opinion, is that of tempo. That of a big, wild river, with its promise of trophy-size fish, sets the stage for spectacular thrills and heady excitement. The small stream cannot compete on these grounds, but the coin of its unique rewards is fascination. I have been fortunate enough to sample both. The reel-screeching run of a salmon or big trout elevates me to a state of wild-eyed ecstasy which has no counterpart. Yet the total absorption which small-stream fishing commands evokes a quiet contentment which I relish in quite a different way, but with equal appreciation.

Once, on the George River in northern Quebec, I managed to circumvent the refusal of Atlantic salmon to take my conventional flies by offering them rough creations which I tied on the scene from swatches of hair shed by migrating caribou. It was a memorable triumph, for I was into twelve- and fourteen-pound fish as soon as I hit on a solution.

This spring, while worming a "secret" little stream for brookies, I was both puzzled and frustrated when I couldn't draw as much as a bite in a pool which had always been good for at least a pair of plump brook trout. I drifted my worm through the hole time and again, flawlessly it seemed to me, but each time it drifted on through untouched.

Confident that the pool held trout, and determined to save face, I retreated upstream, where I looked around for stick caddis. I soon found several clinging to a sunken log. After adding them to my bait box, I snipped the No. 8 hook from my leader, removed the single split shot, and tied on a fine-wire No. 14 hook.

Returning to the head of the problem pool, I shucked one of the caddis larvae from its woody case and carefully threaded it on the tiny hook, trying to preserve its natural appearance as much as possible (I'll have more to say about caddis later in this book). When all was ready, I dropped the tiny unweighted bait at my feet and carefully fed slack as the current carried my line into the pool. I was happy to see that the caddis larvae was sinking nicely, of its own accord, as it disappeared in the three-foot depths of the pool.

Midway of its drift, I saw the line begin moving to one side. When I carefully inched in slack I felt a slow throbbing—the ever exciting message which tells of a bite. Out of respect for the very small hook, I set it with only a gentle lift of the rod tip.

Immediately all was commotion. The stung trout flounced at the surface, a foamy and colorful upheaval which only a brookie can make, a vivid display of orange, black, and white made more startlingly brilliant by the brevity of its visibility. No eight- or nine-incher, this trout, but truly a whopper!

Because a net is an encumbrance on a tangled small stream, and is seldom needed anyway, I was forced to make out without one. After a long and hectic struggle, fraught with many crises, I finally led the tuckered trout to my feet and then scooped it ashore with a lucky sweep of my hand. It was a full thirteen inches long and weighed just short of a pound!

Although the two triumphs were of vastly different dimensions, their components were identical. Making the most of one's fishing is much a matter of recognizing this similarity. Fishing would soon lose its charm and appeal for me if I allowed exotic experiences to become the standard against which all others were to be condescendingly compared.

It is perhaps because of its effect of making small triumphs seem great that I have a special affection for small-stream worm fishing. The opportunity to catch really large trout shrinks steadily. We all dream of catching big trout, but our dreams come true more and more infrequently. The relativity of small-stream fishing is often our salvation. To catch a foot-long trout in a large stream may be satisfying; but if the stream is famed for its rare lunkers, such a catch fails to evoke any feeling of special accomplishment. On the other hand, to take a fish of that size from a small, brush-choked stream is always true reason for pride.

Finally, by my observations, the small brook provides one of the most reliable tests of trout-fishing ability. Among fly fishermen, the difference between mediocrity and a high degree of competence is usually only moderately apparent. Expertise asserts itself, of course, but seldom to a degree which seems almost miraculous. The reason, I suspect, is that larger streams preclude that intimacy between fisherman and trout which allows true trout-fishing genius to flourish to the fullest.

Like the musically gifted and the artistically talented, there are fishermen who instinctively do all the right things at the right times. On the small stream, where they can ply their genius point-blank, the difference between the results of their efforts and those of ordinary mortals often becomes incredibly apparent. In the course of many years I have fished with a scattering of such gifted fishermen, always to my considerable humiliation. All could fish behind me, giving me first crack at every pool, and finish with more and bigger trout!

The memory of these drubbings is always in the back of my mind when I'm fishing a small stream. No matter how well I do, I know that there are others who could do much better, and the knowledge keeps me striving to gain greater insight and empathy. I know that the goal of ultimate expertise is of the carrot-on-a-stick variety, but I pursue it earnestly and happily.

It is impossible to learn from the words of another what one must learn from experience. Nevertheless, I hope that this chapter has identified basic principles which are worthy of brief review.

1. In order to win acceptance, a bait must be responsive to the current and it should tumble along the bottom.

   Means of achievement:

   (a) Keep sinker weight to the lightest minimum that is practical.

   (b) Lower the bait well upstream of the anticipated lie.

   (c) Keep a cushion of slack between rod tip and drifting line.

2. The bait's natural appearance should be retained as completely as possible, and its normal movements should be unhampered.

   Means of achievement:

   (a) Use small hooks. No. 8 and No. 10 for most conditions; No. 12 and No. 14 for tiny baits, and when the water is especially low and clear.

   (b) Hook bait as lightly as possible. When worm fishing, merely bury the barb at the worm's midpoint.

There is ever so much more, of course. Learning to "read" trout water in terms of where the fish are most likely to lie is an art by itself. It is one which must be learned almost entirely from experience. Also, every basic ploy is open to unlimited variation, tiny embellishments which evolve as responses to the ever shifting situations encountered in stream fishing. Each fisherman gradually acquires an exhaustive bag of small tricks, and the longer he fishes the greater the collection becomes.

I have already professed my affection for this most elementary level of trout fishing, and before closing this chapter I would like to elaborate a bit more on its unique virtues.

Two circumstances are widely lamented by trout fishermen. One is the diminishing opportunity to fish for "wild" trout, fish which are the result of natural reproduction and not the output of hatcheries. Preference for "wild" fish may or may not be justified. Nevertheless, the known presence of stocked fish in a stream detracts from its charm and appeal in the opinion of most trout fishermen.

The second lament is the absence of brook trout. Again, when the situation is viewed objectively, there seems to be little reason to rate the brookie ahead of the brown or the rainbow. Yet the brook trout is unquestionably the darling of Eastern trout fishermen, for reasons disassociated from objectivity.

Applying one of the quaint standards of human society, trout fishermen instinctively bestow upon the brookie that special distinction which is universally reserved for the "native" and as arbitrarily denied the "newcomer." Also, the brook trout is generally regarded as the most handsome of all trout, a rating which is probably deserved, and as the best eating, which is debatable.

At any rate, the opportunity to fish for wild brook trout is held in special esteem by most trout fishermen, and I confess that I'm not competely immune to its special appeal. This opportunity no longer exists to any significant extent with respect to our larger and best-known streams, but it *does* exist in the small streams with which this chapter has been concerned. Although our major streams are no longer sufficiently pure to support the delicate brook trout, the clear, cool waters of the many small feeders often hold nothing but wild brookies.

These small streams are open to exploration and conducive to many pleasant discoveries and surprises. To worm a limit catch of colorful brookies from one of these streams is not only an angling accomplishment in every sense of the word, but the exotic nature of the feat makes it one of special magnitude.

Although the basics of small-stream worm fishing can be used to enormous advantage on larger waters, in the more sophisticated pursuit of much larger trout, it is a delightful game in its own right, one which can greatly broaden the scope of trout fishing. I heartily recommend it, not only as a foundation for true trout-fishing savvy, but as an additive from which it is possible to derive much pleasure and satisfaction.

6

DELICATE BUT DEADLY!

IT HAS BECOME something of a fad among fishing writers to explain that they have passed through two unbecoming stages before reaching the ultimate level of trout-fishing sophistication. They speak first of an original desire to catch trout in great numbers with the implied disdain which only reformed sinners can muster. Then they refer to a subsequent preoccupation with trophy fish, as though this, too, were a passing sin of the flesh from which they have gained redemption. Finally, they extol the exalted level to which they profess to have risen, a nebulous stratum in which all gross desires allegedly dissolve. In this bland context, with all avaricious goals finally renounced, they can at last lay claim to angling regality.

Maybe so. Maybe I'm guilty of injustice, but this line of talk always strikes me as a roundabout way of bragging. "Look," they seem to be saying, "I'm such a helluva fisherman that I've grown tired of catching trout. I just fish for exercise and to get the fresh air."

Years ago, when I first moved to the town in which I live, I made my first visit to the local hardware store. The deer season was in progress, and the talk turned to deer hunting.

"Gotcha buck?" I inquired of the proprietor.

"Haven't bothered to go out yet," he answered. "No matter,

though," he added grandly. "I'll go out one of these mornings. Figger to have a deer in the first twenty minutes."

That was about thirty years ago. I know that the store owner has done his share of deer hunting since, but to the best of my knowledge he has yet to bag a buck!

My record as a deer slayer isn't enough better to warrant any claim of prowess. As for trout fishing, there seems little likelihood that my expertise will ever become so devastating that the game palls before it. I'm not out to kill a lot of trout, but I sure as hell fish to *catch* them, the more the merrier and the bigger the better. When the day comes that these twin goals pose no challenge, I'll stash my rods and call it a day!

Because it is my firm belief that most trout fishermen fish to score, I shall devote this chapter to a special method. It has not been widely embraced as yet, but I'm convinced that it has no equal when it comes to taking trout, not only trout in numbers but particularly trout of trophy size.

As we saw in the preceding chapter, the determinants of success in stream worm fishing are the twin abilities to achieve both a deep drift of the worm and its uninhibited response to the varying impulses of the current. This is a tough assignment in downstream worming, calling for a delicate sense of feel and subtle manipulation of rod and line. Presentation at the hands of the most skilled and experienced often leaves much to be desired.

It is obvious that the problem of effecting a convincing drift can be simplified greatly by fishing upstream wherever this is possible. When a worm is cast upstream, it tumbles back toward the fisherman while the slack for an unaffected drift develops automatically. Until fairly recently, however, no really suitable outfit for upstream worm and bait fishing has been available.

While upstream worming can be done with fly rod and fly line, the fisherman is always compromised. Casting is always difficult, for one thing. Any bona-fide backcast usually snaps the tender worm from the hook. Sinkers compound the problem, for any terminal weight is an abomination when casting with a fly rod. The upstream wormer who uses a fly rod is therefore restricted to soft lobs which often fall far short of the desired distance. Moreover, while the weight and bulk of a fly line is helpful in maintaining slack while fishing downstream, it becomes a detriment in upstream fishing, creating a dragging effect upon the drifting worm as the extended line loops back upon itself.

The problem was solved, although inadvertently, by the development of the ultralight spinning outfit. The rig was devised to permit the casting of tiny metal lures, some weighing as little as a thirty-second of an ounce. This called for an outfit that was scaled down dramatically on all fronts: short, wispy rod, miniature reel, and line of very small diameter.

Nearly twenty years ago a tackle company furnished me with one of the outfits for testing. Trout went for the innovatively tiny metal lures with such zeal that I wrote and placed a magazine article about my success with the rig. Although letters poured in, indicating that the piece had aroused considerable interest, ultralight spinning failed to gain widespread permanent popularity. I confess that my own outfit saw less and less use as the aspect of novelty gradually eroded.

Author's fishing partner Pete Terwilliger makes an upstream cast with ultralight worming rig.

He reels in slack to keep pace with freely drifting bit of worm.

As bait comes opposite, he ceases reeling and holds rod high. This allows bait to drift on past fisherman, and the prolongation of drift often pays off in extra strikes.

Then, much more recently, the Orvis Company, of Manchester, Vermont, sensed that with a bit of redesigning the ultralight spinning outfit could become a one-package double threat to trout. They reasoned, and correctly, that if the right balance between delicacy and backbone could be engineered in rod action, the rod would still be sensitive enough to handle the tiny spinning lures and yet have enough guts to lay out a reasonable length of fly line. With the single rod, and at only the slight inconvenience of carrying an extra reel, the fisherman could switch from spinning to fly fishing as conditions seemed to warrant.

When the Orvis Company generously made one of the resulting combination outfits available to me, my flagging interest and enthusiasm immediately reawakened. With the original outfit I was committed to spinning, a mark which I held against it. The ability to shift from spinning to fly fishing at will placed matters in a new and more favorable light.

The expertly combined elements of rod action, reel function, and line weights exceeded my highest expectations. With the single rod and the twin reels, I took trout on metal lures and on dry flies, from the same stream on the same day. When no trout were showing, I teased them with deadly little spinners and spoons. Whenever a hatch developed, I merely switched reels and laid about me with dry flies. All was beautiful.

It occurred to me, however, that I wasn't yet utilizing the outfit's full potential. If it would toss a lure weighing only a tiny fraction of an ounce for a substantial distance, it would do the same for a worm and split shot. I added upstream worming to my ultralight repertoire, and the outfit immediately became a *triple* threat. When one of the three options failed to work, another usually succeeded. I took a lot of trout on spinning lures and flies. But I took even more, including some whoppers, by tossing worms upstream.

My success with the three-way outfit inspired an article which found a home with *True.* After its acceptance, Peter Barrett, then the magazine's Outdoors Editor, called me on the phone. He said that he wanted to illustrate the article with pictures of me taking trout on the outfit, and that he would like to come up and follow me around with a camera. I had no choice but to agree.

But I knew that I had put myself on the spot. True to my trade,

I had made no effort to minimize my successes. In fact, as I reread what I had written, the article seemed to imply that I was the angling counterpart of the twenty-minute deer slayer. It was based on fact, but I hadn't felt called on to temper the truth with overtures of self-effacement.

"Ye gods!" I thought cringingly. "I caught all those trout in May and June, and now it's August. When Pete Barrett shows up with his cameras, I'll be lucky to catch so much as a goddam six-incher!"

Pete arrived at the appointed time, and the next morning we drove to a stretch of stream that I knew held big browns and rainbows. But although I was confident that fish were there, I was anything but certain of my ability to make connections, and equally unsure of my ability to land them if I did. The trout of that stretch tend to take off like rockets when hooked, the current is fast and heavy, and, in accord with the script, my little spinning reel held line of only two-pound test.

While Pete readied a camera, I rigged the little rod with its matching fly reel and line. I cast a dry fly for a spell, but no fish were showing. A good trout finally rose to a blind cast, but either it failed to take at the last moment or I goofed in my attempt to set the hook. The rise had all the appearance of a no-nonsense take, and I had been virtually certain of hooking up when I raised the little rod.

"Just as I damned well expected," I mused dejectedly when the hook failed to connect. "Before this day is over I'm going to eat every last one of all my smart-ass words!"

In accord with the article's theme, I changed to the little spinning reel when repeated casting failed to bring another rise. I tied a No. 12 hook to the two-pound line, pinched on a single split shot about eight inches above the hook, and lightly impaled a squirming worm on the tiny barb. Thanks to the little rod's special action, and to the minimal resistance of the very fine line, I could cast the light bait well upstream.

Each cast resulted in what appeared to be a flawless drift, and following each toss I cranked in slack just fast enough to keep pace with the current. I knew that the sunken worm was getting down near the bottom, and I had every confidence that big trout were eyeing it critically as the current tumbled it downstream. According to all I had written, a bite should have been a brassbound certainty. But the jinx persisted, exactly as I feared. Drift after drift produced nothing.

Wading was precarious, and I had been hard put to gain my position from which I could reach the base of a foaming falls with upstream casts. Downstream, the heavy flow quieted somewhat as it spread over a broad pool that was much too deep to wade. In order to drift my worm into the pool I would have to do it from upstream.

But I had written glibly of a trick for just that situation, and I faithfully followed the text. I reached in my vest for a tiny plastic bobber, hardly bigger than the marbles that kids break out each spring, or did when I was a kid. I snapped it to the line about four feet above the hook. I lobbed out bobber and worm with a cross-stream cast, left the reel bail open, and fed slack through the guides as the little red-and-white bubble danced downstream.

The wispy line exerted almost no restraint on the drifting bobber, and I knew that the latter must be traveling at almost exactly the speed of the current. The worm which hung from it must therefore be doing the same. If I knew anything at all about trout, I reflected, all should add up to a hit. Then I gloomily thought of Pete and his camera and moodily pondered the inexorable perversity of those days when nothing will go right.

Plop! The little bobber chugged under as abruptly as though the line had been caught in a spinning flywheel! I closed the reel bail and then set the hook discreetly as the line tightened against the rod. The reel spool took to buzzing instantly. As the hooked fish raced downstream I could feel those spaced-out undulations which always bespeak a heavy fish.

The run stopped as suddenly as it had started. I put a bit more strain on the fragile rod and felt nothing but unmoving resistance. "Around a cussed rock already," I agonized inwardly. "Wouldn't you *know* it!"

zzzzzzzzz! The reel spool resumed buzzing without warning, then stopped as abruptly as before. Another cautious lift of the rod fetched up against the same motionless and unyielding weight.

After the unlikely performance had been repeated a third time, the truth finally dawned. The trout, undoubtedly a brown, wasn't wrapping the line around rocks. It was just so damned big that it didn't even know it was hooked! The tiny hook in its jaw, and the slight pressure from the wispy rod, registered only as a minor irritation.

I cussed the irony of my predicament. Minutes before, I had been convinced that fate had preordained that I was not to catch a trout worth photographing. Now I had gone and hung one so big that landing it on my frail rig would be nothing short of a miracle.

The fish took off again, then halted with rocklike immobility as before. I tightened the drag a whisker and risked a wee bit more pressure. The line fell slack with demoralizing finality. I reeled in morosely, expecting to find that the line had broken. Instead, the tiny hook had simply pulled out! The whammy which hung over me had even denied me the dubious honor of going down to defeat in genuine battle!

It was time for beer and sandwiches. After lunch, we moved downstream to a proven hot spot. A big, undercut boulder pushes up in the middle of the river, and trout invariably lurk at its base.

I cast my worm well above the boulder, this time without benefit of bobber, and then held the rod high as the deeply sunken worm swept around the near side. Pete was standing alongside, and we both saw the broad flash as a taking trout zoomed out of hiding.

"A two-pounder, at least!" Pete exclaimed.

I agreed, but silently. I set the hook at the flash, and from that time on was much too busy to make audible reply.

This fish was a rainbow. Those who have yet to tangle with prime, wild rainbows in big, quick water have a special thrill in store. Those of the stream I was fishing are particularly dynamic. An abundance of food prompts growth to lengths of eighteen inches or more in just three years, and the same rich supply soups up vitality accordingly.

The hooked fish sped downstream, scarcely slowed at all by the slight drag that is appropriate to two-pound line. I had a job on my hands, but this was no such unmanageable brute as the first fish I had hooked. I knew that I could land it, with a little luck. But on that day, my luck had obviously stepped out for a beer.

With infinite care and attention to details, I weathered a succession of streaking runs, then nursed the slowly tiring rainbow through long minutes of stubborn resistance. At long last the fish turned on its side and hung in the current, directly downstream.

The broad pink stripe along its side gleamed against its silver background. With premature elation, I could already see the vivid colors in print.

Reluctant to drag the fish against the heavy current, I proposed to Pete that he take my net, approach from below, and scoop up the exhausted trout.

Whether from fear of spooking the rainbow into a last dash, or out of a misplaced regard for propriety, Pete refused. "Nothing doing," he said. "You net him."

I tightened the drag gingerly, and began to wind in line ever so slowly. All went well until the spent fish reached back and found a last remnant of energy. It was able to right itself and make one last bid for freedom. It was a feeble flurry, compared to his earlier behavior, but it was enough to maintain the chain of perversity. The tiny barb had worn loose its hold during the prolonged struggle, and once more it came free!

Ostensibly, we were right back where we started, but I knew that the picture was actually much blacker. I had had two chances to come through the hero, and I had flubbed both. A third chance was beyond all reasonable expectations. I rebaited numbly, and listlessly dropped the worm above the boulder once more.

Providence has a way of looking out for drunks and sinners, and apparently it sometimes takes pity on braggarts with their backs to the wall. I watched the line follow the previous path, and as it curled under the lip of the boulder there came another soul-stirring flash.

Bless us and save us! In a trice the little reel was buzzing under the streaking run of a second fish! And finally, as if by a sudden decree of clemency, things began going right. The trout, another fine rainbow, fought until it, too, was completely drained of energy, but it finally wound up in the net. Pete all but wore it out taking pictures, some of which served to substantiate the claims I had made in the article.

"Wanna try for another?" I asked.

"Hell, no!" Pete replied. "Let's go celebrate. I think we've both earned a drink."

The foregoing yarn wouldn't merit space in this book's how-to-do-it context were it not for its pertinent implications. Had I written as extravagantly and glowingly about an innovative fly pattern or a special lure, it's an odds-on bet that it would have made me out a liar if I had tried to prove its efficacy for the camera. Tricks and tackle that work *on occasion* are commonplace. Those that work *on demand* are reason to sit up and take notice!

Before zeroing in on particulars, let me buttress my claim for the deadliness of ultralight worm fishing by adding that some of the pictures which accompany this chapter are of fish also provided on demand. To obtain them I persuaded my longtime partner, Pete Terwilliger, to fish under the lens of my camera. With his ultralight outfit he soon produced a sixteen-inch brown and followed that with an eighteen-inch rainbow, almost as though performing a routine chore.

Pete's skill with the ultralight rig greatly surpasses mine, and closely approaches wizardry. Yet I'm sure that he would be the first to credit the little spinning outfit for a large part of his on-call success, his own expertise notwithstanding.

This hefty rainbow came to net only after a long battle against wispy rod and two-pound test line.

In addition to providing the worm and bait fisherman with a trout-taking means of unprecedented deadliness, the ultralight spinning outfit does much to supply the delicacy and refinement whose lack is deplored by those who take a condescending view of worm fishing. Accurate casting of the almost weightless bait calls for skill and timing, and when the fragile rig is pitted against a fish of substantial size, the ensuing fray is a cliff-hanger from start to finish. The fly-rod user can always release line instantly, whenever the breaking strength of his leader is threatened, but the spinning reel commits the fisherman to the drag tension which he has elected to apply in advance. If he tightens the drag in order to gain line, as he is often obliged to do, the line is then very likely to break if the fish makes a sudden dash. In my opinion, playing a fish to the net on an ultralight spinning rig is at least twice as difficult and uncertain as landing a fish of equal size on a fly rod.

Another plus for the method is that it is conducive to the release of fish unharmed. There is truth to the charge that trout caught on worms and other bait tend to be deeply hooked, but this doesn't hold true in ultralight worm fishing. Surprisingly, most trout caught by the method are merely jaw-hooked. Consequently, the small hook does them no significant damage and allows the fisherman to release them unharmed.

Taking first things first, the ultralight rig that is to be used for upstream worm fishing should be selected with care. Its principal requirement is the ability to cast very light baits, and this ability is not necessarily reflected by the weight of the rod. A rod may weigh less than two ounces, for instance, and yet be too stiff for worm casting. The most satisfactory way of making a selection is by actual testing. Rig the rod with two-pound-test monofilament and pinch a couple of small split shot to the end of the line. If the rod will flip the twin shot a reasonable distance, it has the soft action that's needed. If not, it is too stiff.

The reel is equally important. If you are to parry the rushes of big trout against two-pound-test line, the drag must be extra smooth and it must permit fine shadings of adjustment. That it should be mechanically trustworthy goes without saying, and because of its small spool it should feature a five-to-one retrieve ratio.

The finest ultralight rods are made of graphite or bamboo, but most cost a bundle. By careful shopping, it is possible to buy one of fiberglass for much less and still come up with the needed action.

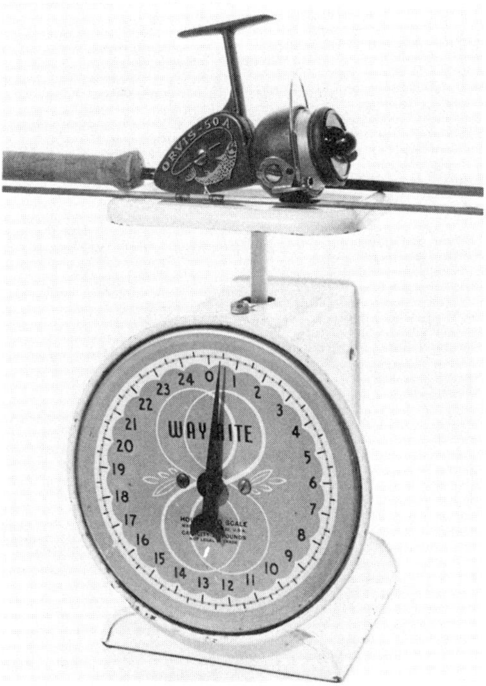

Complete outfit tips scales at less than eight ounces. Rod accounts for only two ounces of total weight.

Ultralight spinning reels are a different matter. The cheaper models are likely to let you down just when it hurts the most. The best bet is to buy the best that a reliable company offers.

Line visibility is of special importance in ultralight worm fishing, for reasons which we will soon come to. Because of this special requirement, my choice is fluorescent Stren. This line is cleverly designed to fluoresce under the ultraviolet rays which go to make up daylight, but this fluorescence ceases at the water line because the rays are filtered out by the water. The result is a line which the fisherman can see clearly, at least the portion which is above the water, but the fish can see only minimally. Other monofilament of two-pound test tends to be very difficult to follow, and against a background of broken water it is virtually invisible.

Since constant and complete line control is vital in ultralight worming, the extra visibility of Stren is a major advantage.

As I have already indicated, I tend to be overly critical in choosing hooks for bait fishing. While my choice for general bait fishing is the Mustad #3399, I prefer the Mustad #3906 for ultralight worming, the hook on which I tie most of my wet flies. The wire is a bit lighter than that of the #3399, and a tapered eye adds further refinement. Delicacy is the name of the game, so I seldom use anything larger than a No. 12, and often drop down to a No. 14.

The fine-wire Mustad #94833 approaches the ultimate in hook refinement, and it may seem to suggest itself for general ultralight use. However, I turn to it only when using extra-tiny baits such as caddis larvae and natural nymphs. The reason is that the thin wire tends to cut free during the frays with hefty fish which are one of the pleasant products of ultralighting. The normal wire of the #3906 reduces this risk—although it is by no means infallible, as we have already seen—and I prefer it wherever its slightly greater bulk is not a significant factor.

Prior to my introduction to ultralight worm fishing, I was resigned to the conclusion that bait fishing for trout became a poor bet after hot weather had set in and water levels had dropped drastically. This period, "hot-weather fishing," is traditionally regarded as a time when only the tiniest dry flies, extra-long leaders, and the finest of tippets can be expected to produce. This belief is essentially correct—with respect to fly fishing. Even then, with refinement approaching the vanishing point, a fisherman usually does well to creel two or three trout over an evening's fishing.

It is also true that the conventional worm fisherman finds everything against him at this time of year. High water temperatures make the trout listless and dull their appetite. Low, clear water provides a context in which the artificial aspects of a baited hook become glaringly conspicuous to the fish. But the resulting high incidence of refusal, often overwhelmingly complete, does not mean that trout subsist only on the few tiny mayflies which hatch, or that they have lost interest in other items of natural food.

The stomach contents of the few trout that *are* caught during this difficult period show clearly that the trout are still interested in food—if it is served properly. Dissection reveals the presence of the usual variety of nymphs, larvae, beetles, ants, etc. But because hunger isn't acute in the warmer water, the trout tend to be especially critical. In other words, the major change has been a sharp tightening of the standards of presentation which will win acceptance.

The truth of this circumstance is evident from the fact that the nymph fisherman who knows his business is not nearly as disadvantaged by hot weather and low water as are the dry-fly fisherman and the conventional worm fisherman. His continued success hints strongly of the ultralight rig's late-season potential. If low-water trout can be fooled by a dragless artificial nymph, it stands to reason that they will also take a worm—if it can be presented delicately and convincingly. The ultralight spinning outfit makes such presentation possible!

Pete Terwilliger, the partner whom I have already introduced, shares my special affection for dry-fly fishing. He also shares my viewpoint that the purpose of fishing is to catch fish. If anything, his dedication to the proposition is even stronger than mine.

Consequently, before spin-fly combination outfits were available, Pete often approached a stream carrying two rigs: a fly rod for preferred use whenever feasible, and an ultralight spinning rig as a backup. He was so armed on an afternoon when we fished together several years ago. It was August, and the water was warm, low, and clear.

When we reached the stream, Pete lay the spinning rig and a worm-filled bait box on a flat rock, and then set off downstream carrying the fly rod. He planned to fish back upstream with a dry fly after moving downriver a few hundred yards. I began fishing upstream immediately, also with a dry fly.

No flies hatched, no fish showed, and my blind casting teased up no rises. Finally, I gave up and dropped back downstream to check on how Pete was doing. When I came to the spinning outfit, my partner was still hidden from view by the first downstream bend.

Pete had praised the virtues of ultralight worming, but at that time I hadn't felt moved to experiment with it. Out of curiousity, I picked up the outfit. Following what I knew to be Pete's recommended approach, I broke a worm in half and hooked it at the broken end so that the half would trail in the current. A single split shot was already clamped to the line.

I flicked the half of worm upstream, closed the bail, and began winding in line to keep pace with the current. The line came

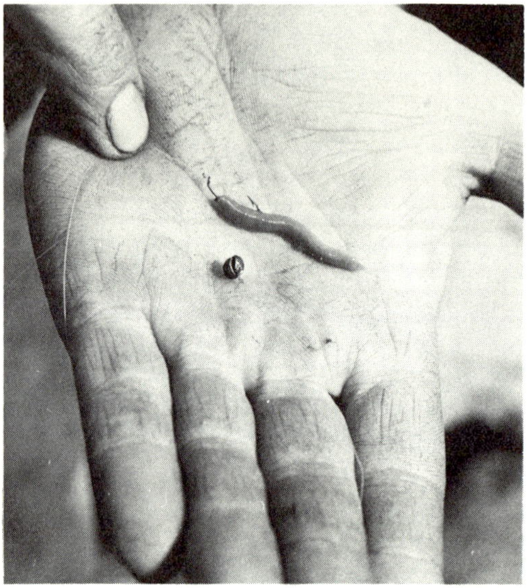

Manner of hooking worm section is important. Pete shows method on which he relies for most fetching presentation.

opposite me, and I held the rod high to maintain line control. Suddenly the line checked.

I remembered Pete's warning that unless the hook was set almost instantly, striking fish would be gone. I acted accordingly, and made instant contact. A fine, foot-long rainbow shot into the air, then raced downstream in a run which buzzed long yardage from the little reel. When I finally brought the fish to the net, I noted that it was merely hooked in the jaw, exactly as though taken on a dry fly. Without lifting the rainbow from the water, I tweaked the No. 12 hook from its jaw. A backhand flirt of the net gave the trout its freedom. I felt that the pin-pricked fish would promptly be as good as new.

Pete soon joined me. He, too, was both fishless and strikeless. Against our twin failures, the deadliness of the ultralight rig stood out in bold relief. Each of us had cast dry flies for at least a half-hour without the hint of success. Yet it had taken only a single cast with the little spinning rod to produce a foot-long rainbow!

My friend Pete has not been the only fisherman on the local scene to adopt the ultralight spinning rig for bait fishing. Our town clerk, a young trout-fishing wizard by the name of Gordon DeLong, does all of his trout fishing via the ultralight route. A natural-born trout fisherman, he has utilized the method's unique virtues to hone his inherent expertise to a state of near-genius. Other local trout fishermen look on him as a breed apart. "Gordon DeLong? That guy is something else," they say. "He can even catch trout where they *ain't!*"

I have picked Gordon's brains at some length on the subject of ultralight bait fishing. Because he fishes to catch trout, but not necessarily to kill them, he has been quick to point out that trout caught by this method are usually lightly hooked and can be released unharmed.

"Lots of times, on Furnace Brook, I have put back twenty or thirty trout without harming any of them," he told me. "It's like fly fishing in that respect."

Like Pete, Gordon has found that half a worm is usually better than a whole one. When conditions become stringently demanding, they reduce the half to a mere pinch.

"I fish whole worms in the spring," Gordon told me, "but I use only a small piece when the water gets low and clear and the trout are really fussy. Seems to work better."

My experience has confirmed this opinion. Neither of my two authorities has ventured a reason, but there must be one.

Food items tend to become smaller as the season advances. Hatches are of tiny mayflies, and the slackened current no longer brings the more substantial articles of forage common to springtime water levels. If my guess is correct, trout adjust accordingly. As soon as the larger items become anomalous, the aversion to all that departs from the norm asserts itself. Items which are foreign to low-water conditions are therefore regarded with suspicion, even though the same items are snapped up eagerly in season. By August, when trout fare has been reduced largely to small tidbits, their tolerance adjusts to embrace only those items which fall into that category.

If this sounds farfetched, it is because my repeated references to a trout's inborn aversion to anomaly have failed to convince. It may seem illogical to insist that a trout will refuse a whole worm, yet will snap up a tiny piece of the same. Yet I can report from experience, and from the testimony of two fishermen of much greater expertise, that a little dab will do it when the whole thing will go begging. A mere fragment of worm is an anomaly in one sense, of course, but in this instance it is also a conformity, and thus acceptable. (I'll have more to say about this in the next few pages.)

The mechanics of ultralight worm fishing, like those of so many other unobtrusive arts, are simple but subtle. Simple, for all that's needed for starters is an upstream cast, and once a feel for the ultralight outfit has been acquired, casting is just that. Subtlety enters the picture the instant the worm starts drifting back toward the fisherman.

Line control is of the essence. If too much slack accumulates, bites will go unnoticed. Or, if they are detected, the slack will make it impossible to set the hook at the instant the bites occur. If the line is reeled at too fast a pace, this will affect the worm's behavior and thwart the goal of a free and dragless drift. It is here that the high visibility of fluorescent Stren is such a boon.

Guiding the worm through each drift is more nearly a "nursing" process than anything else. I have stressed the need to have the worm tumble along the bottom, but this incurs constant risk of snagging. The preventive, or at least partially so, consists of reeling to match the pace of the current as exactly as possible and of giving the rod light tosses repeatedly. The tosses serve to keep the worm dapping along the bottom, rather than dragging over it, but do not seriously affect the illusion of free drift.

It is best to stop reeling as the worm draws opposite. Slack is best controlled at this point by raising the rod high as the worm drifts by, and then lowering it to gain extra drift after it has passed. The prolongation sometimes accounts for fish that wouldn't have been taken had the slack been reeled in completely with the effect of terminating the drift at a point directly opposite the fisherman.

I have pointed out the necessity of setting the hook the instant the line checks from a strike. This is an interesting feature of ultralight worming, one which does not seem to follow and which seems worthy of speculation.

The worm fisherman's first response to the bite of a trout is usually to "let him have it"—give the biting fish time to take the bait well into its mouth. This simply won't work in ultralight worming, although there may seem every reason to believe that a trout would tend to retain a piece of worm, once it had grabbed it. Instead, a biting trout is usually gone in a flash unless the fisherman sets the hook instantly. It ejects the tiny bait as speedily as trout eject the dry fly to which they have risen.

I haven't been able to deduce a thoroughly satisfactory explanation, but I can vouch for the phenomenon's reality. Since it does occur, and since there must be a reason, I have tried to find a logical answer. The best I can submit is the following.

Trout either rise to a dry fly with complete confidence or they don't rise at all. They rise because deception has been complete; they would refuse the fly if they had the slightest doubt that it was anything but an actual mayfly. Their attitude toward the drifting piece of worm is quite possibly identical. It behaves so naturally (when all goes well!) that it arouses no suspicion, and it is taken in the absence of reservations.

In each case, an awareness of irregularity registers the instant contact is made. Since it was totally unanticipated, it comes as a shock, and the fly or baited hook is instantly ejected. I have no way of telling if I have actually hit on the truth, but at least I have the small satisfaction of thinking that *possibly* I have.

At any rate, the check of the line resulting from a bite must be acted upon instantly, otherwise the trout will be long gone. This, like the other unique features of ultralight worming, places the method in a separate category and adds to its challenge.

I have pointed out the special help which Stren provides in maintaining proper line control. But even with the aid of this remarkable line I'm no match for Pete at the task. He is blessed with vision which enables him to see with the naked eye almost as well as I see with the help of a binocular. To help me follow the line in fast water, I have experimented with the tiniest bobbers I can find. Not only do these help me to follow the course of my drifting bait, but I believe that they enhance the quality of the drift wherever conditions are suitable for their use.

I do not recommend the use of a bobber in quiet , shallow water. The splash of their descent is small, but sufficient to put trout on the alert. But where the water is swifter and deeper, the bobber's slight impact on landing seems to have no adverse effect. Moreover, certain advantages become manifest.

Since the bobber furnishes sufficient weight for casting, sinkers can be eliminated. This results in an immediate advantage, for as I have stressed repeatedly, the use of a sinker is always a compromise. In all but the most violently churning currents, the sinkerless worm will hang straight down from the bobber throughout its entire drift, much as an airborne housefly maintains its relative

BOBBER SIZES USED BY AUTHOR
Always use the smallest bobber that will do the job.

position in a rapidly moving railway car. This ultimate quality of congruence is not lost on the trout. They assess it as evidence of the normality upon which they so strongly insist.

It is undoubtedly because the nearly perfect presentation of tiny bait can be achieved with its help that the ultralight rig accounts for such a high percentage of large trout. Ever in jeopardy, modern trout can grow to trophy size only by exercising a degree of self-restraint that would put an ascetic to shame. In order to reach their large size, they have had to develop an immunity to all conventional advances and temptations, and the chances are mighty slim that any individual fish of this select group will lapse sufficiently to fall for any of the offerings which it has learned to fear and which it has seen and rejected hundreds of times.

A mere dab of worm, drifting with no discernible restraint, falls in none of the familiar categories. Consequently, it is not automatically scorned as a routine measure of self-defense. Instead, it is an innovation which must be surveyed and judged on its own merits. If it appears to be completely innocuous, it may be sucked in by a three-pound brown, a brown which has long since learned to resist temptation in the forms of juicy nightcrawlers, lifelike dry flies, and enticingly provocative metal lures.

Thus, ultralight worming constitutes a double-barreled threat to big trout safety: Very small baits can be fished with exquisite realism, and these minute offerings fall outside the category of things to be rejected automatically. The field of tiny natural bait is wide open for exploration. Trial and error will sometimes turn up those which have especially powerful appeal.

A year ago, I declared war on a colony of hornets which had built a nest in my raspberry patch. The besieged insects put up a valiant defense, inflicting wounds which, if not lethal, were certainly painful. But I manfully pressed on, taking no prisoners, and finally annihilated the colony with the help of a flaming torch on the end of a long pole. When I finally removed the charred nest it was surprisingly heavy. I broke into it, and found it crammed with white, plump larvae. Always alert to exotic bait possibilities, I transferred the larvae to a large coffee can, clamped on the plastic cover, and tucked it in the freezer for future experimentation.

To my enormous gratification, the appeal of those hornet larvae proved to be directly proportional to the difficulties and suffering inherent in their acquisition! Because of their "secret-weapon" characteristics, I forced myself to use them sparingly in order to space out their effectiveness. Each time I used the ultralight rig I'd put a half-dozen in a plastic tube, but no more, and tuck the tube in a pocket of my fishing vest.

They would have been gone soon had I used them indiscriminately, for there were run-of-the-mill trout waiting to snap them up eagerly in every pool. Instead, I carefully reserved them for spots which suggested big trout, and even then I resorted to them only after my dab of worm had failed to bring results.

No bait or lure is surefire, but those hornet grubs came close. Wherever I could manage a good drift, through or alongside a particularly secluded retreat, lurking trout seemed very hard put to resist them. The bites I got in these selected spots generally came from larger-than-usual trout, and in a gratifying number of instances some real busters greedily gulped the juicy tidbits.

I have already indicated that the larvae of the caddis fly are another very deadly trout bait. Fortunately, they can be gathered far more easily, to say nothing of much less painfully, than can hornet grubs! By some mysterious means they encase themselves in woody material from which only their heads and short legs protrude. They anchor themselves to sunken rocks and logs, always in plain view and but thinly disguised by the sticklike appearance which results in the name "stick caddis." They can be picked up by the dozens in most trout streams of the Northeast.

To the best of my observation, stick caddis do not constitute a major item of trout diet, probably for two main reasons. First, the larvae usually cling to objects in the shallows and backwaters which trout seldom invade. Second, it seems likely that the trout take a dim view of the woody casing. Examination of stomach contents reveals that trout occasionally gulp them, case and all, but it is very rare to catch a trout whose stomach is jammed with them, as would certainly be the case if trout fed on them eagerly.

Trout indifference swaps ends instantly, however, when the larvae are shucked from their cases. Naked, they appear as tiny white grubs, a mere half-inch in length. If care is used, a single grub can be threaded on a No. 14 hook of fine wire without suffering serious disfigurement. Although they may appear to be almost too tiny to have significant appeal, they are among the most deadly of trout baits when presented with a delicacy geared to their very small size. The ultralight method is made to order for their proper presentation, and the result is an offering of devastating effectiveness.

Grasshoppers and crickets make wonderful bait in season. Their populations peak in August and September. Wherever streams wind through meadowlands, a significant number of hoppers are constantly splatting down in the streams as the result of ill-fated flights. To a lesser extent, crickets also wind up in the drink by jumping one way when they should have jumped the other. As soon as they appear regularly, trout await them hungrily, waiving their late-summer aversion to all but the minute as more substantial fare once more predominates.

Although tumbled-in grasshoppers and crickets ride the surface, it is not necessary that they float when used as bait. Once trout begin feeding on them regularly, they seem to develop an especially strong liking for both insects. Accordingly, they will gather them in avidly at almost any level, provided that they drift without serious drag.

Gordon DeLong has a photograph in his office which shows him holding an eight-pound brown trout.

"Whadja take him on?" visitors ask invariably.

Gordon delights in telling them the truth—that he caught the monster on a single salmon egg!

The inquiring visitor usually thinks that Gordon is pulling his leg, merely exercising his fisherman's right to be devious. But Gordon sees no need to employ subterfuge. In this case he can tell the unvarnished truth without fear of proselytism, for no one actually believes him. Their "common sense" tells them that no eight-pound brown would ever show interest in anything as tiny as a single salmon egg.

Any who may be inspired to take up ultralight bait fishing for trout will discover that the foregoing brand of "common sense" is usually an unreliable criterion. The old theory that "the bigger the bait, the bigger the fish" may have the ring of logic, for which reason it so often suggests itself. It has application in fishing for nothern pike, largemouth bass, and other rapacious predators, and under certain circumstances—a quick rise of water, for instance—it applies to trout fishing. But an overriding faith in big bait prompts the inverse, a belief that small items will attract only small trout. This is anything but true. The purpose of this chapter has been to make clear that one of the surest ways to go loaded for lunkers is with seemingly trivial tidbits and ultralight spinning gear.

In closing this chapter I want to make it plain that I'm not making the kind of pitch that county-fair hucksters make for their various gadgets. The ultralight outfit will perform no miracles by itself; it can be no better than the fisherman who uses it. But in the hands of those who have served honest apprenticeship, fishermen who have gained true trout-fishing insight and empathy, it is effective. It can lead, if not to miracles, to successes which often seem miraculous when compared with the results of traditional methods.

7

TROUT IN STILL WATER

IN THE PREVIOUS two chapters we have dealt with what I believe to be the most important basics of bait fishing for trout in streams. The quest for trout is not limited to streams, of course. It spills over to include lakes, ponds, beaver flowages, spring holes, and bogs. Here the water is motionless, save for the waves which may exist at the surface, with no shifting currents to contend with in striving for natural presentation.

Seemingly, the lack of current should simplify the problem of innocent presentation, but the truth is that it tends to complicate it. The trout of quiet waters can afford to be deliberate. They don't have to make snap judgments about items which appear suddenly, borne by swift currents, and which must be snapped up quickly if they are to be gathered in at all. Instead, there is always time for critical study and scrutiny, and the wary trout of lakes and ponds tend to make the most of this opportunity.

Although there is no current against which to assess the bait's conformity and naturalness, you can be sure that the trout's powers of discrimination are not significantly lessened by this lack. They simply turn to other standards for a backdrop. Lake and pond fishermen soon learn that these are often even more stringent than the standards applied by stream trout. As a result, catching trout in lakes and ponds, even in those where trout are plentiful, is often exasperatingly difficult, and it sometimes borders on the impossible.

The treatment of trout, to this point, has been less than complete on yet another front. Care has been taken to picture trout as elusive creatures which can be caught only by satisfying their exceedingly discriminating sensitivities. It is a true picture, up to a point, for this innate shyness, with its accompanying aversion to all that is strange, is the principal obstacle which the trout fisherman must overcome.

Yet there is another side to trout nature, more recessive than dominant, but nevertheless present. It is surprising, almost to the point of paradox, for it is the antithesis of the furtiveness which dominates throughout trout behavior. The following incident, lifted from early experience, illustrates a moment of its extreme manifestation.

When I was very young, and sadly lacking in all but enthusiasm, I haunted a small brook with unflagging design on the brookies which it held. Although I fished with enraptured determination, it was with guileless dependency on luck. I fished for trout much as I "fished" blindly for cardboard fish in the toy fish ponds much in evidence in those days and to which I often fell heir at Christmas and on birthdays. I innocently assumed that there was little I could do to engineer success beyond dropping my baited hook in the water, and I acted accordingly.

One day, as I boldly approached the head of a pool, I spotted a trout which I knew was at least an eight-incher, an in-context whopper which set my pulse to racing. The trout lay motionless, save for the gentle finning required to hold its position in the gentle current. I'm certain that it saw me as plainly as I saw it. Yet for some unknown reason it didn't turn tail and flee.

I proffered my worm-baited hook. The current nudged it along the gravel bottom until it was within inches of the trout's nose. Quite understandably, the trout refused to have anything to do with it. Less understandably, it still failed to take flight. I retrieved the bait and offered it again. Again, no soap. Repeated submissions yielded the same disappointing results. It was an obvious standoff.

Finally, in exasperation, I aimed the tip of my battered steel rod at the trout and jabbed at it savagely as though the rod were a lance. The jab startled the trout, thereby carrying out my spiteful intent, but it also imparted sudden action to the worm-baited hook lying on the bottom. The trout dodged the thrust, and then be damned if it didn't dart in and grab the suddenly activated worm! I swung the rod aloft with a whoop of triumph and arced the solidly hooked trout far back into the puckerbrush!

NIGHTCRAWLER ON HOOK

Despite the common practice of hooking worms through the "collar," I prefer hooking at midpoint. In my opinion, it permits slightly better presentation and results in surer hooking.

The episode has stuck in my mind ever since, a reminder of that no-man's land which lies between truth's ostensible and actual limits. Until that time I had come to accept trout shyness as an unvarying characteristic. Suddenly, I had been served dramatic notice that beneath their inherent shyness lay the ingredients of excitability and belligerence! Did they exist in all trout, I wondered, or was the one in which I had provoked their display an exception?

I soon discovered that the same latent tendencies did exist in all trout, and not just the one. The discovery came about inadvertently, precisely as empathy with the outdoors is gained by kids who are free to roam the woods and to explore the streams.

A small river ran through town, and one of its deepest pools served as a swimming hole. One side was of gently sloping sand, providing safe wading for tads and other nonswimmers. The opposite shore was a sheer cliff, and the water at the base was eight or ten feet deep. Niches in the cliff provided diving platforms of varying elevations sufficient to accommodate the different degrees of daring and foolhardiness possessed by older swimmers.

High above the deepest part of the pool was a shelf which had long served as the ultimate test of bravado. Within the rather short span of my memory, only one lad had dared to take the death-defying plunge. He had gone off to college shortly thereafter, and thence to the obscurity of adulthood. Needless to say, however, the echoes of his heroism lingered after him, evoking the grudging admiration accorded those whose feats are of such daring that they discourage emulation.

Early one morning, purely by dint of aimless roaming, I found myself on the high shelf. Although my belly squirmed as though inhabited by eels at the very thought, I pretended to wonder if eventually I would gain sufficient courage to take the dive and thereby win the same lasting fame. The speculation brought me little comfort, for I knew in my heart that it was pure sham. No incentive, then or later, could neutralize the horrible dread which the mere thought of doing any such thing aroused.

I abandoned that disturbing train of thought and transferred my attention to the water below me. How clear it was! I could see every detail of the bottom, even though I knew the water to be nearly a dozen feet deep at that particular point. As though to affirm the depth, I picked up a thin wafer of shale and dropped it into the pool. Its prolonged, fluttering descent was attesting to the depth eloquently when the twinkling bit of shale suddenly became the center of an attack launched by a huge rainbow trout, a leviathan which had come from nowhere to flash green, silver, and pink in the clear, clear water. The big rainbow proceeded to circle the fluttering chip in a series of lightning-fast swirls and thrusts, much in the manner of a terrier harassing quarry brought to bay.

The trout's clear show of belligerence came as an incredible shock. As I stared in amazement, it darted in and grabbed the pulsating scrap of shale, only to release it. Yet when the released flake resumed its erratic descent, the reborn action excited the big trout anew, and it once more took up its swirling attack. Twice more it dashed in and grabbed the shale before the thin piece of rock finally reached the bottom.

The incident forced me to revise previously formed convictions. I had goaded one trout into taking my bait by jabbing at it deliberately. Now I had aroused another to a state of atypical rashness by an equally unlikely means. Clearly, trout could be stirred to aggression by subjecting them to unorthodox stimuli!

The discovery haunted me, for it fairly begged exploitation. Yet I was stymied, by the lack of appropriate means and by the lack of sufficient ingenuity to devise any.

Long in advance of the availability of spinning tackle, I had stumbled on that unique vulnerability in trout which the spinning outfit would eventually exploit. It excites me, even now, to speculate on the probable results had I been equipped to offer that big rainbow a trout-size spoon or wobbler!

When spinning was first introduced in this country, shortly after the end of World War II, trout seemed hard pressed to resist the innovative little metal lures which danced and darted so provocatively. They proved to be so deadly, in fact, that many feared that their continued use would be the ruination of trout fishing. Although the fear seemed warranted at the time, it failed to take into account the well-demonstrated ability of trout to tighten their defenses against new angling threats as they evolve.

Like many other trout fishermen, I made some fantastic catches of trout when I first began using spinning hardware, but the "slaughter" was of short duration. Trout soon made the necessary defensive adjustments, and spinning lures promptly lost their special effectiveness. Nowadays, the small spoons and wobblers which created such havoc initially have become lures of dubious worth. Their widespread use, often less than inspired, has educated trout almost to the point of categorical refusal.

Yet a latent excitability reposes beneath the sense of caution which dominates trout nature, and it remains open to appeal. Where trout have become almost prohibitively critical of ploys geared to conformity, they can sometimes be taken by discreet exploitation of this dormant characteristic. This brings us back to lake and pond fishing, and to trout which are all but immune to the best efforts of the most skilled bait fisherman.

The metal spinner undoubtedly owes its creation to one who witnessed, as I did, the fascination which a fluttering object holds for trout and other fish. This observer, unlike me, had the ingenuity to put what he had seen to practical use. The spoon and the wobbler must have been similarly inspired.

While all three are more alike than different, spoons and wobblers are complete lures by themselves. Certain spinners fall in this category, too, but spinners are more commonly used as attractors, employed in combination with separate lures and especially with natural baits.

The effectiveness of spoons and wobblers in trout fishing usually is the inverse of the degree to which trout have been exposed to them. I know from heady experience that they are peerless killers when used among the unsophisticated brook trout, ouananiche, arctic char, and lake trout of virginal subarctic waters. But as I have already related, I have observed the rapid diminution of their effectiveness which occurs with their repeated use. Their appeal is directed to what must be regarded as an oddity of trout nature, a quirk which runs contrary to a much stronger sense of caution. While the novelty of first exposure to flashing spoons and wobblers may provoke indiscretion, stronger instincts quickly reduce the incidence of imprudence whenever exposure becomes repetitive and poses a serious threat to survival.

Although the spinner is also used to arouse interest and capture attention, its pitch to trout excitability is more moderate and less direct. This is evident from the fact that while trout will strike a spoon or wobbler, they strike an unadorned spinner much less frequently.

The chief virtue of the spinner lies in the fact that trout will come from a distance to *inspect* it. They are aroused and excited by the whirling blade, but not sufficiently to strike it directly. Nevertheless, the excitement is sufficient to cause their normal sense of caution to lapse momentarily, and if the spinner is trailed by a nightcrawler or minnow they may be sufficiently moved toward rashness to dart in and grab it.

As I have already confessed, I am by no means a purist despite the fact that I'm an ardent dry-fly fisherman. Consequently, as in all my fishing, I strive to broaden the base of my trout fishing, rather than try to effect its convergence at some point of special preference. In this attempt I have done considerable experimenting with "hardware" and bait combinations, particularly in recent years. My findings have been profitable. I have discovered that by combining spinner and bait it is possible to fish productively, the goal I set above all others, in lakes and ponds where other methods tend to go begging.

SPINNER-AND-CRAWLER COMBINATION
Worm gang is shown rigged with single nightcrawler to show manner of hooking clearly. I like a single 'crawler for trout, but for walleyes and smallmouths I prefer to string on a pair. To achieve hooking shown, it is necessary to reverse hook when introducing it. In other words, direction of hooking should be toward trailing tail section. When barb is drawn clear, entry point will be nearer eye of hook than point of exit. This allows 'crawler to stretch out fully when trolled. Hooking in the opposite direction creates sharp bends in bait which cause it to wad up when under way. Vary weights as depth increases or decreases.

In capitalizing on this "discovery" I have learned to assemble my own spinners, and am thus able to experiment with various designs, colors, combinations, etc. This fascinating hobby, the bait fisherman's counterpart of fly tying, will be the subject of a future chapter. Directions for creating effective trout hardware will be included therein, rather than in this chapter.

I gained my first insight of the bait-and-spinner answer to stubbornly poor trout fishing nearly twenty years ago. I was fishing Attean Lake, in Jackman, Maine, under the tutelage of a seventy-year-old guide named Walter Wilson. I stubbornly stuck to flies throughout an entire day, casting dry and wet flies at the mouths of inlets, and trolling streamers just under the surface the rest of the time. It was too late in the season for surface fly fishing, and I knew it. Yet I persisted despite my failure to stir up a single rise or strike.

Walter withheld comment until late afternoon, but at last he spoke to the subject.

"You ain't gonna catch trout on flies."

I felt an obligation to argue the contention on general principle, but I couldn't find any suitable ammunition.

"My wife hasn't had a trout to eat all season," Walter went on obliquely. "She *loves* trout," he added.

"Then we'd better catch her some," I said.

" 'Twon't be on flies," Walter warned.

"No time to stand on ceremony when a woman's starving for fish," I replied. "Tomorrow we fish for the table, any way you say."

Walter seldom allowed his emotions to show, but for once his habitual scowl lifted long enough for the hint of a triumphal grin to shine through. I felt pretty sure that his reference to his wife's love of trout had been a gambit contrived in the interest of my education, rather than a real effort to satisfy her alleged craving. Knowing Walter, I wouldn't have been surprised if his wife actually despised trout.

Walter showed up the next morning with a spinning outfit and a can of worms. He reached in his ragged knapsack and pulled out a terminal rig which consisted of a large spinner and a plastic rudder. He tied a snap swivel to the spinning line and snapped it to the rudder. He tied about a foot of monofilament behind the spinner and attached a single hook. After clamping a heavy sinker to the line, just ahead of the rudder, he draped three squirming worms on the hook.

He adjusted the outboard motor to trolling speed and made a long cast astern. Finally, he handed the rod to me.

"See that point up ahead?" he asked. "Bar runs out from it.

Spinner should just clear the bar. Likely to be a trout or two atop it."

The canoe moved slowly past the point and I readied myself for a strike. I got one, but only in the form of a couple of tentative pecks. To Walter's obvious disgust, I tried to set the hook and failed to connect.

"Yanked it away from him, dammit," my guide chided. "Shoulda told you. You feel a bite, don't yank. Trout's only pecking away at the ends of the worms. Shove the rod back toward him. Trout sees the worms slow down, he'll grab 'em good. *Then's* the time to yank!"

Walter brought the canoe around and pointed it back toward the sunken bar. The rod tip danced as the spinner and worms came over the magic spot, but this time I thrust the rod in the direction of the nipping trout. The line fell slack momentarily, but when it retightened, it was against gratifying resistance. I set the hook with a decisive yank. Some moments later, Walter scooped up a fat, beautifully colored brookie that would have weighed at least a pound. He lifted it from the net and held it high for our mutual inspection.

"That should make your wife happy," I said.

"Should *what*?" Walter asked. Obviously, my question had caught him off balance. Just as I had suspected, his wife's love of trout, if indeed it actually existed, was a matter for which he had little immediate concern.

"Whaddya mean?" I demanded. "You told me your wife *loved* trout. I merely said that she oughta like that one."

"Oh, yeah, yeah," Walter agreed, finally remembering his original ploy. "But let's we catch her some more. For a woman she has a helluva big appetite!"

"Catching her some more" involved nothing more demanding than recrossing the bar repeatedly and yanking at the right time. When our catch neared the legal limit, I voiced the opinion that we had fulfilled our obligation to Mrs. Wilson's yearning for the taste of trout, and Walter could do little but agree.

I was impressed by Walter Wilson's easy solution for the hot-weather doldrums, but at the time I felt uneasy concerning its acceptability. I was more snobbishly inclined in those days. My desire to catch trout often played second fiddle to the fear that I would somehow lose status if I let practicality take priority over purism. Only when I matured sufficiently to fish to catch fish, and to hell with decorum or protocol, did I finally cash in on the lesson taught me many years ago.

When I set out to fish a lake or pond for trout nowadays, I go equipped with a fly rod and a supply of dry flies, wet flies, and streamers. If trout are showing at the surface, I rejoice and lay about me with the dry flies. If the surface layer is still cold, and it is reasonable to expect trout near the top, I give the wet flies and streamers their chance when no trout are rising. But I also go prepared to go down after them with spinner and worms whenever fly fishing proves to be all but hopeless. Walter Wilson's method works as well now as it did that day when we allegedly fished to feed his wife, and I like to think that I have even improved on it a bit.

Walter depended on his lifelong familiarity with the lakes of his region to lead him to the spots most likely to hold trout. I'm not that well acquainted with many of the lakes I fish, so I rely on a little hand-held depth finder to tip me off to the reefs, bars, dropoffs, and other irregularities that suggest the presence of trout. The instrument is not sensitive enough to spot individual fish, but by laying bare the contours of the bottom it remedies the blindness which otherwise is often a frustrating element in trolling. Instead of hit-or-miss probing, potential hot spots can be located and then concentrated on.

Hot-weather trout almost always lie well below the surface, and getting a worm-and-spinner combination down to them always exacts a compromise. The necessary weight combines with water resistance to make trolling less than pleasant. Worse, the same factors hamper fish that are hooked and thus detract from the fun of playing and landing them.

A fairly recent innovation, the downrigger, solves both problems, and it will be discussed in a chapter dealing with technological advances. It is highly specialized gear, however, and I doubt that more than a minority—the most serious devotees of deep trolling—will go to the expense and trouble of owning and operating it. What follows are ways in which the majority can minimize the unpleasant effects of conventional deep trolling.

I have found that small spinners are sufficient to attract trout. If maximum flash and glitter are needed, several small spinners in tandem will provide it without creating as much drag as a single large blade. Use of the small spinners reduces the danger of line twist. This eliminates the need for a rudder, and thus cuts down resistance further. I merely tie a snap swivel to the end of my line or leader and attach this directly to the eye of the spinner.

One way of getting worm and spinner down to the trout-holding level is with the same terminal rig used to bump bottom for walleyes. This rig consists of a thirty-inch "lead" or leader, an eight-inch dropper, a bell sinker, and a three-way swivel. Tie the dropper to one of the swivel's three stations or eyes. Tie a snap swivel to the end of the dropper and engage the bell sinker with the snap. Tie the thirty-inch lead to a second station of the swivel. (Dropper and lead should be eight- or ten-pound-test monofilament.) Attach a snap swivel at the end and hook this to the spinner. The spinner can be rigged with a single hook or a two- or three-hook worm gang. Finally, connect trolling line and troll by means of a third snap swivel tied to the end of the line. When this rig is trolled, the bell sinker drags the combination down, while the spinner and worm trail behind, a little higher than the sinker. Depth is controlled by sinker weight, the length of line that is trolled, the nature of the spinner, and the speed of the boat. Obviously, sinker weight should be no greater than is required to get the spinner and worm down to the proper depth—at normal trolling speed and when using a reasonable (manageable) length of line.

The foregoing is a very efficient combination, but the concentration of weight near the spinner and worm creates a drag on the rod. If trout are on the small side—a foot long or less—the sinker will place them at an added disadvantage when they are hooked.

Trolling can be made pleasanter, and fish allowed to give better accounts of themselves, if a lead-core line is used. If the choice of line is one of eighteen-pound test, the diameter will be small enough so that enough for most trout trolling can be wound on the spool of a large fly reel, and its weight and drag are slight enough to permit the use of a fly rod. The line should be rigged with a fairly long leader of monofilament. (I like to use at least ten feet.) Tie leader to line with a nail knot (tying instructions are given in a later chapter) so that the connection will slide easily through the guides when landing fish.

Lead-core lines are given contrasting colors over each ten yards of their length. Finding the "number of colors" necessary to take the lure down where the trout are is largely a matter of trial and error. The fisherman seldom knows the exact depth at which his lure is running, but this isn't necessary. He knows all he needs to know when, for example, fish start hitting when he trolls five colors.

Trolling a lead-core line is never as pleasant as trolling an unweighted fly or spinning line, but the difference is not markedly objectionable when the light-test line is used. The small diameter holds friction to a minimum, and weight becomes a less significant factor by virtue of its distribution over the entire line.

I am an inveterate tinkerer and experimenter, and I have hit on a way of deep trolling which exacts even less compromise. This involves the extremely fine stainless-steel wire which orthodontists use. This wire has a breaking strength of around eight pounds and "mikes" only a hundredth of an inch in diameter. Enough can be wound on an ordinary fly reel to reach the bottom of the Grand Canyon, or so it seemed from the number of turns it took to fill the spool of one of my fly reels.

I carry this wire-filled reel in my kit as a back-up to my fly-fishing aspirations. It has meant the difference between a good catch and a skunking on many occasions, days when soaring temperatures had driven trout and salmon to depths quite beyond the reach of conventional lines.

In the foregoing I have used the term "deep trolling" rather loosely, for it would be more accurate to refer to *relatively* deep trolling. Trout go only deep enough to reach conditions that are to their liking, usually far short of the extreme depths of the lakes in which they live. In fact, they usually avoid the latter because of their lack of sufficient oxygen.

Each spring, northern trout lakes "turn over." Water reaches its maximum density at forty degrees Fahrenheit, and as the surface layer warms to this temperature it sinks accordingly. It is replaced by colder water, which warms and sinks in turn. The process continues until the water, from top to bottom, stands at forty degrees.

From then on, the water at the top warms in accordance with the weather, soon soaring well above the temperatures which trout and salmon can tolerate. The bottom layer remains at the forty-degree level, and it tends to stagnate. Sandwiched between the two layers is a relatively thin layer in which the temperature drops sharply with each foot of descent, but which, at the same time, contains the oxygen that trout and salmon require. This layer is called the thermocline, a fact of considerable unimportance to almost everybody. It is this layer which holds the trout, however, and that is of *great* importance to hot-weather trout fishermen.

The depth of the thermocline may vary from lake to lake, but it is within fairly easy reach in most, usually no more than twenty-five or thirty feet beneath the surface. Consequently, it is seldom necessary to go much deeper in most lakes to take trout and land-locked salmon during hot weather. Lake trout tend to be a different proposition, sinking to considerably greater depths in search of the lower temperatures they require.

It is important to realize that trout do not simply spread out over the entire thermocline. Instead, they congregate at favored spots. These spots are usually those places where the bottom either pushes up into the thermocline, or drops sharply into it. These sites—bars, reefs, sunken islands, and drop-offs—are the hiding and breeding places of baitfish, insects, and crustaceans, and trout and other fish are attracted by the pleasant combination of food and comfortable temperatures. My old guide Walter Wilson may not have known this in so many words, but he sure as the devil knew it from experience, which is "knowing" in the preferred way when it comes to catching fish.

While I prefer to troll flies, wobblers, and spoons at a fairly fast clip, the spinner-and-worm combination should be trolled very slowly. Barely enough speed to make the spinner blade revolve is sufficient and best. It is important to understand the goal: to combine the spinner's power to attract and excite with the worm's appeal as food. A rapidly moving spinner will attract and excite, but the trailing worm will be avoided if it is zipping along at excessive speed. Strikes come only when the spinner's influence and the worm's natural appeal strike a balance which falls within the limits of trout tolerance.

I have concentrated intentionally on lake and pond trout fishing when it is most difficult, for it is at this stage that special measures are called for. The coin has its bright side, however, for during the early part of the season the trout of still waters respond well to worms and other natural baits.

This happier phase of lake and pond fishing warrants little added discussion or comment, for it is nothing more than a projection of the small techniques and ploys which I have recommended in fishing for panfish. Simply do all the same things, only do them much more carefully and with maximum regard for small details.

All natural baits can be used successfully—worms, grubs, minnows, etc.—but it is wise to keep all baits small and fish them as delicately as possible. Take special pains to keep sinker weight to a minimum, and use no sinker at all whenever feasible. The greater flexibility of light leaders and light monofilament lines helps to effect a more natural presentation, and this is especially important in winning over trout. My choice for lake and pond bait fishing is four-pound test. But when all is said and done, just pretend that you are fishing for perch with college degrees. You'll fool plenty of trout in May and June.

Unfortunately, the majority of vacationing fishermen take their licks at trout long after optimum conditions have come and gone. They schedule vacations for July and August, and they usually run into the difficult conditions that I have described. My purpose has been to suggest antidotes for fishing that can be frustrating otherwise. I, for one, refuse to go fishless merely because flies won't work. If a spinner-and-worm combination will put trout in the creel, as it will, I don't hesitate to resort to it. I'm betting that the majority of fishermen share my sentiments.

8

BASS

DURING EACH of the past dozen or so years I have made at least one fishing trip to Maine's West Grand Lake Region. The area is justly famed for its exceptionally fine smallmouth bass fishing and also for its equally good landlocked salmon fishing.

I try to arrive about the middle of June. If all goes well, and seasonal weather prevails, the bass will be along the shorelines and the salmon still near the surface. This circumstance affords two exotic choices: that of working the shorelines with fly-rod bugs for smallmouths and that of trolling streamers at the surface for salmon.

In my earlier days I would have concentrated on the salmon. They are rare, and thus exotic. Landlocks hit a streamer with electrifying jolts, and when hooked their dynamic leaps and lightning-fast dashes are incomparably spectacular. Rounding out their glamour is their beauty—sleek, streamlined, and silvery, each color and contour a badge of aristocracy.

By first-glance comparison, the smallmouth seems bound to the peasantry, a rough, muscle-bound commoner. Yet long association with both now impels me to rank them as equals. Whatever the smallmouth may lack in explosive verve and physical beauty, it makes up in sheer brute strength and extraordinary endurance.

The landlock strives for freedom, and often wins it, by sheer razzle-dazzle. The smallmouth is capable of dishing out the same, but it relies to a much greater degree on unembellished power. Its command of the latter approaches the unbelievable, as each and every three- and four-pounder promptly demonstrates when hooked. Whenever it gains solid leverage against restraining tackle, whether by happenstance or angling incompetence, something usually busts!

During one of my earlier visits to the West Grand Lake Region, I fished the Grand Falls Flowage of the St. Croix River, under the guidance of Val Moore. The Flowage results from a dam which floods many acres of what once was north-country wilderness, and it is still studded by the stumps and weathered skeletons of water-killed spruce, pine, and cedar trees. Rafted driftwood, "dry-ki" in northern terminology, chokes the coves and lies along the shorelines. The bottom is jackstrawed by more of the same, which has become waterlogged. It constitutes a context in which smallmouths not only flourish, but in which they enjoy a major advantage when hooked.

Out of respect for the many sunken snags, and also because of the presence of pickerel which were prone to chop off bass bugs, I was using a leader whose tippet tested a full fourteen pounds.

We rounded a point and Val slid the canoe within casting range of the edge of a wide apron of dry-ki. I was preparing to drop my bug along this edge when I spotted a small pocket of open water in the otherwise solid mat of driftwood. It was a made-to-order retreat for a big bass, and I worked out line preparatory to casting to the far side of the pocket. The move was logical save for a single circumstance: a large log lay across the mouth of the pocket, a seemingly prohibitive obstacle if I should hook a bass of size and substance.

As I lengthened line, Val asked the obvious question: "You hook one in there, what are you gonna do with him?"

It was an unanswerable question, but I didn't let it deter me. The bug landed in the pocket. I let it lie a moment, then gave it a twitch. A big buster of a smallmouth pounced on it savagely, almost as though it had been standing guard against any such intrusion.

I yanked the hook home, and my rod plunged as the bass sounded. But it was in the air so quickly, gills a-rattle, that it seemed as though it must have met itself coming down on its way to the surface. It then proceeded to *stay* in the air, tailwalking along the surface as only an enraged smallmouth can. As luck would have it, it "walked" toward the canoe—and right over the problem log!

"Now we've got him!" Val exulted, hurriedly sculling the canoe backward away from the driftwood and toward open water.

Alas, he spoke too soon. The bass finally dove again, and this time I felt the line fetch up solidly; the sounding bass obviously had wrapped it around one of the many sunken logs. I eased up with the rod, but no hooked bass took up slack. The line was firmly around the log, and I felt sure that the bass had used the leverage to tear free of the hook.

Val put me directly over the snag, and I took the fly line in hand and pulled straight up. It began slipping, and I retrieved it gradually. I expected to bring in my empty bug, along with line and leader, but the bug was long gone. That smallmouth, a fish which weighed four pounds at the most, had had the strength to break a fourteen-pound-test leader, once it got a solid pull against it!

Although I was amazed, I really shouldn't have been. I had witnessed similar shows of smallmouth strength, beginning when I was a kid.

My uncle owned a farm which bordered the Connecticut River, and when I was of grammar-school age I often spent weekends at his farm. He was no fisherman, but he kept a long cane pole under the corn barn for my personal use.

The river held a variety of fish, ranging from fallfish, despised for their abundance and their pin-cushion boniness, to smallmouths, which were accorded top priority and among which existed some veritable giants.

On one memorable trip to the nearby river, an eight-inch fallfish grabbed my worm-baited hook the instant I lowered it. Instead of tossing it back in disgust as usual, I was seized by inspiration. I removed the hook from the fallfish's mouth and slid the point under the skin of the back, just ahead of the dorsal fin.

A few yards upstream, a huge granite boulder jutted into the river, breaking the current and forming an eddy on its downstream side. I moved to a position opposite the boulder and carefully lowered the still-lively fallfish into the pocket, reaching out as far as possible with the cane pole.

The line promptly began moving off to one side, and my first impression was that it was being towed by the big bait. But when the line tightened against the cane pole, the tip was inexorably drawn after it. I waited until the tip touched the water, and then gave a mighty heave.

One of the biggest bass I have ever seen instantly flung itself high into the air, its indignation so evident as to be almost palpable. It fell back with a mighty splash, then sounded with the same show of outrage that it had displayed in leaping. I applied all the upward pressure I could command, and the bass did the same but in the opposite direction. The weathered cane pole quickly took on a strain which far exceeded its endurance, and after a few audible and ominous groans of protest it shattered to a broomtail of splinters at its midpoint.

I had spiraled the line back toward the butt as a precaution against just such an emergency, but to no avail. The snubbed line could no more stand the terrific strain than could the pole, and it broke with a demoralizing "tunk" as soon as the bass bulled directly against it. The effect was shattering, almost as though that huge smallmouth had risen up and smashed my tackle just to put me in my place.

Smallmouths stand ever ready to do the same for anybody rash enough to employ stiff-hitch methods in trying to subdue them. Only a policy of give and take will succeed when they are hooked on conventional tackle. It is largely because of this extraordinary fighting ability that I divide my time equally between bass and salmon when I fish in the West Grand Lake Region. The two species have few characteristics in common, but each, in its own way, is a superb game fish.

Bass differ from trout in the same ways in which they differ from landlocked salmon, and these differences must be taken into account when fishing for them. As has been stressed in the preceding chapters, the chief problem in trout fishing is that of convincing the quarry that all is kosher, down to the smallest detail and to the nth degree. While it is true that trout can be provoked to moments of rashness and belligerence, this is the exception rather than the rule. As a result, a provocative approach must follow a thin line or it is likely to frighten far more trout than it excites and arouses.

It would be stretching things to say that bass behavior is precisely the opposite of that of trout, but it is true to a significant degree. Where trout are inherently poised for flight at the introduction of anomaly, without pause for study or reflection, bass do not seem to have the same instinctive fear of all that is abnormal. This doesn't mean that they aren't alert to all obvious signs of danger, but they tend to be more tolerant of mere deviations from the norm. Trout are programmed to retreat at the least show of oddity; bass tend to size up the pros and cons of a new circumstance or situation before deciding what to do about it. They are very shrewd, indeed, but they are not deterred by some slight show of artificiality—the aspect of "drag" to which trout are sensitively attuned, for example—in a desirable item which is judged to be intrinsically harmless.

A recent Lake Champlain incident serves to illustrate this basic difference between bass and trout temperaments. Mike and I were fishing with nightcrawlers and minnows for anything that would bite. When our first choice of location failed to produce, we moved on to another. I guided the boat into a small cove while Mike stood ready to drop anchor.

Suddenly, about fifty feet ahead of the boat, a fish made a shambles of the calm surface. I would have given a pretty to have had a surface plug ready to drop among the widening rings, but I didn't —and time was of the essence. One of my spinning rods was rigged with bobber and minnow, and I had placed the hooked minnow in the bait bucket to keep it alive while we changed places. As quickly as I could, I grabbed the rod and let ding with what seemed to be an outlandishly inappropriate offering.

Minnow, bobber, and sinker splashed down with what appeared to be a prohibitive commotion. But the bobber had scarcely righted itself when it was rudely yanked under and went streaking off to the side. I wasted no time in setting the hook in what proved to be a smallmouth which weighed a bit better than three pounds.

Had the rising fish been a trout, even one of equal size or greater, the effect of the violent and unexpected descent of any such ill-matched conglomeration would have been nerve-shattering. The trout would have streaked away in frenzied flight, and probably would have lost all interest in food for hours. The hungry bass had obviously responded quite differently. It waived the implications of the minnow's unorthodox appearance on the scene, and acted on the theory that minnows are innocuous by definition.

The basic differences between bass and trout undoubtedly stem from the fact that trout rank as "primitive" on the evolutionary scale, while bass are rated as "advanced" species. The ratings have nothing to do with fighting ability, beauty, food value, or any of the other standards by which fishermen judge game fish. Instead, the term "advanced" relates to evolutionary gains which facilitate survival under present-day environmental conditions. Most of these gains have been physical. In bass, for example, they include a protective armor of heavy scales, sharp fin spines, and the ability to tolerate relatively high water temperatures and degrees of impurity which would be fatal to trout. Also, at least by my fisherman's observations, bass seem to manifest an increase in what, by point-stretching, can be called intellect. I think that it is largely because of this difference in "intelligence" that trout fishing and bass fishing are such markedly different propositions.

Ironically, it is largely the trout's lack of brains that makes it so darned hard to catch. Its instinctive aversion to oddity constitutes a more impregnable defense than could be erected by conscious appraisal. On the other hand, the same lack of brains accounts for trout vulnerability.

This apparent contradiction arises from the fact that while the inherent sensitivities of trout become sharper and more discriminating with increases in fishing pressure, these changes are not accompanied by the power to deduce the deadliness of the devices used against them. Although trout may become increasingly critical of the drag of a dry fly, for example, they lack the ability to categorize the dry fly as an object to be steadfastly avoided because of its lethal properties. Instead, while they may reach the point of demanding nothing less than perfect presentation, they will *still* rise to dry flies whose behavior they judge to be flawless. It is for this reason that skilled fishermen are always able to take at least a few trout from the hardest-fished waters.

Because bass tend to act more from deduction, and less from instinct, they are usually easier to catch. The reason, of course, is that to act from "thought" is to run the risk of error. The smallmouth I used as an example "thought" that it was safe to grab the minnow despite the unorthodox manner of its arrival—and thereby committed what turned out to be a fatal mistake.

Bass would soon be extinct, of course, if they consistently acted that rashly. Fortunately for them, they do so only up to a point. Beyond that they quickly do a double take. When they do, quite unlike trout, their "reasoning" penetrates to the true source of danger—the lure itself. Therefore, excessive fishing pressure may not make bass merely *hard* to catch; it may make the cagey cusses *impossible* to catch!

While the wariest trout can still be conned by flawless presentation, "educated" bass are not to be so fooled. They "know" damned well that the *lure itself* is as deadly as a rattlesnake, and wouldn't dream of touching it under any circumstances: It is for this reason that heavily fished bass lakes are sometimes thought to be "fished out" when, in reality, they hold bass that are just too shrewd to fall for the best efforts of the best fishermen.

I once was a guest at a cottage on the shore of a heavily fished lake. A diving raft was moored offshore, and while we were sunning ourselves on it my host invited me to peer down through a crack in the planking. There, just under the surface and calmly finning away the time, were upward of a dozen enormous smallmouths. They had lived there all summer, my friend told me.

It is illustrative of bass boldness that the daily swimming and diving obviously gave them no cause for concern. In their unique "wisdom" they had it doped out that human presence was not, in itself, a threat to their safety. This shrewdness was further demonstrated by the fact that while those bass had no fear of humans per se, not one throughout the entire summer was known to have made a pass at any of the lures flung daily by a veritable armada of bass fishermen. The bass weren't merely critical of the lures; *they "knew" full well what they were!* They were no more likely to be taken in by any of them than a sophisticated New Yorker would fall for an offer to buy the Brooklyn Bridge.

Fortunately for fishermen, bass reach a stage of immunity only when fishing pressure is extremely excessive, usually in small lakes where heavy fishing results in complete and continuous coverage. Under average conditions they learn caution, but they remain catchable. They can be provoked to indiscretion by tantalizing lure action, and their appetite can be appealed to successfully by the use of tempting baits.

With respect to the latter, I think that it is correct to say that bass are easier to catch on bait than are trout. I have already called attention to what I believe to be the reason. A trout concerns itself with a bait's behavior and its authenticity; bass tend to demand only that the bait be the real thing.

I caught my first smallmouth, a lusty two-pounder, when I was only six years old. My tackle consisted of a cane pole, trimmed to a length I could manage, a coarse cotton line, a chunk cut from a piece of lead pipe for a sinker, and a large hook to which I looped a nightcrawler without regard for finesse. Many years passed before I caught a *trout* of two pounds, an accomplishment which required a much higher order of skill, to say nothing of far more sensitive and refined tackle.

While I felt justified in devoting much space and wordage to the subtle ins and outs of bait fishing for trout, I'm not going to pretend that comparable subtlety must be employed to catch bass on bait. In fact, successful bait fishing for bass is largely a matter of meeting two requirements. The first is to find the spots where bass hang out. The second is to have available the bait which has the greatest appeal at the time.

In order to meet these requirements it is necessary to distinguish between largemouths and smallmouths. The two species differ greatly in their choice of haunts, and markedly, if not as greatly, in the food items which they prefer.

Although largemouth bass and members of the pike tribe are miles apart in most respects, they share a liking for the same kind of retreats. Like northerns and pickerel, largemouths like the shallows where they can lie hidden among weeds and under pad beds. Where floating mats of vegetation extend outward from the shoreline for considerable distances, largemouths will often lie far back in this cover, sometimes in water only a couple of feet deep.

Largemouths find sunken weedbeds equally attractive. Here the depth is greater, usually six to ten feet. The weeds grow to a height of several feet, but do not reach the surface. The bass take cover in the weeds themselves, particularly along the fringes, where they watch for prey.

Thanks to this liking for shallows and weeds, spots that are likely to hold largemouths are comparatively easy to locate. The largemouth's special liking for shade should be taken into account. Look for them at the base of, or under, anything that casts a protective shadow: stumps, fallen trees, leafy overhangs, etc.

The smallmouth's choice of location is quite different. It seldom hides up in weeds, and is usually found over a "clean" bottom—one free of vegetation. It is attracted to gravel, and it especially likes a bottom that is jumbled with boulders. It is no stranger to shoreline shallows, but, in general, the smallmouth is to be found at considerably greater depths than those frequented by largemouths.

Both species spawn along the shorelines when water temperatures rise into the sixties, usually in late May and early June in northern states. They spawn in circular "beds" which they scoop from the bottom. Smallmouths prefer to spawn over gravel, and the brightness of their newly prepared beds makes them readily visible in clear water. The largemouth prepares its bed in the mud bottom which it generally prefers. This, coupled with the fact that largemouth water is often murky, makes largemouth spawning beds much less noticeable.

Many states now permit bass fishing during the spawning season, but usually on a fly-casting basis only, and subject to drastically reduced daily limits. It is possible to make tremendous catches of smallmouths on fly-rod poppers during this period. I have caught as many as fifty in a single day on lakes in Maine and New Hampshire. Although I hope that it is unnecessary, I hasten to add that all were released, with damage confined to their loss of dignity.

It would seem that largemouths would be equally vulnerable during their spawning period, but I have never caught them in any such numbers while they were on their beds, nor have I ever heard of others doing so. I am at a loss to explain why this should be so.

Inasmuch as bait fishing for bass is not usually permitted or undertaken until spawning is completed, the foregoing puzzle is outside our immediate concern. What should be heeded is the fact that smallmouths tend to move into greater depths, and to offshore locations, once they have spawned, while largemouths may still frequent the shorelines.

Consequently, one of my favorite largemouth fishing locations is along the edges of matted vegetation which extend outward from the shoreline, and which may cover entire coves. The greater the covered area, the more likely it is to hold bass. Such a weedy retreat invariably attracts baitfish, and is usually well populated with frogs. Crayfish thrive among the roots, while a wide variety of aquatic insects and crustaceans cling to the stems and the underside of the leaves. The "jungle" may look too tangled to hold large fish, but this is seldom the case. If the water caters to largemouths, it's a safe bet that some of the biggest will be lurking in the weedy thicket, feeding on the rich fare which it affords.

It is a mistake, one often made, to expect the lurking bass to emerge for any great distance to gather in a proffered bait, for this is contrary to their nature and opposed to the mechanics of the situation. The forage exists in the depths of the tangle, and the bass know it. Consequently, they direct their attention inward, and are not distracted by what goes on on the outside.

In the face of this circumstance, it is imperative to anchor so that the bait can be lowered at the *very edge* of the vegetation. Proximity is of the essence; largemouths will accept offerings if they are within mere inches of their retreat, but tend to refuse the same items if to gather them in they must leave their cover for only a few feet.

In this situation, patience becomes especially important. It is virtually impossible to anchor properly in such a spot without creating a disturbance whose effect will persist for a significant period. Thus, action should not be expected immediately. It will come only after things have returned to normal and your intrusion has been forgotten.

Weedbeds may appear to be a solid mat at first glance, but closer inspection will usually reveal small pockets of open water at varying distances from the edge. These are always worthy of a try, but again patience is a requirement.

Forcing the boat to one of these small pockets will disturb all the fish in the vicinity. In fact, it is likely that you will see the swirls of alarmed fish as you progress. Once you are in position to reach the small opening it is wise to wait ten minutes or so before lowering the bait. Results are often well worth the wait. The many bass that lie far back in the weeds are seldom disturbed by fishermen. Consequently, they are usually quick to grab a bait, once all commotion has died down.

My second choice of spot for largemouth bait fishing is a sunken weedbed. It will draw as many bass as do the shoreline weed mats, but it is usually harder to fish.

If I can locate a definite edge, a distinct break between vegetation and open water, I prefer to try there. It is as important to fish close to the edge here as it is when fishing alongside top-water vegetation, and for the same reasons. If I can't locate a clear-cut edge, and must fish from directly over the bed, I always try to lower my bait through the weeds until it is only a short distance above the bottom. This is usually a frustrating business, for the bait is forever tangling in the weeds. Yet it must get down to where the fish are if it is to draw bites, and almost invariably they are near bottom.

At one time or another, I have caught largemouths on many kinds of natural baits: nightcrawlers, minnows, frogs, crayfish, hellgrammites, tadpoles, grasshoppers and more. I can say the same about smallmouths, but it applies quite differently. As we shall see when we get to them, smallmouths display an ever shifting preference which covers the range of all available baits. They're likely to favor nightcrawlers one day, hellgrammites the next, and so on, never really settling on definite favorites. Largemouths differ in this respect. While they don't draw the line at anything that is edible, it is my opinion that they show a distinct preference for minnows and crayfish.

Of the two, minnows are my choice as bait. I don't think that this reflects bass sentiment, for examination of stomach contents will reveal fully as many crayfish as bait fish. But although the two may be equally attractive to bass appetites, it has been my experience that minnows will draw more bites, mainly, I suspect, because they advertise their presence and thus attract maximum attention.

A live minnow struggles constantly. Its efforts to escape are highly visible, and probably are audible as well. The crayfish's instinct is to hide, and amid weeds it often manages to do just that. Thus, while bass may like one as well as the other, the constantly pulsating minnow is far more likely to draw a hungry largemouth's attention.

What I believe to be a common mistake made in minnow fishing for largemouths is that of using bait that is too small. Although the largemouth is not equipped with the sharp teeth which so clearly mark the pike as a savage predator, a five-pounder has a mouth that can engulf a baseball, or at least looks as though it could. You may be sure that nature endowed the largemouth with its enormous maw with every intent that it be put to practical use. Fishermen tend to look on six-inch chubs and suckers as suitable bait only for northern pike, but the truth is that they are equally effective when used for largemouths.

MINNOW ON HOOK
Hook just under the skin and let barb emerge. Avoid deeper hooking, which will either kill bait or hamper movement and shorten its life. Hooking ahead of dorsal fin makes for surer hooking of the taking fish. This is especially true when largest baits are used. Also, the larger the bait, the larger should be the hook that is used.

Mike and I learned this important truth inadvertently. When we're fishing for "anything that will bite" we always hang a six-inch chub or sucker on one rod. Sometimes we fish it straight down and other times we let it tow a bobber around, depending on which we think will do the most good in the immediate situation. Originally, we hoped that the big bait would lead eventually to a tussle with a big northern, an old bruiser of a bowfin, or perhaps a fifteen-pound catfish.

The big baits produced a gratifying number of just such frays. To our surprise, however, they also accounted for unexpected set-tos with big largemouths. But it wasn't just the lunkers that went for our big suckers and chubs; run-of-the-mill two-pounders obviously preferred them to the three- and four-inch minnows which we fished at the same time.

There may be tricks of manipulation which will help persuade bass to take a big live minnow, but I know of none. I'm inclined to believe that the best bet is to put on enough sinker to drag the bait down—it may take several buckshot—and then snap on a bobber and let the minnow drag it around. I'm inclined to believe that the jigging ploy—raising the bait and letting it fall back—which works well on other species, is more likely to dissuade than persuade in this instance. It takes patience just to sit and do nothing; but when my bobber is finally snatched under by an old lunker of a largemouth, I like to believe that I outwitted the shrewd old devil by simply outwaiting him.

Although I greatly prefer minnows to crayfish, I do not intend to imply that crayfish are anything but excellent bass bait. Crayfish molt, as do lobsters, shedding their entire shells and then growing new ones to accommodate growth. While they are "between shells" they are soft and vulnerable, and are usually referred to by bait dealers and fishermen as "softshells" or "shedders." They are doubly effective as bait when they are in this stage, and any opportunity to acquire and use them should not be neglected. The devil of it is, their molting can neither be induced nor predetermined. As a result, their availability is always a matter of happenstance, and one which cannot be relied upon.

CRAYFISH ON HOOK
Slide point of hook under first tail segment and draw barb free. Make hooking as shallow as possible to prolong life of bait. As with minnows, change hook size to match bait size. Here a No. 2 hook is used.

Some fishermen hook crayfish through the hard body shell, some toward the tail, and others midway between. My preference is to slide the point of the hook under the segment of the tail closest to the head, and then draw it free.

Because of the crayfish's tendency to hide, and because it does little to advertise its presence, it is not wise to leave it undisturbed as I have recommended be done with large minnows. Instead, "stir it up" frequently by raising it a couple of feet and then letting it fall back on a slack line.

Because largemouths are not highly critical of small details, it is both feasible and wise to use relatively coarse terminal tackle when fishing for them with bait. In open water, very large fish can be subdued on very light lines and only tiny hooks, but this doesn't hold true in the presence of weeds. By virtue of their chosen habitat, largemouths are a sure bet to plow through heavy growth when hooked. There is nothing the fisherman can do to prevent or relieve the drag and friction which build up, with the result that fine leaders invariably break and small hooks tear loose.

In order to avoid such demoralizing developments, I use stout leaders and relatively large hooks. For a leader I use about four feet of monofilament in fifteen-pound test, whenever I fish with fly rod and fly line. If I'm using a spinning rig, I use a spool filled with the fifteen-pound mono. When using big minnows I vary hook size among Nos. 2, 1, and 1/0, depending on the size of the bait. I like the No. 2 when using large crayfish, but drop to a No. 4 if the crayfish are of medium size.

Although a line or leader of fifteen-pound test may sound heavy by old-time standards, advances in technology have altered things markedly. I have just "miked" a strand of fifteen-pound monofilament—a mere two-hundredths of an inch. The bass of my youth didn't take exception to fabric lines of several times that diameter. I'm therefore quite certain that the stout mono exacts no penalty while effectively guarding against line breakage in thick weeds.

We are about to move on to smallmouths and their somewhat more complicated ways, but it seems timely at this point to deal with a facet of bait fishing for bass that applies to both species equally. This has to do with readying tackle for anticipated bites, and setting the hook when they materialize.

Once smallmouths and largemouths decide to take a bait, they are straightforward, no-nonsense biters. There is seldom any preliminary testing or nibbling, as is almost always the case with walleyes, perch, and other delicate biters. A bass simply gulps the bait calmly, an act which may not even register against the rod, and then swims away. It is quite unaware of its mistake to this point, but the fish is instantly alerted if line tension develops. It reacts violently; the rod tip plunges into the water, the reel screeches, and the fish is usually long gone before the fisherman can do anything about it.

Consequently, advance precautions should be taken to prevent the development of tension immediately following a bite. I usually fish with two rods which I prop in position so as to fish on both sides of the boat. If I'm using a spinning outfit, I leave the bail open. This eliminates the danger of tension, but line flows from a spinning reel so easily that slack will be drawn from the spool by a lively minnow, or even by current, waves, or wind, if nothing is done to prevent it. My method is to draw a loop of slack from the reel and trig it lightly atop the boat seat. A quarter or half-dollar serves nicely. Or a pocket knife, a line spool, or any other light object can be adjusted to serve the purpose. The small object holds the line in place until a bite develops but lets it slide free so easily when a bite occurs that the biting fish is not alerted. Line flows from the reel without resistance, and the fish continues to believe that all is well.

When I'm fishing with a fly rod, I strip six or eight feet of line from the reel and coil it on the bottom of the boat, or on a seat, so that it will pay out easily. The weight of the fly line is usually sufficient to keep it in the boat until a fish bites, but it can also be trigged in the same manner as the spinning line if necessary. In the case of a bait-casting reel, it is usually sufficient to leave it on free-spool. The spool's slight inertia will hold the line in place, but will yield to a bite without significant resistance.

The theory has long prevailed that the trick of hooking bass on live minnows consists of letting the biting fish make a first run before any attempt is made to set the hook. According to the script, the bass will make the first run, come to a halt, finish swallowing the minnow, and then move off again. It is alleged that to try to set the hook during the first run is very likely to be abortive, while a hook-up is almost certain if the attempt is postponed until the second run materializes.

Maybe so, but the bass I deal with seldom run true to form. The run-pause-run pattern is more myth than fact, and waiting for it to develop is too much like waiting for flushed woodcock to become the easy targets they are supposed to be by allegedly springing aloft and then pausing above the cover before departing. Both theories would simplify things greatly if only bass and woodcock would conform, but those of my experience seldom do.

In my opinion, which is not necessarily more valid, far more biting bass are missed because the fisherman is caught off balance than because of his failure to set the hook at the right time. If the above precautions are taken, and all else goes smoothly, a sudden bite—most *are* sudden and unanticipated—has no effect but to draw out the slack as already planned. The fisherman has plenty of time to pick up his rod while slack line continues to pay out. Since it feels no tension, the fish is not aware of its mistake. Unalarmed, it usually takes the bait well into its mouth at the outset.

Instead of waiting for the pause which so often fails to materialize, I prefer to either close the bail or squeeze the fly line against the grip—whichever may be necessary to set the stage for snubbing—and then try to set the hook an instant before the departing slack comes taut against the tip of the rod. Needless to say, I don't always connect. But I believe that I hook a higher percentage of fish by following this routine than by fiddling around in the hope that biting fish will follow the book, which they do all too seldom. Trying to wait them out merely gives them time in which to become suspicious, which they often do, and then immediately drop the bait.

For as long as smallmouths are along the shorelines, nothing could persuade me to fish for them with bait. No prejudice enters into my sentiments. They arise from the fact that bass bugs and fly rods will account for more fish at this time, and that bass bugging, in my opinion, is by far the most exciting form of bass fishing. But as already mentioned, smallmouths don't hang to the shorelines and shoreline shallows throughout the season, and I don't hesitate to turn to bait fishing when they have moved outward to deeper water.

As with bait fishing for largemouths, there are two main requirements: find the fish and then offer them what they want. In general, these requirements become harder to meet when the goal shifts from largemouths to smallmouths.

The task of locating productive smallmouth grounds is made

difficult by the comparative lack of obvious clues. Unlike largemouths, smallmouths are not attracted to weedbeds. They tend to move into much deeper water than that preferred by largemouths, and the greater depth further precludes the advantage of visible clues.

It certainly seems logical to conclude that smallmouths move to deeper water in search of lower temperatures, and that because they go deeper than largemouths they are less tolerant of high temperatures. This appears to be borne out by the fact that while largemouths often flourish in waters so shallow that the summer temperature becomes uniformly high from top to bottom, smallmouth lakes are almost always of sufficient depth to allow the stratification already alluded to with respect to trout.

As in hot-weather trout fishing in lakes, the task of locating smallmouth grounds involves discovery of the depth of the thermocline—that layer in which ample oxygen and comfortable temperatures coexist—and then finding spots within that stratum which have special appeal for the bass.

There is one basic difference, however. Because smallmouths have greater temperature tolerance, they are not as inexorably bound to the thermocline as are trout. Once trout "go down" they tend to stay in the cool thermocline until fall weather lowers the surface temperatures to tolerable levels. Smallmouths, on the other hand, may move in and out of the thermocline daily. They often move into the shoreline shallows after sundown, for example, and they may shift about during the day for reasons that are less apparent. Consequently, the hot-weather smallmouth fisherman enjoys more latitude than his trout-fishing counterpart, for even if he fails to locate bass directly in the thermocline he may be lucky enough to intercept them as they come and go.

An understanding of water stratification tends to prompt the conclusion that locating summertime smallmouths (and trout) should be reducible to scientific exactitude. In truth, it isn't that easy. Too many variables exist to upset attempts to go about the job too scientifically.

While it may seem most logical to try first to determine the depth of the thermocline and then look for fish, it is more practical to find the fish first by educated trial and error. It is not easy to determine the precise depth of the thermocline, and any error will result in a subsequent search for fish at the wrong level. However, if you find the fish first, it is an easy matter to determine the *exact* depth they are using, and this also determines the true depth at which further searching should be conducted.

While trial and error are involved, the search for the fish-holding level need not be undertaken blindly. As with trout, smallmouths do not congregate just anywhere in the thermocline. Instead, they tend to gather where the bottom lies within the comfort zone and also is of the type they favor: gravel, boulders, shale, etc. Again like trout, they are attracted to spots where suitable bottom either rises up into the thermocline from greater depths or plunges sharply into it from above.

In view of the foregoing criteria, the underwater extension of a rocky point would be a likely choice of site. Begin fishing at about a depth of fifteen feet and move toward deeper water gradually. If the bar drops away suddenly and sharply, zero in on the drop-off. Note the depth at which bites finally occur as accurately as possible. Center all future prospecting around this depth, for this is the level which will hold the most fish.

A bass-holding spot can be one of considerable area—a broad reef, for example—or it can fall within narrow limits, as along the edge of a sharp drop-off. In the latter case, the point at which the anchor is dropped is often of critical importance. If necessary, successive tries should be made until bait can be lowered precisely over the edge of the drop-off. If there is sufficient wind to swing the boat to and fro, use a stern anchor to hold the boat in position. Otherwise, the movement may be just enough to prevent you from cashing in on a spot that is high in potential but small in area.

The second requirement—offering the bass what they're looking for—is considerably more of a problem in smallmouth fishing than in fishing for largemouths. Smallmouths are exceedingly omnivorous, but their preferences are ever-shifting and largely unpredictable. The solution, of course, would be to have every conceivable bait at hand, but this is virtually impossible.

Fortunately, although smallmouths feed on dozens of different items, their preferences usually fall among a smaller list of baits which can be regarded as more or less standard. The following fall in this category: nightcrawlers, garden earthworms, minnows, crayfish, hellgrammites, frogs, grasshoppers, and crickets.

Although smallmouths are much bolder than trout, and less inclined to quibble over small flaws in bait presentation, they tend to be considerably more critical and questioning than do largemouths. Therefore, while I more or less "let dangle" while fishing for largemouths, I strive for natural presentation when I'm after the fussier smallmouths. Here again, the basics of worming panfish can be put to advantage, to say nothing of the greater degree of finesse employed in trout fishing.

Although the smallmouth bass packs more power and pizzazz per pound than any other freshwater fish, bait fishing for smallmouths does not require the heavy terminal tackle recommended for largemouths. When they are in deep water, where bait fishing is usually undertaken, obstructions rarely exist and there is little danger of snagging and resulting line breakage. Not only does the use of light terminal tackle and small hooks abet natural presentation, but it allows hooked fish to take their best shots at getting off.

For smallmouth fishing my choice of line or leader is one of eight-pound test. The diameter of the eight-pound Stren which I use is only eleven thousandths of an inch—fine enough to assure sufficient flexibility for live minnows to move around with but minimal restraint. I use No. 6 hooks (Mustad #3399) for small baits, No. 4 for the in-betweens, and No. 2 for the largest.

Trying to list smallmouth baits in order of effectiveness is futile, simply because that which is "best" one day is all too likely to fall from top favor the next. However, while I don't rate nightcrawlers as more than mediocre bait for largemouths, my first bid of the day for smallmouths is likely to be a squirming 'crawler impaled lightly on a No. 6 hook and carried down by a single buckshot.

It is perhaps important to point out that while I favor nightcrawlers over small garden worms for smallmouths, I have caught plenty of smallmouths on the latter, but few if any largemouths. This illustrates one of the major differences between the two species. Smallmouths often show a troutlike liking for tidbits, while largemouths are seldom interested in anything but substantial items.

If nightcrawlers go begging, I usually turn next to minnows. Smallmouths are quite capable of engulfing the six-inch chubs and suckers preferred by largemouths, and on occasion they do just that. On the whole, however, they seem to like the smaller sizes better, those that run around four inches long. Lively, vigorous minnows produce the most bites, so hook each bait as lightly as possible and change to a fresh one when the first becomes drained of wiggle.

Incidentally, the bobber which can be used to advantage in largemouth fishing is only an encumbrance when you're using minnows for smallmouths in deep water. In shallow largemouth water a bobber encourages the minnow to swim here and there, tempting fish which may be hiding at various points. In smallmouth fishing the aim is to be anchored directly over fish, and in this case you don't want the minnow to wander. Equally objectionable is the fact that the bobber must be removed before a hooked smallmouth can be worked in from a depth of twenty or twenty-five feet, and nobody who is fast to a rampaging smallmouth has time or opportunity to fiddle with a bobber!

The hellgrammite, as a smallmouth bait, is much like the little girl with the curl: awful good when it's good, but a disappointment otherwise. Hellgrammites can result in fantastic fishing on days when the bass hanker for them, but there are as many days when they have little or no appeal. Because they can be a needed ace in the hole on occasion, the fisherman who can acquire them should carry a supply by all means. Unfortunately, they are usually hard to come by—difficult to obtain by netting and seining because of their comparative rarity, and only infrequently available from bait dealers for the same reason.

They are mighty tough critters, however, with single specimens often accounting for several bass before they are stolen or become hopelessly mangled. They will stay alive indefinitely if hooked under the hard shell which lies just back of the head. They should be fished close to the bottom, but like crayfish, they will burrow into the mud or hide under debris if they are allowed to reach bottom. Jig them frequently to make sure that they stay clear of the bottom where bass can see them.

It has long been my opinion that crayfish make better bait for smallmouths than they do for largemouths. It is usually a mistake, however, to try to tempt smallmouths with the king-size crayfish which seem to hold the most appeal for largemouths. The small and medium sizes will draw plenty of bites when the bass are crayfish-minded. When they are especially fussy, a tiny crayfish on a No. 10 hook may prove to be what's needed. The only trouble with the smallest of crayfish is that panfish relish them, too, and they may snap them up while the bass are making up their minds.

HELLGRAMMITE ON HOOK

In this shot, thumb and forefinger indicate size of bait. Point of hook should pass under shell immediately back of head, and then come out free. This bait is incredibly tough—it will live on hook indefinitely, and will often account for several fish before tearing free. One of the top baits for smallmouths.

Frogs make good bait for both bass species—big ones for largemouths and smaller ones for smallmouths—but I can't write about their use with real enthusiasm. I caught many bass on frogs in my younger days, but the mellowing effect of age has made me increasingly aware of a frog's pathetic struggles to free itself from the hook. I can't use them in good conscience, or with peace of mind, and have discontinued the practice.

It probably is silly, or at least inconsistent, to make any sentimental distinction between the use of live frogs and live minnows. Honest reporting obliges me to declare their worth and importance, and to advise from experience as to their most effective use. Because frogs are essentially creatures of the surface, it seems logical to assume that the most strikes would result by merely letting them swim and struggle near the top. Curiously, I have never had much luck when I have fished them in this manner. Much better, by my experience, is to hook them through both lips, add enough sinker to take them down, and fish them just above the bottom. Incidentally, big tadpoles are as effective, if indeed not more so, when hooked through the base of the tail and fished at the same deep level. With continuing inconsistency, my aversion to the use of live frogs does not carry over to the use of tadpoles. I'm sure, however, that the tadpoles are no more cheerfully resigned to the practice than are the frogs!

When grasshoppers and crickets are available, the smallmouth fisherman can get in some deadly licks with these insects. Best results derive from hanging a single hopper or cricket on a No. 10 or No. 8 hook and lowering it into bass territory with the help of only a single split shot. This, again, is a ploy aimed directly at the smallmouth's liking for naturally presented tidbits.

The list of potential smallmouth baits is open to indefinite expansion: grubs, all other types of larvae, salamanders, nymphs, beetles, etc. Most are difficult to come by, but all are worth a try whenever the opportunity arises. There's no telling what may have special smallmouth appeal on a given day, so there's the chance of hitting the jackpot with an offbeat offering.

At the very least, the smallmouth fisherman should stand ready to offer both nightcrawlers and minnows. Supplies of crayfish and hellgrammites will beef up his chances. Frogs, if he can bring himself to use them, are another item of proven worth. These five baits cover the choices that usually are available. They won't blanket the entire range of smallmouth whim, but they will serve in the great majority of instances. In other words, it is only on exceptional days that one of the foregoing five items won't produce if they are where smallmouths congregate.

Many bass-buggers and plug-casters claim to have their best luck during the early morning hours and after the sun has gone down. My experience has not followed this pattern. If anything, I have had my best luck with artificial lures after the sun is well up, and before it sets.

Bait fishing has been a different matter. I don't rate the after-sundown hours as anything special, but I rate the very early morning ahead of all other times of day.

When I was much younger, and had the will to arise at whatever ungodly hour was necessary to get the best fishing or hunting, I planned to be anchored along the edge of a proven drop-off not merely by sunrise but just before the first hint of gray showed in the east. Such early rising is a painful price to pay, but it can buy the sufferer some mighty fast fishing. Smallmouths, at least those of the past, were frequently so ravenous at daybreak that they snapped up my nightcrawlers and minnows as fast as I could lower them.

I feel certain that smallmouths still tend to bite eagerly at the first show of light, but I'm not about to prove it. Although I retain my youthful enthusiasms to a considerable degree, I will no longer get up at three a.m., even to watch an ant eat an entire bale of hay!

Up to this point we have dealt only with the bass of lakes and ponds. Largemouths are seldom found elsewhere, at least in the region with which I'm most familiar, but smallmouths sometimes live in fast-moving streams where it is not unusual to find them sharing the water with trout. Unfortunately, for reasons unknown to me, the smallmouths of quick-water streams tend to run to small size, and I must confess a personal disinterest in small bass. This is purely from prejudice. I'm in heaven whenever I can catch ten- or twelve-inch trout, and a ten-inch smallmouth gives as good, or even better, account of itself on light tackle as does a rainbow, brown, or brook trout of equal size.

Others of fairer mind do enjoy fishing for small river smallmouths, and all power to them. Many use artificial lures, but for those who may wish to try bait, I direct them to the chapter on ultralight worm fishing for trout. The method, as described, is as deadly on river smallmouths as it is on trout.

The main difference between ultralight bait fishing for trout and for smallmouths is the difference between the positions usually preferred by trout and those generally taken up by bass. There is some overlapping, of course, but in the main, smallmouths tend to prefer those protected pockets of slack or "easy" water which seldom attract trout. Once the knack of deducing the likely spots has been acquired, the ultralight bait fisherman can take river smallmouths by the dozens, whenever conditions are normal. I wish I could promise a limit of trophy-size fish with equal assurance, but unfortunately I can't. In the bass rivers of my experience, the fast-moving one, that is, a foot-long smallmouth, usually rates as a whopper.

For reasons unknown, bass fishing has never inspired the cult-like adulation which for so long has been lavished on trout. Aspiring trout fishermen often hold trout in reverence even before they have caught one, all because trout are accorded regality by definition.

Bass do not evoke the same degree of charitability. They must *earn* respect and admiration, which they do ever so eloquently by tearing up the pea patch at the first jab of the hook. A fisherman has only to hook his first three-pound smallmouth to discover that the smallmouth's brand of pea-patch up-tearing is really something to behold!

9

THE EASY ART OF SPINNER MAKING

I COUNT MYSELF among those least qualified to moralize, but it seems evident that in order to derive maximum satisfaction from any enterprise, a person must invest in it his own labor and creativity. If a hunter buys a professionally trained bird dog, for example, he may enjoy good shooting; but never can he claim personal credit for his dog's flawless performance. On the other hand, the dog an amateur handler trains from a pup may be lacking in polish; but the owner's deep involvement in the pup's development will more than compensate for the lack.

For the same reasons, fishing is always most absorbing and fulfilling when the fisherman stands or falls by his own hand: his physical efforts, his personal savvy, and, to the fullest extent possible, his own handiwork. The distinction is relative, of course. When a guide puts me among trout or salmon I glory in what follows, even though success may be largely the guide's doing. Nevertheless, when I slog through quaking bogs, endure the torment of bloodthirsty blackflies, and finally discover a hidden beaver dam teeming with brook trout, I relish a sense of personal accomplishment to which I can never lay claim while a passenger in a guide's canoe. If my efforts result in a modest catch of wild brookies, I take more pride in this small triumph than I can take in far more spectacular catches made with a guide's assistance.

It is undoubtedly the gratification to be gained by personal involvement which inspires so many fly fishermen to tie their own flies. Fly tying is a pleasant hobby by itself, particularly for those like myself whose powers of creativity are distinctly limited. Yet its chief charm is that of making the fly fisherman more clearly entitled to undiluted credit for his successes and more directly responsible for his failures.

When I take a finished fly from the vise on a January evening, I often delay before adding it to the stockpile to speculate on the returns I may realize from my efforts. It is quite conceivable that my labors of the past ten minutes may come to naught—I may hang the fly beyond reach on the first backcast and be forced to leave it to deteriorate near the tip of some high branch overhanging the stream. Yet as I study the finished fly I know that at some point during the coming season there will be an apex of triumph, the moment when I bring to net my biggest trout of the year. The trout will break no records, nor will it even remotely approach any. But within the context of my commonplace existence it will loom as exceptional, and at some unknown point in my winter's fly tying I will create the fly which will result in its capture. I take a last look at the fly in my hand before dropping it among the others, and wonder if it will be the one to turn the trick.

When the moment finally arrives, and I have what promises to be the best trout of the season safely in the net, I wonder what my feelings would have been could I have anticipated the responsible fly's special destiny at the moment of its tying. At the same time, I realize that such power of foresight would be self-defeating. It is the uncertainty of outcome, rather than foreknowledge, that inspires my investment of time and effort.

Bait fishermen seldom enhance their fishing pleasure in this way, largely because no creative avenue comparable to fly tying suggests itself. Yet within the past few years I have discovered one. When I first became aware of the special effectiveness of bait-and-hardware combinations, I relied for a time on store-bought spinners and attracters. Then, with much pleasure resulting, I learned to assemble my own.

Catalogs offering fishing tackle and fly-tying materials have always fascinated me, and I tend to study them until I know many of the sections by heart. Yet I tended to skip over the pages devoted to the materials of spinner making: wire, spinner blades, beads, spacers, clevises, and more. When I became more interested in bait-fishing hardware I began to regard the neglected sections with interest. The materials for making every type of spinner were abundantly available. Not only that, the abundance of components opened the door to limitless experimentation.

Only one obstacle stood in the way: a means of handling the tough steel wire used in spinner making. I had tried, with ordinary pliers, and had failed. The neatly wound eyes, the locking coils, and all the rest seemed to bespeak the need of highly specialized tools and equally specialized skills.

Then, in the fascinating catalog put out by the Netcraft Company of Toledo, Ohio, I saw advertised a simple little gadget which was alleged to make wire winding easy. The illustration attested to its mechanical simplicity, and the price at the time was under five dollars. Both characteristics made me skeptical, but I decided to order one. I was probably being a sucker, I told myself. Like all cheap and glowingly described contraptions, it would undoubtedly fail to live up to its billing.

When the little gadget arrived, I screwed it to my tying bench. Then I turned to the accompanying book of instructions, "Tackle Tricks with Wire," written by Netcraft owner Herb Ludgate. I read the opening paragraph and immediately detected what I took to be a ratty smell. "With practice a spinner eye can be made in ten or fifteen seconds," it read reassuringly. But this qualifying warning followed: "But be prepared to take half an hour on the first one."

Just as I suspected, I thought; the old how-to-play-the-piano routine: nine easy lessons and then one hard one. I figured right then that I had wasted the price of a fifth of bourbon.

But I went on to learn that I was dead wrong. Unlike the hucksters of unworkable gadgetry, Herb Ludgate greatly overemphasized the negative. I followed his written directions, fully expecting them to lead to a botched attempt. To my surprise and delight, I created a round and neatly wrapped eye on the first attempt, and in only a matter of moments.

I pressed on to other operations: open eyes, coils for sliding sleeves, spacer coils, wire snelling of hooks, various linkages, and more. In almost every instance I was able to turn out a professional-looking job on the second try, if not on the first. I was both impressed and elated.

Since acquiring the magical little wire winder, I have stocked up lavishly with spinner-making materials. Just as I have enough

Wire winder (foreground) and essential tools and materials: wire, pliers, wire nippers, beads, and instruction book. Lazy Susan holds spinner blades, clevises, split rings, hooks, etc., etc. Cabinets contain reserve supplies.

fly-tying supplies to tie flies for all the trout fishermen of the Northeast, I now have the means of supplying them with spinners as well. Laying in all those materials has been an interesting diversion, for various supply houses (see the classified ads in the outdoor magazines) offer a fascinating and irresistible array. Spinner blades are available in a wide range of shapes, designs, sizes, and finishes. Beads of all colors, finishes, and sizes are available, in choices of metal, glass, and plastic. Spring-steel wire of different weights can be bought in economy-size coils. There are metal bodies for weighted spinners, in a wide choice of design, and of course the clevises from which the blades are hung are offered in all needed sizes.

Beads, one of the chief ingredients of spinner making and one of the main means of achieving innovation, are also available from other sources. I have enlarged my stock by visiting craft and hobby shops, and by ordering from my wife's catalogs of decorative supplies. I'm a sucker for all colors, sizes, and materials, and if all the beads which I own could be strung on a single string, it would encircle the asylum to which I should be committed.

Just as in fly tying, I am not guided by need but by the pleasure I get from turning out creations of my own. As a result, I have more spinners than any ten men could use, and they're still coming off the production line. Fortunately, I can report that this excessive enthusiasm has a way of paying off. I have found that fish response to differences in spinner design can be as erratic and unpredictable as their fickle response to other lures and baits. Just as a certain fly, plug, or natural bait may be a winner one day and a loser the next, preferences shift as regularly over the range of spinner design, color, finish, etc. Although this fact is not generally recognized by fisherman, it should come as no surprise. It would be much more surprising if fish preferences fluctuated only with respect to certain lures but held steadfastly consistent when it came to spinners.

There is a weedy shallows in Lake Champlain, a sunken delta which spreads outward from the mouth of a creek, where Mike and I often take pot luck. The water over the flat is little more than six feet deep during normal water levels, and a tangled weed growth comes to within half that distance of the surface. Many baitfish hide and breed among the weeds, and this circumstance is not lost on the larger fish of the surrounding waters. Each species visits the area more or less regularly, often in rich combination. Consequently, Mike and I never know what the next bite or strike will bring, for it can be one of an impressive list: northern pike, chain pickerel, calico, smallmouth, largemouth, yellow perch, walleye, bowfin, bullhead, catfish, or eel. The spot is no purist's paradise, but Mike and I list it high among our assets. We have fished it for many years, frequently to the tune of heavy catches and wide variety. I have referred to it here for a particular reason, however. It was over these grounds that the peculiar effectiveness of the bait-and-spinner combination was first brought forcefully to my attention.

We routinely fished from our anchored boat with nightcrawlers and minnows. We caught fish, but the weeds were a constant nuisance. If we held our baits clear of the tops, few fish would leave the retreat to gather them in. In order to take fish we had to lower our worms and minnows close to the bottom, but then our lines were weed-fouled more of the time than they were clear.

One day, after clearing the weeds from his hook for the umpteenth time, Mike rebelled. "There *must* be a better way than this," he declared.

He opened the tackle box and studied the contents gravely.

"You're looking for something that ain't there," I said.

Mike ignored the remark and finally selected a spinner. From another compartment he took a three-hook worm gang. He tied a swivel to his spinning line and snapped it to the closed eye of the spinner. He rigged the worm gang to the open eye at the other end and secured it with the coiled locking sleeve. Finally, he strung a fat nightcrawler over the three hooks.

"You might take a walleye on that, if you could run it along the bottom," I said critically. "But you've gotta retrieve it above the weeds. Nothing's gonna come up for it."

Mike has long since learned to put little stock in my predictions and pronouncements. So have I, for that matter. The only difference is that I have learned even better, for I've been at it longer. Consequently, he paid no attention to my voiced pessimism, and flipped out the worm and spinner as far as he could cast handily. He let the combination settle, then began reeling slowly.

I watched disinterestedly as he cranked and twitched the sunken bait back toward the boat. Apparently he was holding it above the weeds, for it continued to come in without snagging.

"Aha!" The ring of triumph in the sudden exclamation was unmistakable. Mike had yanked the hooks into a striking fish—and the fish promptly yanked back with a pulse-quickening show of strength.

"What were you saying about nothing hitting?" Mike asked pointedly as he tended his arched and throbbing rod.

The water where we were fishing was clouded with clay. Accordingly, the nature of the hooked fish could not be determined until Mike finally worked it up to the net and I boosted it clear.

"A walleye!" I marveled, gazing at the thumping three-pounder. "I'll be damned!"

Mike didn't even take time to rub my nose in my refuted prediction. Instead, he rebaited quickly and made another cast.

"Man gets lucky, anything can happen once," I warned dolefully.

Mike cast and reeled as before. And again, in mid-retrieve, he set the hooks in another fish with a second grunt of deep satisfaction. His rod took on even more strain than before, and again I readied the net.

A lively give-and-take ensued, but at last Mike brought the fish within netting range. I dipped and lifted, expecting to bring up a whopping walleye. Instead, a northern pike of at least five pounds flopped mightily in the bag of the net.

"A northern!" I exclaimed. "I *will* be damned!"

"You said that before," Mike reminded me happily.

He cast a third time. This time the strike, and there *was* one, was from a fish which didn't require netting—a deep-bodied yellow perch which was at least a foot long.

In the meantime, my two rods, one baited with a nightcrawler and the other with a lively minnow, hadn't relayed so much as the suggestion of a nibble. This, as opposed to three strikes on as many casts, clearly implied that Mike had hit on something important. I decided that it was time for me to begin thinking positively and try to get a piece of the action.

"Hand over that tackle box," I said after Mike had unhooked the perch.

I rigged up with a duplicate of Mike's combination. Incredibly, I, too, was fast to a hard-fighting fish on the very first cast. When it turned out to be a two-pound largemouth, the sweeping appeal of the spinner-'crawler combination became forcefully apparent.

The action tapered off, of course. But when we anchored again in a new location, we were right back in business. We wound up with a catch that was as notable for its wide variety as for its numbers.

The next time we returned to the spot we had high hopes of taking up exactly where we had left off. We rigged up confidently and cast as before, but only a few scattered strikes resulted and these only from yellow perch.

"Looks like they aren't here," Mike said finally.

"Looks like," I agreed. "On the other hand, maybe they're here and just ain't hitting," I speculated. "You suppose the trouble is in the spinner?"

To test this possibility I tried several spinners of my own making in unproductive succession: nickel, copper, and brass blades; single blades and double blades; beads of various colors. Finally, I snapped on a twin-bladed job. The forward blade was concave and nickel-plated, while the second, of polished brass, was flat with a bent-down lip to make it spin. Red beads separated the two blades.

My very first cast with the rather unorthodox assemblage donged up a scrappy chain pickerel. Two or three casts later I was hooked up with a walleye.

I have learned that it pays to make several spinners of each new design, so Mike was able to switch to an exact replica of the type I was using. It turned the trick for him, just as it had for me. Again we went on to make an exceptional catch. But this time only because my zeal for spinner making had produced a wide variety—and a variety which included a type which was accorded special preference on that particular day.

The instance just related illustrates the importance of carrying a variety of spinners. It also shows that the spinner-and-bait combination really adds up to more than just the sum of its parts. For example, nightcrawlers by themselves are almost worthless as bait for members of the pike family. Only in extremely rare instances will a pickerel or northern take an unadorned 'crawler, and even then it is usually when the bait is being retrieved rapidly or given provocative action in some other unthinking manner. A simple spinner works better, but it is never the equal of the spoons and wobblers whose erratic darting action pike find so hard to resist. Yet when the two were presented in combination—spinner and worm—northerns and pickerel slammed into them, right along with the walleyes, bass, and perch, which have a distinct liking for the big worms. Apparently, the whirling blade creates sufficient excitement to transcend the normal indifference to the usually scorned bait.

The wide variety of manufactured lures that is available seems to make the chance of improvement or important discovery by the home craftsman extremely remote. Yet the shadings of whimsy among game fish more than match the many differences of lure design, so the creation of an especially deadly homemade lure is always an exciting possibility.

It is in the hope of achieving this rare but possible outcome that I whittle and sand plugs, hammer, grind, and polish spoons, experiment with fly patterns, and assemble experimental spinner combinations. I derive satisfaction from shaping my angling destiny with my own hands, so to speak; but in the back of my mind is the

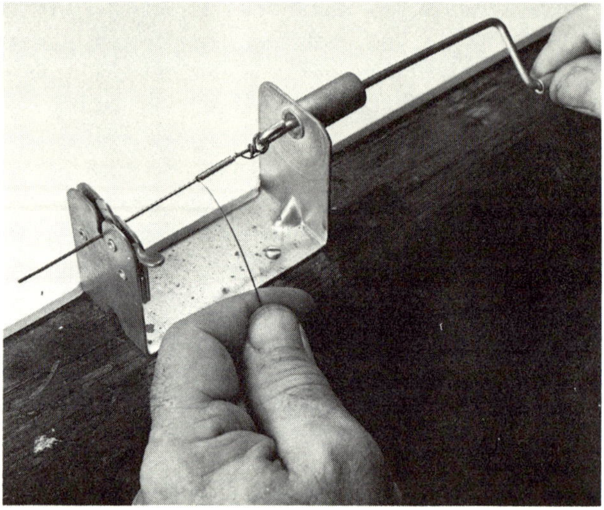

Photo shows method of making a continuous winding which can be cut as needed for locking sleeves and spacers.

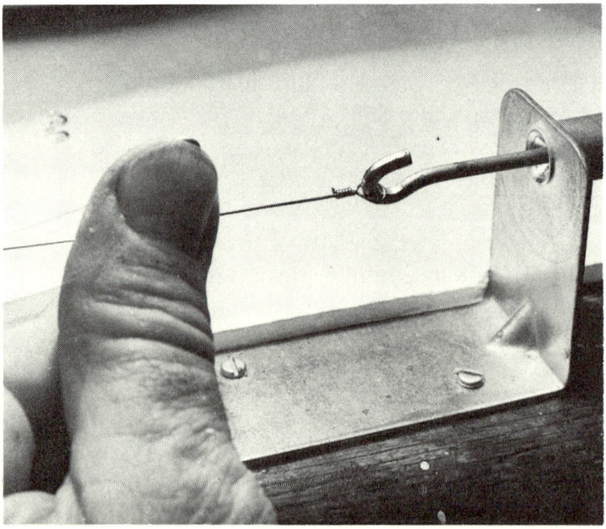

Eyed loop has been pulled back from winding station (under thumb) for viewing. Finished loop is then slipped off hook.

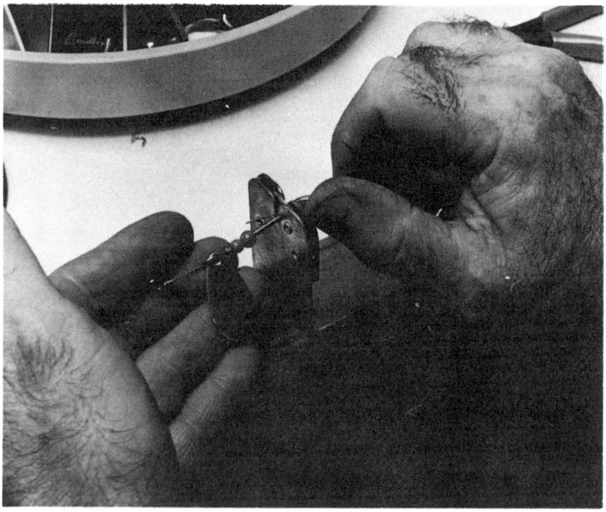

Open eye is formed on completed spinner by pressure on lever. Loop can be locked by coil already on shaft.

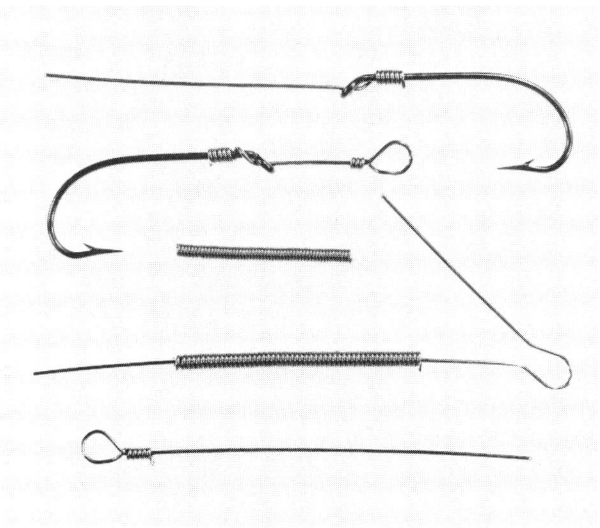

Top to bottom: *Wire snelled to hook; snelled hook with closed loop or eye; coil for locking sleeves or spacers; open loop with locking sleeve; length of wire with eye wrapped by wire winder. Linkage can be achieved by interlocking wrapped eyes as desired.*

hope of hitting the jackpot with a homemade lure of extra-special appeal. This hope is sustained by past experience. In rare instances I have whittled, ground, tied, and assembled so as to achieve contours and combinations which have resulted in super fish-takers. Unfortunately, my efforts to duplicate these lucky accidents of creativity have almost always failed. Those which follow may resemble the originals, but they inevitably lack the subtle chance peculiarities that made the originals so successful.

The variations of originality do not assert themselves among manufactured spinner blades, of course. However, as already illustrated, fish-taking uniqueness can be arrived at by varying the manner of assembly. Furthermore, I have discovered a natural source of spinner blades among which no two are ever precisely alike. The differences are small, but it is from just such subtle variation that lures of special distinction sometimes emerge.

It is standard procedure to "bump bottom" when trolling for walleyes. In Lake Champlain, where I do the bulk of my walleye trolling, it is not unusual for a freshwater clam to clamp tightly to the bell sinker as it bounces along the bottom. For a long time, like other walleye fishermen, I cussed the hitchhiking clams, pried them loose, and tossed them overboard. But there came a moment when I was struck by their natural concavity and the inner iridescence of the twin shells. Both suggested the makings of spinner blades.

I discovered that when the dark, rough exterior was removed with a grinding wheel, the pearly nature of the shell stood revealed. After the shell had been ground to the desired shape on the same wheel, it could be brought to a high luster with a buffing wheel and buffing compound. After a hole was drilled in one end to accept a clevis, I had a blade of exceptional beauty. More important, it was one whose curvature had no exact counterpart.

Since no two clamshell spinners were exactly alike, there seemed reason to believe that among them there would be occasional blades of superior effectiveness. Experiments with these blades of my own making have borne out the contention. All will help to take fish when used with natural baits, but a treasured few have clearly demonstrated outstanding powers of persuasion.

This difference raises an interesting point for all who are concerned with the mysteries of fish behavior and the part it plays in fishing success and failure. Certainly, spinners attract and excite

Rough clam shell at start of grinding.

Same shell ground to shape of spinner blade.

Hole is drilled in end of blade to admit clevis.

Blades have been polished on a buffing wheel and made into spinners. No two are exactly alike. Lucky "accidents" sometimes result in spinners of rare appeal.

fish by the flashes which they emit. In view of the day-to-day whimsy which is a recognized game-fish characteristic, it is conceivable that a spinner of polished brass might prove to be most attractive on a given day while one with a nickel finish might be favored the next. Yet there is another determinant. On a particular day, spinners of the same finish may not be equally attractive. If they are of different design, one may greatly outperform the other.

A whirling spinner blade not only gives off reflected light, but its passage also sets up vibrations. The nature of these pulsations are determined by the spinner's design, and it seems logical to assume that fish may be more powerfully drawn to some vibrations than they are to others. An understanding of fish sensitivity suggests that the difference need be no more than slight to alter greatly a spinner's appeal.

Perhaps this is why my most valued string of "cow bells" is one made from clamshells. For those not familiar with the term, "cow bells" refers to a tandem arrangement of as many as a half-dozen

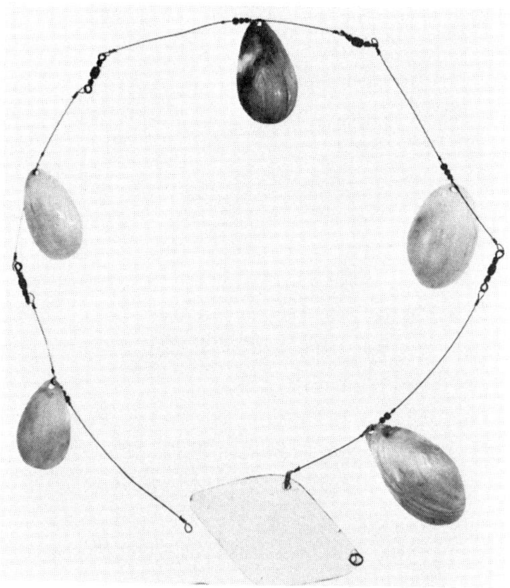

"Cowbells" of clam shell spinners rigged in tandem. This particular string has proven to be especially effective in deep trolling.

spinner blades, usually of graduated sizes with the largest positioned farthest from the bait. The rig is most often used in deep trolling where maximum flash is needed to attract the attention of lake trout and landlocked salmon.

My string of clamshell "cow bells" has demonstrated what I believe to be marked superiority, and I attribute this to the variation of design among the individual blades. Each gives off a unique pulsation, and the composite creates greater excitement than the unvarying vibrations created by a string of spinners of uniform design.

I cheerfully admit that such reasoning is farfetched, but I recommend theorizing of this nature as an additive which enhances the pleasures of fishing. Furthermore, who can say where the truth may lie? With respect to fishing it often reposes outside the limits of "common sense," and to seek it out one often has to take pot luck in areas where human logic does not necessarily apply.

My main purpose of including this chapter is to alert fishermen to the special, but oft neglected, appeal of spinner-and-bait combinations, and to the ease with which they can create all the necessary "hardware." The intent stops short of step-by-step instructions, for these are supplied clearly and in detail by Herb Ludgate's "Tackle Tricks with Wire,"* which he furnishes with each Netcraft wire winder. The directions contained therein are so complete that I can add only a few supplemental suggestions.

One is to point out the value of a soldering gun in achieving special effects. Most important of these is that of providing stops at the proper intervals when positioning spinner blades in tandem on a single wire shaft. The blades can be separated by spacers which can be wound with the winder, but a much neater job results from a series of tiny soldered stops.

My original attempt consisted of winding a spacer coil or spring and then cutting off about three turns with my wire nippers. But when I threaded the tiny coil on the shaft, I found that the solder just wouldn't bond. I found a bottle of acid in a hardware store which purportedly prepared stainless steel for soldering, but even with its help I couldn't get a solid union.

Finally I tried winding my stops from fine copper wire. When I slid these into position and applied the acid, the solder took hold firmly. A drop of solder transformed the three turns of fine copper wire into a tiny metallic bead, unobtrusive but enough to trig clevises and plastic beads and thereby separate the spinner blades.

I also use the soldering gun to cover and smooth the windings after snelling a hook directly to the wire shaft. This also firms up the connection, for while it will jam tightly against the hook eye on a forward pull it will slide back along the shank when the force is reversed. Soldering results in an immovable joint.

Incidentally, hooks selected for snelling must have turned-down eyes, but those with tapered eyes usually break from the strain. The Mustad #3399 has a ball eye which is stronger and will not break when the force of winding is applied.

Inflation has had its effect on the cost of fishing tackle, perhaps to an even greater degree than on the cost of many other products. The cost may be justified where skilled hand labor is involved to a significant degree, but the prices asked for spinners that are easily assembled from low-cost parts and materials are often

*Available from Netcraft Company, 3101 Sylvania Avenue, Toledo, Ohio 43613.

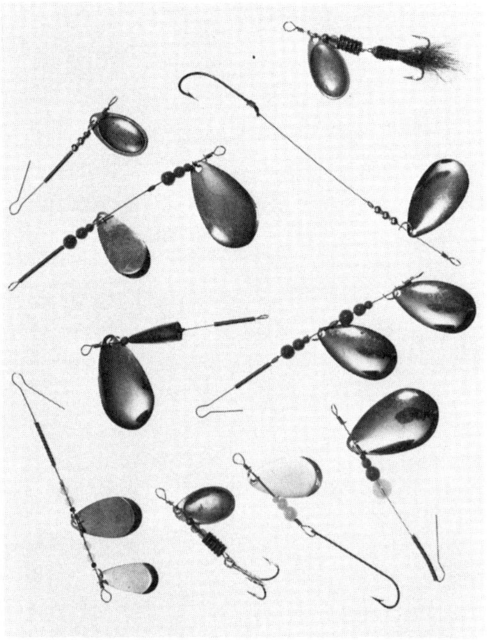

Various spinner combinations that can be wound and assembled quickly and easily.

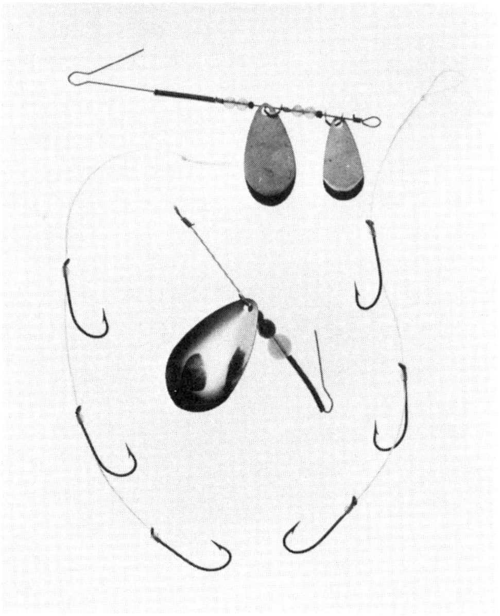

Open-ended spinners and hook gangs. When nightcrawlers are strung on gangs, the spinner-worm combination will account for trout, salmon, bass, walleyes, perch, and even northern pike and pickerel.

excessive. For those who are cost-minded, let me point out that spinners which now sell for over a dollar can be duplicated in a matter of a few minutes from parts and materials which can be bought for fifteen cents or less.

The foregoing savings can be accomplished without compromise in most cases, for components identical to those used in the assembly of many of the most popular spinners are available at relatively low cost. I, for one, welcome this opportunity to economize.

When spinners are used in conjunction with natural baits such as nightcrawlers, a hook gang (hooks snelled in tandem) should be used, both to set off the bait to best advantage and to ensure hooking when fish strike. Inspection of a worm gang may suggest that snelling hooks in tandem must be difficult and complicated, but this is not the case. Full directions for snelling hooks and tying worm gangs will be given in the next chapter.

10

THE "SECRET" OF SNELLING

ONE OF THE MOST maddening and demoralizing things that can happen to a fisherman is to lose a big fish because of a weak knot or one that slipped during a moment of truth. The advent of nylon monofilament truly revolutionized fishing, but among its many virtues nylon has one troublesome characteristic: it is slippery stuff to tie. This does not mean that properly tied nylon is treacherous. It does mean, however, that care should be taken to select the most efficient knots, and equal pains taken to tie them correctly.

This short chapter will not be concerned with the many knots available to the fisherman. There are manuals and books devoted to this important subject, prepared by those who are much better qualified to deal with it than I. Instead, it will deal with one knot in particular, and the ways in which it can be put to profitable use because of its unique characteristics. It is a knot with which every fisherman is familiar, but one which very few learn to tie. It is the snelling knot, which has been very much a part of the fishing scene for a long, long time.

When I was a kid, I looked on snelled hooks as items of refinement quite beyond my means; they cost no less than a nickel apiece! In those older versions, gut snells were attached to eyeless hook shanks by thread wrappings, a means of attachment that was beyond my ability to duplicate. Later, when nylon became available, the snells were tied to eyed hooks with a knot of such professional appearance and perfection that to copy it also seemed beyond ordinary capabilities.

I tied hooks to my leaders and spinning lines with the simpler turle and clinch knots, but I still looked on the snelling knot with admiration and yearned to be able to tie it. Often, I pondered the expertise which it seemed to demand: a smooth, blind wrapping of the hook shank which bypassed the cutting effect of the hook's eye.

I'm sure that most other fishermen do the same, admiring the perfection of the snelling knot without ever learning to tie it. This seems borne out by the fact that while countless quantities of snelled hooks are still used, I have never seen a fisherman use this highly efficient knot in attaching hooks directly to his line.

In my case, I made no serious attempt to learn to tie the knot until I began experimenting with spinner-and-worm combinations. Then the need for hook gangs arose, and these can be made only by snelling two or more hooks to a single strand of monofilament. The trick of snelling a single hook had always seemed prohibitively difficult. That of snelling three in tandem seemed triply so.

But I was stymied by the odd unavailability of hook gangs. Cards of snelled single hooks grace the shelves of every tackle shop, but for some strange reason it is virtually impossible to buy prepared hook gangs. A few mail-order houses carry them, but the choice of hook size and snell diameter is limited. I wanted gangs of large hooks on heavy monofilament, small hooks on strands of small diameter, and the gradations between. Yet I searched in vain for tying directions in all of my numerous references. There were instructions for tying almost every other kind of knot, but not a single reference to the snelling knot.

I have since doped out the method on my own, and like so many seemingly complicated tasks, the snelling knot has emerged as one which is easy to tie after the proper moves have been deduced. Once I mastered it, an amusing truth became apparent.

In recent years, the so-called "nail knot" has come in for a lot of attention. For those who may not know, it is a knot used to tie a leader butt directly to a fly line with a smooth wrapping which will not trig when drawn through the guides of the rod. It also abets delicacy of presentation by minimizing bulk in the connection between line and leader. For both reasons, I recommended its use in previous chapters whenever bait fishing is done with fly line and leader.

Directions for tying this highly touted knot *are* contained in several of my references, but both the directions and diagrams are so complicated that the first impulse is to abandon all thoughts of learning to tie the damned thing. A first try does nothing to dispel this impression; the drawings and instructions are even more difficult to follow than they are to grasp in the abstract. Yet the truth is that the "innovative" nail knot achieves the same thing as the snelling knot that has been kicking around for many decades. Furthermore, it can be tied easily, in only a few moments, when the snelling technique is substituted for the finger-defying manipulations which are generally believed to be required to tie it.

TYING THE BASIC SNELLING KNOT

Although the finished snelling knot appears difficult to tie, quite the opposite is true. The "secret" lies in forming a loop with the snell. Once this is done, no difficult manipulations are required. The pictures and instructions below take you through the procedure step by step.

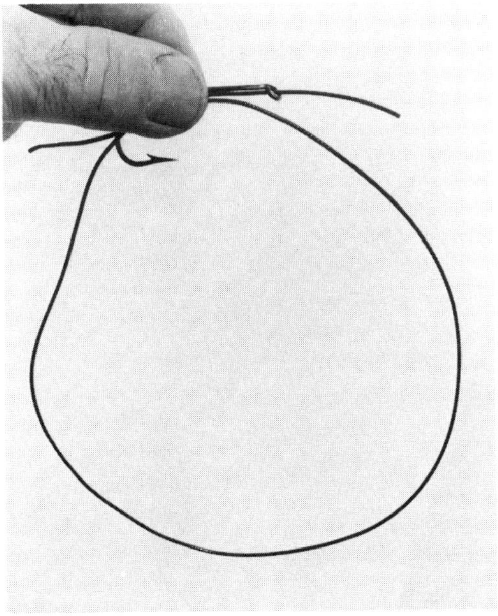

Form a loop with about twenty inches of the snelling material. Thread one end through the eye of the hook as shown, allowing only a short length to extend beyond the eye. Grasp loop and hook shank between thumb and forefinger of the left hand.

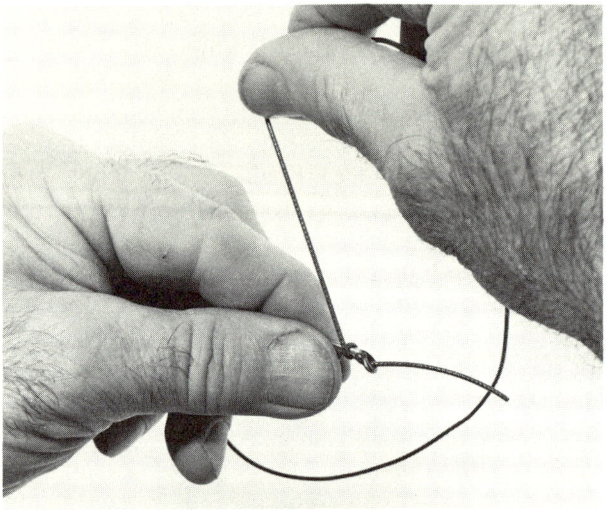

Grasp the snell between right thumb and forefinger a few inches below the eye and carry it over the shank of the hook. Note that two strands of snell lie along the shank. Both must be wound under. The photo shows the line crossing itself at the completion of the first turn.

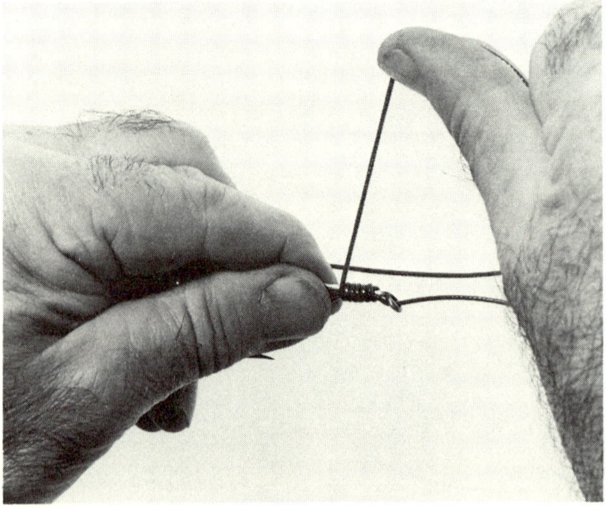

Continue winding evenly toward the bend of the hook. Make at least five complete turns. Opposite ends of the snell are now bound tightly against the shank.

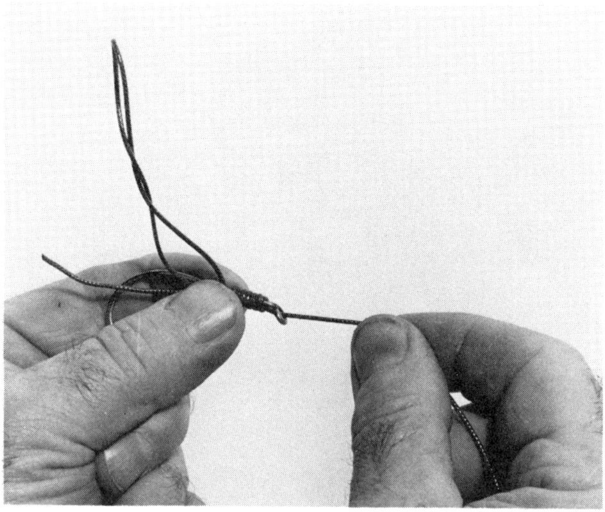

Hold completed windings in place with left thumb and forefinger. Pull slack tight with right hand.

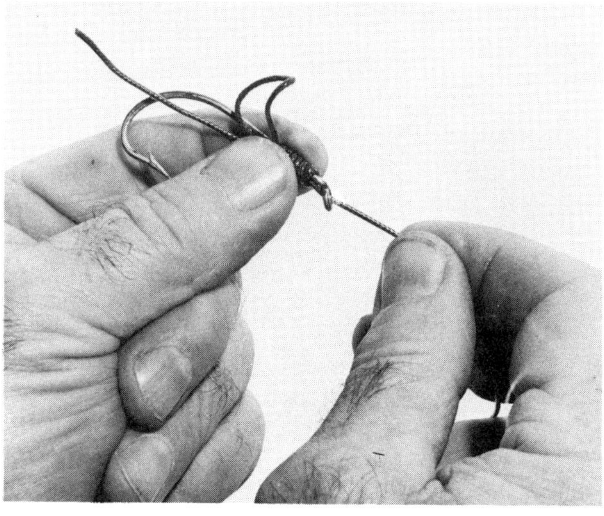

Photo shows loop of slack diminishing as it is pulled through the knot.

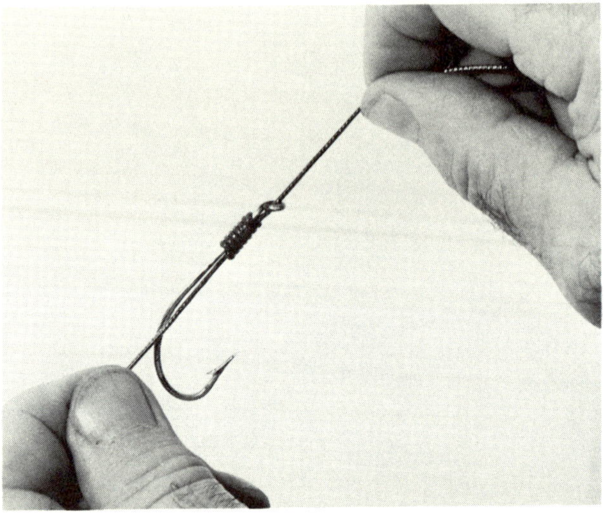

When slack has been snugged against windings, tighten the snell against the hook shank by pulling on the two ends as shown.

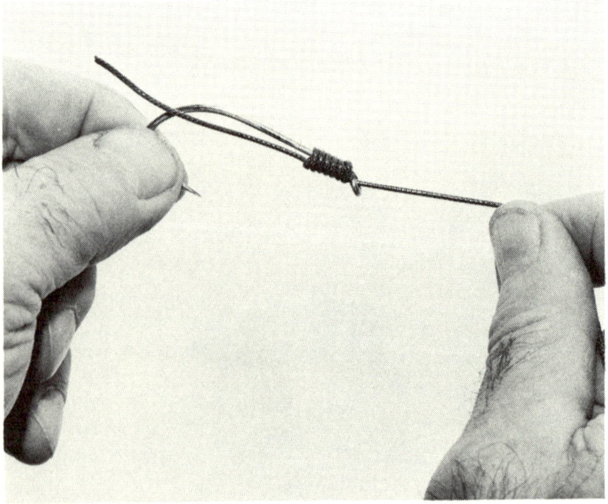

Jam knot against eye by pulling on hook and end of snell.

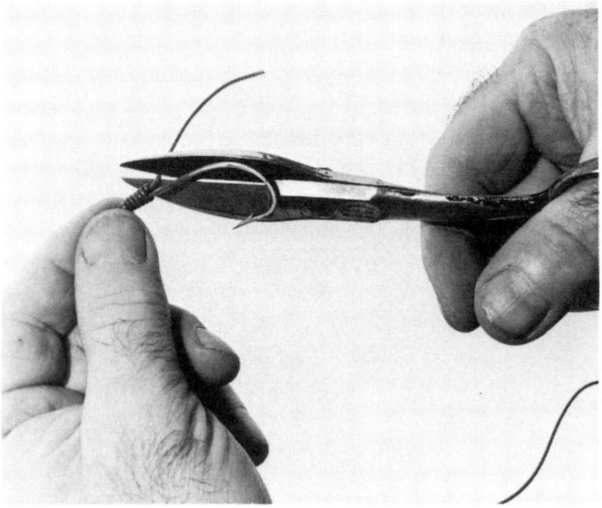

Trim the loose end.

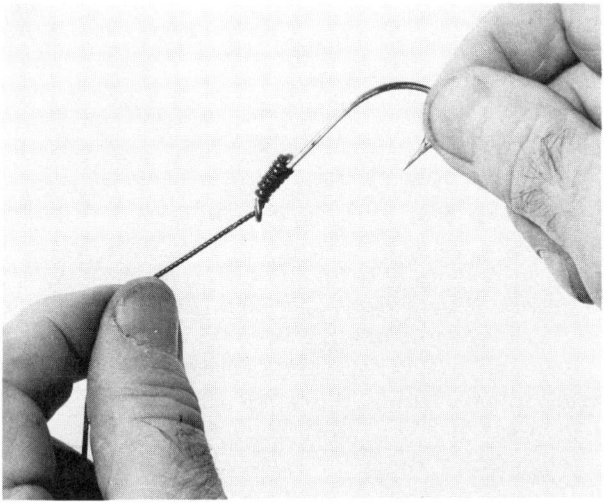

Photo shows completed knot. Tie loop in snell to give desired length.

As is evident from the photos and directions, the secret of tying the snelling knot is to work with a relatively short length of line that can be formed into a loop handily. As soon as I hit on this kink, I could soon tie single snelled hooks, hook gangs, and nail knots quickly and easily. What I *couldn't* do was snell a hook to the end of my line or leader, for here I had only one end to work with. The problem had me stumped for a while; it seemed impossible to complete the necessary turns around the hook shank without also twisting the line around the continuous length leading back to the rod and reel.

I finally found the answer by reversing the hook and employing the manipulations used in fly tying to create what is called a "whip finish." These manipulations are little more than alternate twists of the wrist which cause the palm of the hand to turn upward and downward as the line is wound over the hook shank. The movements are shown in the photos and explained in the directions. They can be learned with only a moderate amount of study and practice.

The benefits are well worth the effort, in my opinion, for I have found the snelling knot to be absolutely slip-proof, and it retains virtually all of the line's tensile strength.

Both virtues gain in importance as hook size and line diameter are reduced. Ultimate benefit is reached in ultralight bait fishing when lines testing as little as two pounds are used in conjunction with No. 12 and No. 14 hooks. It takes extra practice to learn to snell a No. 14 hook to a two-pound line, but it is well worth the special effort, for the retention of breaking strength becomes imperative when you have only two pounds going for you at the outset.

Other knots are as efficient in theory, but they are tied directly to the eye of the hook, which, as already pointed out, serves as a cutting edge and thus reduces holding power. The cutting effect increases as the hook size decreases, and the strength loss is prohibitive in ultralight bait fishing. When hooks are snelled to the line, the eye's adverse effect is bypassed; the line passes through the eye but is not tied to it. Rather, it is secured to the shank by multiple turns. Tension tightens the turns around the shank with no loss of strength resulting.

The advantages of using the nail knot to connect fly line and leader have been pointed out: minimum bulk and smooth passage through the guides. Both are as important to the bait fisherman as they are to the fly fisherman. It should be noted that difficulty will be encountered if the attempt is made to tie a long leader to the fly line with the nail knot. Fortunately, there is no need to do so. Instead, tie a two-foot section of heavy monofilament to the fly line, following the photos and directions. Following that, extend the leader to any desired length by adding smaller-diameter monofilament by means of a barrel knot. Directions for tying the barrel knot are so readily available that none are required here.

The only reason that I have devoted space to the snelling knot is that when I needed it in my business—tying my own worm gangs—I couldn't find directions for tying it. Now that I've learned the "secret," I use the knot to great advantage on a much broader front. In retrospect, it is hard to believe that I fished for half a century before learning to tie it. Equally incredible is the fact that the same inability is virtually universal. Fishermen learn to tie knots by the dozens, just as I did, yet for some strange reason the snelling knot is almost never among them.

The knack is well worth learning. Now that I have acquired it, I wouldn't be without it. Also, for any who may be interested, ability to tie the snelling knot carries with it a certain amount of prestige. Demonstrate to a group of fishermen that you can snell a hook directly to a line, or tie a nail knot in only a few moments, and I guarantee that you will immediately become the center of attention!

11

WALLEYES

THE WALLEYE'S formidable array of sharp teeth suggests a predator of pikelike ferocity, but the walleye displays little of the northern's innate savagery. Although the fish is often called a "walleyed pike," it is not a pike at all but, rather, a member of the perch family. Consequently, its habits are more perchlike than pikelike.

On the other hand, nature didn't give the walleye its impressive dental equipment for nothing, for the walleye is indeed a predator. Yet if there can be such a category, it is a "gentle" predator. It is also a gentle biter, a tester and nibbler with a well-earned reputation as a bait stealer. Finally, it has a very unpikelike liking for nightcrawlers.

The walleye has never attained a glamorous reputation, largely because it is not a savage striker or a spectacular fighter when hooked. Yet its many virtues add up to an impressive whole by my count: It grows to large size under favorable conditions; it will take almost every kind of natural bait and artificial lure at one time or another; walleyes travel in schools, which makes for fast fishing when the fish are in a feeding mood; it is ranked near the top of the list as a food fish by almost all who have sampled broiled walleye fillets. Finally, it deserves special honors for its willingness to bite the year round, spring and summer, fall and winter. I am personally indebted to the walleye for this last trait alone.

Although a hooked walleye doesn't leap like a salmon or unleash the brute strength of the smallmouth, I find it hard to fault the strong, stubborn battle a big one puts up before coming to the net. Although its show of muscle may not be overwhelming, it must be played with skill and care because of the ease with which hooks tear loose from its tender mouth tissues. For this reason alone, the issue always remains in doubt until the fish is in the net.

Because I have fished for walleyes with rod and reel and through the ice during each of the past thirty years, I have logged an impressive total of hours in pursuit of this fish. My experience has been confined largely to Lake Champlain, however, so while I can lay honest claim to local acquaintanceship with walleyes, I cannot lay equal claim to widespread familiarity on a geographical basis. Therefore, what follows will relate to the walleyes I know, with the cheerful admission that it may not hold true of the walleyes of other regions.

Anybody who is foolish enough to write about fishing from a how-to-do-it angle doesn't deserve sympathy, for he knows from the start, or at least he *should* know, that the fish will do their damnedest to make a liar out of him. Yet a measure of self-pity moves me to mention the circumstance that while the poor boob is trying to write authoritatively about the fish of his experience, those of other regions are doing everything possible to refute his learned words.

One regional difference which never ceases to plague me is that while ice fishermen of other areas than mine have good luck jigging walleyes, my efforts to jig Champlain walleyes have long been fruitless. Even on days when they're tripping tilts like crazy all around me, I cannot get them to take a jigged lure or bait.

Some years ago I appealed to the Dickey Tackle Company of Land O' Lakes, Wisconsin, an outfit which puts out an interesting catalog of ice-fishing supplies. Matt Lee, one of the brothers who own and operate the company, sent me some jigging lures which he said would often outfish a whole string of tilts. I used them with renewed hope, carefully following Matt Lee's directions, but I still caught nothing.

I reported this failure. Word came back: The lures were proven walleye killers; the fault *had* to be mine. I couldn't be following directions.

I redoubled my efforts, taking special pains to follow to the letter every step and nuance of the recommended presentation. I still keep at it, for jigging is one way to kill time between tripped tilts. But in five years of trying I have jigged exactly one walleye, and that one wouldn't have weighed a pound. I have talked with other local ice fishermen, and their unanimous conclusion is that Lake Champlain walleyes just can't be jigged through the ice.

I'm sure that I never convinced Matt Lee of this "truth." I'm equally certain that his faith in jigging lures is well founded. The difference is, or so I believe, that "his" walleyes are different critters from "mine," despite the fact that they belong to the same species. If other fishermen can jig the walleyes of his region, I think that I could jig at least a few—and sure would love to try. I'm sure that he still thinks that Lake Champlain walleyes *can* be jigged, but I'm equally certain that he couldn't jig them if we traded localities.

Fortunately, especially for the fishing writer, generalities do exist, and they usually outnumber the regional exceptions. For example, the spinner-and-nightcrawler combination is universally effective on walleyes. It is the standard offering on Lake Champlain, and judging from what I read and hear, it will "work" wherever walleyes exist. This is not surprising, for the walleye is a natural prospect for the combination. The flash of the spinner prods the walleye's predatory instinct, while the trailing 'crawler constitutes one of its favorite items of food.

The terminal rig for walleye trolling should be made up exactly as the one described in the chapter covering trout fishing in still water. I use twelve-pound-test monofilament in tying mine, mainly to save loss of tackle to snags.

Most walleye spinners come rigged with Indiana-style blades, but as I have pointed out previously, it is wise to have a variety of blade styles, finishes, and sizes with which to experiment on days when fish come hard. The spinner should be followed closely by a three-hook gang. I use No. 4 hooks in tying my walleye worm gangs. A single 'crawler strung over the three hooks will suffice, but I prefer to use a pair. Hook them so that the heads are closest to the spinner.

Successful walleye trolling consists of meeting three basic requirements: find the fish; bump bottom; troll very slowly.

In spring and early summer, before the water has warmed excessively, schools of walleyes meander over an established

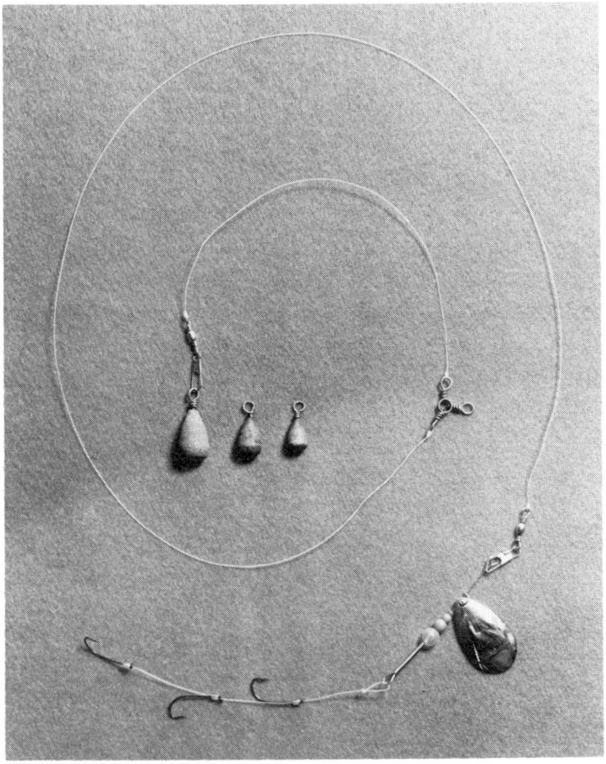

DEEP TROLLING RIG
Photo shows standard rig for bottom-bumping for walleyes, and for trout and bass when they seek deep water. Specifications: *thirty-inch strand of ten-pound (can vary) monofilament between three-way swivel and terminal snap swivel; eight-inch strand of same mono between three-way swivel and snap which holds bell sinker. Worm gang is made up with No. 4 hooks, which is a good size for walleyes and smallmouths (see Chapter 10 for tying directions). Smaller hooks, No. 8, are better for trout of modest size. Spinner shown (Indian blade) is always a good bet, but other styles and sizes should be tried if action is slow.*

course. Finding them is largely a matter of trial and error, for a school may be in a given spot one day and move to another the next. In general, they travel parallel to the shorelines. They are not likely to be found in deep water at this time of year, nor do they invade the weedy bays and other spots which attract northerns and pickerel.

I prefer to prospect for a school by starting within casting distance of shore. If I find nothing along a half-mile or so of shoreline, I move out another cast or so and reverse course. I continue working outward until the depth reaches fifteen feet or so. This establishes a belt or zone which will vary in width according to how sharply the bottom falls away from the shoreline. It may contain entire shallow bays, or it may shrink to a narrow band along steep shorelines. Wide or narrow, it usually holds the bulk of early-season walleyes.

Certain shoreline characteristics sometimes offer clues to where fish may be schooling: jutting points, wave-washed bars, etc. I take these into account during my shoreline prospecting, and sometimes the habit pays off. Yet it is almost as probable that the first school will turn up a hundred yards or more offshore, in water which lacks any visible features or characteristics of note.

In any event, wherever a first walleye is hooked the chances are excellent that there are others in the vicinity. For this reason it is a good habit to carry a float—a plastic jug, for example—with a line and weight attached. If the first walleye is caught a substantial distance from shore, pinpoint the spot by tossing the float overboard immediately. Following this, rework the immediate area thoroughly.

Fish hooked near shore can be marked as to position much more easily. It should be done accurately, however, for a relatively large school may be concentrated in a remarkably small area. Once the spot is marked down, whether by float or landmark, drag through it repeatedly. If you have it marked correctly, it is likely to be good for a fish or a strike on each of a succession of passes.

The matters of bumping bottom and trolling slowly are intertwined, for you can hardly do one without doing the other. When all is going as it should, the bell sinker can be felt "tunking" along the bottom. In water that is about eight feet deep, the sinker will bounce, and the spinner-'crawler will barely clear the bottom, if the length of line trolled is that which can be lobbed out comfortably with a spinning outfit and the motor is throttled down until it is only ticking over. Line must be shortened in lesser depths and more payed out where the water deepens. The trolling pace should be a crawl at all depths.

The proper pace is sometimes hard to maintain when moving against a strong wind. If the motor is revved up enough to provide steerage way, the pace is likely to be too fast for the walleyes. If the proper trolling speed is maintained, the bow will fall off, first this way and then that, resulting in an erratic course and the need for constant maneuvering. Yet the seesawing results in better water coverage, and the lure action is often more fetching than when the boat chugs along a straight course in calm water. At least, it seems to me that many of my best catches have been made while bouncing first this way and then that, in the face of a strong wind and a heavy chop.

The wind can be used to advantage whenever it is gentle enough so that drifting with it results in an acceptable trolling speed. More often it is too strong, moving the boat too fast. Therefore, unless I'm fishing in only a mild breeze, I troll into the wind as far as I desire and then run downwind and begin over again.

There is not much to be achieved by rod manipulation while trolling for walleyes, for a slow, steady pace, with the spinner churning evenly, seems to get the best results. Pike, pickerel, trout, salmon, and other species are often responsive to erratic lure behavior, but walleyes are not favorably moved by such strategy. To the contrary, they tend to shun a spinner-and-worm combination that alternately darts ahead and falls back under impulses from the rod.

As nearly as I can tell from what I feel from my rod, a walleye's manner of taking a trolled nightcrawler is to close in slowly from behind and merely close its jaws over all or part of the 'crawler. Only rarely is there the sensation of a strike in the sense in which the term is generally applied. Instead, there comes a slowing or sagging back with an equally slow buildup of pressure, much like the pressure which develops when the hooks strike a snag. As a result, many "strikes" turn out to be snags. More happily, "snags" frequently prove to be hooked fish.

It would seem impossible for a fish to grab a couple of nightcrawlers on a three-hook gang without becoming solidly hooked, but walleyes are experts at pulling off the stunt. More often than not, their first move is to nip at only the trailing ends of the 'crawlers. The fisherman who tries to set the hook prematurely stands a fifty-fifty chance of missing.

My answer to the first hint of a take is to lower the tip of my rod and thrust it back toward the fish as far as I can reach. This creates a moment of slack, during which the worm comes to a halt. This serves to reassure the nipping walleye, for it is no great lover of motion. In the short interval of immobility, it takes the 'crawlers more completely into its mouth, along with one or more of the worm gang's hooks. I wait until the line retightens and then sweep the rod upward.

If the walleye has taken the bait, and is of respectable size, the first impression is that of having set the hooks solidly in a snag, for a hooked walleye is usually slow to react. Disgust quickly turns to elation when the fish realizes that it is hooked, swaps ends, and puts a throbbing bow in the rod.

A spinner-and-minnow combination will draw plenty of strikes from walleyes, but the rates of missed strikes and stolen bait increase greatly. Walleyes are not strongly attracted to a minnow which has been sewn or laced on a hook so that it "rolls" behind the spinner. They will come much more readily to a four-inch minnow which has been hooked through both lips and merely "swims" behind the spinner without revolving. Here again, however, the walleye moves in cautiously and deliberately, nipping at the tail of the minnow preparatory to actually engulfing it. This usually tears the minnow from the hook, and the tug is often so slight that the fisherman never knows that he has had a strike.

If yellow perch are present, as they usually are, they will use the same tactics to strip minnows from the hook with frustrating regularity. They are often pesty when you are trolling with nightcrawlers, nipping at them constantly, with or without getting hooked, and necessitating constant rebaiting.

When this becomes too much of a problem I remove the hook gang and replace it with a single hook, and on the hook I hang a three-inch strip of squid which tapers from a width of half an inch to a pointed tail. The strip is almost as tough as preserved pork rind, and neither nipping perch nor tail-grabbing walleyes can strip it from the hook. Unlike the preserved rind, the strip has the taste and smell of fish, for I cut the strips from fresh squids which I buy in fish markets and then keep frozen. Incidentally, a strip of fresh squid can be used whenever a lure needs to be doctored up with a fluttering tail, and its taste and smell make it greatly superior to pork rind in my opinion.

Walleyes will not only grab this saltwater bait when it is trailed behind a spinner, but they will swallow it as they do a nightcrawler if they are given a moment of slack and inaction. I'm certain that they prefer the 'crawlers to pieces of squid, but I've caught enough walleyes on squid strips to know that they like the taste of them, too. I've also caught enough to know that the strips offer a happy compromise when perch are cleaning the 'crawlers from my hooks almost as fast as I can rebait.

Although the May-June trolling season is the most popular among Champlain walleye fishermen, many fish are caught earlier when they enter tributaries to spawn. Here, for the most part, trolling is forsaken in favor of other methods.

Where the water is fairly swift, fishermen anchor their boats and fish with live minnows. The minnows are hooked through both lips so as to create minimal resistance in the fast current. The live minnow is lobbed out gently in cross-stream casts, with several buckshot clamped to the line to take the minnow close to the bottom. It is "jigged" through a downstream arc, keeping just enough tension on the line for a bite to register. In this case the walleye doesn't close in from behind to grab the minnow by the tail and tweak it from the hook. The minnow is carried toward the walleye and the fish merely closes its mouth over the bait. A check of the line signals a bite. The fisherman may feed a little slack, but not much. The current quickly picks up the slack, and the walleye is likely to become suspicious and drop the minnow when it feels the additional tug. Therefore, the common practice, and the wisest, is to set the hook as soon as a bite is suspected.

Where the current in the spawning stream is moderate or slow, many fishermen prefer to drift, probing bottom as they move slowly with the current. Some use live minnows, this time hooked ahead of the dorsal fin, but the majority prefer nightcrawlers. Enough sinker should be used so that the bottom can be felt almost constantly and the nightcrawler dapped along it.

Walleyes tend to be hard to hook because they are such light biters, but in this drift fishing they come as close to being easy to hook as they ever do. Since the boat moves at the speed of the current, the jigged bait does the same. This aspect of naturalness is not lost on the walleyes; they tend to gulp the current-borne 'crawler much more confidently and forthrightly than they do one which is being trolled behind a spinner. Quite often, after sucking in the nightcrawler, they merely drift along with the current. The fisherman may not know that he has a bite until he lifts his rod and feels resistance.

Another phase of walleye fishing develops after hot weather sets in and the walleyes leave the shallows and seek the cooler temperatures of greater depths. They don't require the cold water which trout and salmon do, but they do abandon the shoreline shallows where they are plentiful in spring and early summer. Their favorite midsummer spots are reefs which rise up from deep water to form sunken plateaus. Here they respond to trolled spinner-and-'crawler combinations exactly as they do along the shorelines earlier in the season.

The big problem, of course, is to locate the reefs over which they congregate, for the presence of these is seldom betrayed by visible clues. An electric depth finder can be a help in finding such spots, but the location of a walleye reef is one fishing "secret" which cannot be kept for long. Any fisherman who plies his boat back and forth in a specific area for a significant period is bound to have company very shortly. A pair of boats working the same spot will soon attract a dozen. For this reason, the productive reefs of most walleye lakes are both well known and heavily fished.

These hot spots continue to produce, year after year, for the walleye is remarkably prolific wherever its habitat is favorable. Finding them is largely a matter of keeping an eye out for a concentration of slowly trolling boats.

The water over walleye reefs usually runs between twenty and thirty-five feet in depth, so it is a bit more difficult to get the spinner and bait down to the pay-dirt level than it is in the springtime shallows. A one-ounce bell sinker and a longer length of line may be required to reach the proper depth. The rules of springtime trolling still apply: Keep the sinker bumping along the bottom and troll very slowly.

Before closing this chapter I should point out that while trolling with spinner and nightcrawler is usually the surest way of making contact with walleyes, there are days when this does not hold true. On these days, for reasons known only to the walleyes, they will have nothing to do with what is usually their favorite bait. This should be the signal to experiment with artificials: sinking plugs, spoons, wobblers, etc. Stick to small lures and continue to roll slowly along the bottom. Limiting out is always a possibility, for somewhere in the tackle box there is likely to be a lure that will prove to be king for a day when it is finally given a try.

Over the long haul, however, the spinner-and-nightcrawler combination is almost a sure bet to outfish all other lures. Troll slowly, bump bottom—and enjoy!

12

NORTHERN PIKE AND PICKEREL

NORTHERNS AND PICKEREL can be caught on almost every type of artificial lure: spoons, wobblers, spinners, plugs, and what-have-you. They show little or no interest in small flies, but they will hit big streamers savagely, and they rise to large popping bugs with a commotion that is a sight to behold!

When it comes to natural bait, however, you can forget all else but minnows and other baitfish. Pike and pickerel are strictly fish eaters, and it's largely a waste of time to try to tempt them with anything else.

As pointed out in a previous chapter, they *will* hit a spinner-'crawler combination, but mainly because they are excited to rashness by the whirling spinner blade. But the worm-and-spinner is aimed at a broad clientele, and while it will take members of the pike tribe along with other species, I do not recommend it as a specific for northerns and pickerel.

When I concentrate on pike exclusively, I usually go after them with artificial lures. I prefer a bait-casting outfit, for it will handle the big spoons and plugs that are most effective. I usually take along a fly rod and some king-size popping bugs as well. These won't account for as many pike as the metal and plastic lures will, but the awesome eruptions that accompany surface strikes from big northerns more than make up for the difference. Yet there are days, by no means rare, when pike show little or no interest in artificial lures. On these days I don't hesitate to switch to live bait. If this doesn't turn the trick, you can be sure that the fish are off their feed and virtually invulnerable.

Pickerel are quite generally distributed throughout the New England states, but northerns are relatively scarce. My home territory is an exception, for northerns are much more common than pickerel in Lake Champlain, and in the warm-water lakes and streams of the Champlain Valley.

Otter Creek, the longest river contained entirely in Vermont, flows through the town in which I live, wending its sinuous way through miles of meadowland to join Lake Champlain some forty or so miles to the north. It is a sluggish stream over most of its length, with many snags, stumps, and secluded pockets which afford hiding places for fish. It holds many northerns, some of which grow to large size. These characteristics—slow flow, interesting cover, and big fish—add up to exceptionally fine float fishing, of which Mike and I take frequent advantage with the help of my thirteen-foot Grumman canoe.

We drift and cast to the shorelines for the most part, but always in the canoe we have a bait bucket and a can of worms. If the action is slow, or sometimes for the sake of variety, we tie small hooks to our lines and catch a few of the fallfish which abound in the stream and which furnish rich fare for the pike.

For the information of those who may not be familiar with fallfish, they are members of the minnow family which sometimes grow to considerable size. Mike and I must take them as they come, of course, but the half-dozen we save for the bait bucket are six-to-eight-inchers.

It is worth mentioning that fallfish are excellent bait for all predatory game fish. They come in for relatively little use only because they are relatively hard to come by and are even harder to keep alive for any appreciable length of time. But those we catch on the scene can be counted on to live long enough in the minnow bucket to satisfy our purpose.

Once we have a small supply, we pull into the first eddy or backwater, and there we drop our sashweight anchor. If possible, we tie the opposite end of the canoe to a snag or overhanging branch to keep it as steady as possible.

I tie on a large hook, impale one of the fallfish by the skin of its back, and then let it tow a bobber around the eddy at will. Mike usually prefers a different approach. He lowers his bait beside the canoe where he can keep an eye on it.

There are reasons for both methods. I figure that a traveling bait is more likely to drum up business than a stay-at-home. Mike is well aware of the logic in my line of reasoning. Yet he prefers to keep his bait within view to enjoy the thrill of actually seeing a pike take it.

This can be a nerve-tingling experience, especially if the pike is spotted before it takes the bait. One moment there is nothing in view but the struggling fallfish. Suddenly, there is an ugly snout in the picture, its brutal appearance bespeaking the epitome of malevolence. Its utter indifference to the plight of the poor fallfish is a chilling reminder of nature's merciless unconcern for the unfortunate creatures which it designates to serve as prey.

The pike is likely to study the fallfish for many minutes on end, during which the fallfish redoubles its efforts to escape for reasons which are easy to understand. After prolonged scrutiny, the chances are that the pike will disappear, demonstrating that fish are not lunkheads and accounting for the fact that they have not all been caught long since.

But there is also a chance that the pike will take, and when it does it is invariably with incredible speed. One moment the long fish is lying there like a length of waterlogged driftwood, the fallfish cavorting frantically within a yard of its cruel jaws. Suddenly, there is movement so swift that the eye cannot follow it. All it can report is that both pike and prey have vanished. All that remains to serve notice that the drama was real and not imaginary is a slowly settling cloud of silt that was raised from the bottom by the turbulence set up by the pike's swirling attack and departure.

But while the visual evidence may be sketchy, the line that immediately streams from Mike's reel is eloquently palpable.

"I'm gonna let him have it," Mike says wisely, leaving the bail of his spinning reel open while monofilament flows from it by the yard.

There is good reason to let a pike work on a big bait. While northerns have maws of enormous capacity, they seldom gulp a bait as bass are inclined to do. Instead, if my deductions and observations are valid, their first intent is to kill their prey by grabbing it in a crushing grip. I know their power to be viselike by reason of a once victimized thumb and the anguished distress messages which immediately issued therefrom. I also know the latent power of a pike's jaws from much bug-fishing experience.

I bug fish for northerns with huge poppers which I tie from deer hair. When bass grab a bug they usually take it well into their mouths, but pike grab it between their jaws and sharp teeth as I have indicated. When the fly rod is yanked vigorously in an attempt to set the hook, it fetches up solidly and this gives the impression that the pike is firmly hooked. The illusion continues as the pike moves off and puts a mighty strain on the fragile rod. But just as a ding-dong battle seems a certainty, the line often falls slack and the bug floats to the surface.

This has happened to me so often that I have come to realize that it is because I haven't hooked the fish at all. With the hair bug squeezed as though in a vise, no yank of a limber fly rod is going to move it so much as a fraction of an inch. Consequently, it cannot engage. The pike is not alarmed by the yank. Instead, it regards it as the bug's natural effort to escape and simply clamps down all the harder. Only when the fish feels certain that it has squeezed the life from its prey does it relax its grip preparatory to swallowing its prize. It is then that the line pulls the bug free.

Much the same thing happens when the bait fisherman tries to set the hook while it is still outside the pike's mouth, although in this case there is no impression of hooking up. Instead, the hook simply tears free from the bait, moving the fisherman to bitter self-recrimination and futile cussing, and providing the pike with a free snack. Here, as opposed to bass fishing, it *is* important to pay out line in the hope that the pike will eventually pause and swallow the bait. It may, and again it may not. It may feel the drag of the line, drop the bait, and go streaking away. If it does halt, timing the hook-setting bid is always a judgment call. The ratio of misses is always high enough to assure the uncertainty which makes fishing a challenge and keeps it interesting.

Except during our float trips, our bait fishing for pike and pickerel is done on days when we're fishing for anything and everything that's in the mood to bite. In a bid to cover all bets, each of us fishes two rods, one baited with a nightcrawler and the other with a live minnow. We carry a bucket holding dozens of small and medium-sized minnows, but in another bucket we keep a much smaller supply of bigger baits—suckers and chubs of up to eight inches in length which we keep in a separate cage in our minnow pond. The 'crawlers and smaller minnows are our bread-and-butter bait. The big baitfish constitute a bid to tangle with something hair-raising.

Most of the time one of us has one of the big baits on one of his rods, and usually before the day is over one or more epic struggles can be attributed to the king-size offerings. Sometimes we tangle with a trophy-size largemouth. Or a big old brute of a bowfin may latch onto one of the big suckers or chubs. More often, however, the heavyweights of a given day will be northerns which can't resist the appeal of what would seem to be a hearty meal.

Actually, of course, an eight-inch sucker is *not* a hearty meal for a big pike; more accurately, it is little more than a snack. A six- or eight-pound northern can swallow a foot-long fish with ease, and it often does. I have long suspected that the use of foot-long bait, or even longer, would bring spectacular results. But baits of that size are hard to obtain and are harder to keep alive. Finally, it is difficult to fish them properly on ordinary tackle. But if eight-inch bait is a compromise, which probably it is, it is a happy one. The heavyweights give our eight-inch suckers and chubs enough of a play to keep things interesting.

With suitable bait at hand, there are few tricks to pike and pickerel fishing. The main requirements are to seek out the type of water the closely related species prefer and then present the bait in the manner best calculated to attract their attention.

One of the spots I look for is the edge of reeds, the tall ones which come up through several feet of water to extend another three or four feet above the surface. Pike and pickerel lie in wait among the sunken stalks, in what amounts to an underwater forest. There they hold themselves in readiness to pounce on baitfish which cruise along the edge.

Yet to make the most of such spots it is important to know something of pike nature. Although they lie in wait, hair-triggered to pounce, they almost invariably refuse to break cover for any but very short distances. Instead, they play what is strictly a waiting game, refusing to strike until their prey approaches to within easy reach of their tooth-studded jaws.

Because Mike and I know the critical importance of proximity, we often spend an inordinate amount of time jockeying for precisely the right position, often anchoring and reanchoring several times until wind and restraining anchor combine to bring the boat to rest where we can lower our minnows within a foot or two of the outer edge of the reeds. For those who seek to catch pike and pickerel on live minnows, the importance of such careful maneuvering cannot be overemphasized. It has long been apparent to Mike and me because of the following fact. With our boat properly located, minnows fished from the side of the boat closest to the reeds will bring strikes from pike and pickerel. Fish the same minnows on the *opposite* side and neither will leave their hiding places the relatively short distance required to gather them in. Minnows fished on the far side will account for bass and other species more given to cruising, but not pike or pickerel. They're programmed to wait for their prey to come to them, and there's no changing them.

Where tall, deeply rooted reeds are not in evidence, I look for sunken weedbeds. Pike often lie under weeds and pads which show at the surface and which usually denote quite shallow water. But it is my experience that these spots tend to hold small pike and very few lunkers. The beds which I refer to grow in water which is six or more feet deep, with the tops of the weeds a substantial distance beneath the surface. These beds usually cover a relatively large area, so exactitude of location is never as critical as when fishing the edge of reed growths.

The important thing here is to keep the bait swimming as close to the tops of the weeds as possible. The pike lie deeper, of course, using the weeds as concealment. Again, they are reluctant to move any significant distance in pursuit of prey. They will flash up to grab a minnow which barely clears the weed tops, but are likely to ignore one that hangs a couple of feet higher.

The best means of keeping the bait within tantalizing proximity is to use a bobber and enough sinker to drag the minnow down the full length of the supported line. After adjusting the bobber so that the hook will barely clear the weeds, I open the reel bail and allow the big sucker or chub to tow the bobber wherever it pleases. This brings the bait to the attention of the pike of a considerable area, and also makes for fascinating fishing.

I love the suspense of watching a dry fly come over the lie of a feeding trout, and the thrill of seeing the fly disappear in the center of a broad swirl is one of the most exciting moments in fishing. I find similar fascination in watching a bobber while a big, lunker-tempting sucker drags it erratically over what I know to be pike-holding water. It may cruise this way and that without interruption, but no matter how long the wait I can't tear my gaze from the dancing and dipping float, nor does my feeling of expectancy diminish. When, at last, the bobber picks up speed and reflects suddenly inspired action on the part of the bait, my pulse quickens. I know that a pike has closed in and the sucker is trying desperately to escape. I know full well that all may come to naught, but there's a good chance that the inspecting pike will take. The suspense becomes delectable!

The bobber continues to dance and dart, activated by the sucker's frantic struggles. Suddenly, the minor tremors give way before a vicious yank, which jerks the bobber under with a violent finality that bespeaks the end of the sucker's earthly troubles. The bobber goes streaking away, deep beneath the surface, and line flows from the open spool of my spinning reel.

The only black mark against a bobber is the resistance it sets up as the biting pike tows it away. Sometimes this is enough to arouse suspicion and cause the fish to drop the bait. But a northern is a bodacious critter, and once it makes up its mind to grab a baitfish it is not easily deterred. Besides, even though omission of the bobber might result in a higher percentage of hooked fish, the bait, in its absence, must be held above the weeds by the rod, which confines it to the area immediately surrounding the boat. I prefer to advertise as widely as possible. Also, I guess that I'm a natural-born bobber-watcher.

Baitfish can be used to take pike and pickerel in another way which is largely overlooked. This consists of rigging a large dead chub or sucker on one or more big hooks and then casting and retrieving it exactly as one casts a plug or spoon. If the hooks are adjusted so that the dead bait turns and wobbles during the retrieve, the result is compounded appeal: strike-stirring action, to which pike and pickerel are inordinately susceptible, plus the allure of a genuine food item.

The element of tantalizing action can be enhanced by adding a single-bladed spinner ahead of the revolving bait. This combination not only will take pike and pickerel whenever they're in the mood to go for spoons and plugs, but it will continue to score during those interludes when neither species can be persuaded to hit artificial lures.

I know from long experience with both species that the days when they are disinterested in plugs and hardware occur with considerable frequency. Those are the days when it pays to sweeten the ante with something that's for real: a sucker or chub that doesn't *imitate* a baitfish, but actually *is* one!

Another deadly pike and pickerel bait is the strip or slab of perch belly that used to be so popular with cane-pole fishermen. The traditional bait was a three-inch section of perch belly, cut so as to include the bright-red ventral fins. A single large hook was stabbed through the strip between the fins. This is still a good bait, but a strip cut from the belly of a pike or pickerel will do as well. The fins are not included in this case. Instead, just slice a narrow strip from the white belly which is three or four inches long. It should taper from a width of about an inch to a point at the tail. The front end should be trimmed to a blunt point, and the hook should be placed near the forward end.

Old-timers flipped out these baits with their long cane poles, then "skittered" them across the surface in an arc. After the strike, always an exciting swirl, the pickerel or pike was given time to swallow the bait before the hook was yanked home. Stories have it that whenever a pickerel or pike was big enough to threaten line breakage, the cane pole was heaved overboard and the fish allowed to tire itself out by towing it around!

I can't vouch for the truth of the last allegation, but I have caught pickerel by "skittering" with a cane pole, and can attest to the fact that it is an exciting way to fish despite the primitive nature of the tackle employed. I also know from experience that a belly strip is a fetching pike and pickerel bait when cast and retrieved with a spinning outfit, or when lobbed out with a fly rod and brought back in erratic spurts. Again, action is combined with the real taste and smell of actual fish, a combination which the members of the pike family are always hard put to resist.

Both pike and pickerel are often held in contempt by fishermen who concentrate on more glamorous species, but such poor-mouthing is richly undeserved. No fish strike more savagely, and the chain pickerel puts up a fight which, for its size, needs no apology. Although northerns run to much larger sizes, they are sometimes disappointingly sluggish when first hooked. But when you have them alongside, watch out! They may appear to be completely played out; but when you reach for them with the net they're likely to explode with a fury which has broken many a rod and snapped many a line.

Because their inertness is always dangerously deceptive, never lift a live pike from the net and lay it in the bottom of the boat or canoe. It is likely to come alive in an outburst of convolutions which will lay waste to everything not nailed down!

Always keep a club handy, and subdue any big pike that you intend to keep by batting it over the head while it's still in the net. By the same token, remove the hooks from those you plan to release while they, too, are still safely in the net. Never, never reach inside a pike or pickerel's mouth, even if it is stone dead. Use pliers to remove hooks to spare yourself badly cut fingers.

Needless to say, I'm not among those who downgrade pike and pickerel. I owe them far too much, for their widespread availability, their willingness to hit and bite throughout the entire year, and for the added scope which these characteristics add to my fishing.

13

BAIT

ONE OF THE BIGGEST "SECRETS" of worm fishing, or of bait fishing of any kind for that matter, is to have bait on hand at all times. Those who must depend on bait dealers are often stymied, for dealers have a demoralizing habit of being "fresh out" just when a fellow can shake free to fish. In general, bait is usually in good supply in the spring, but then becomes scarcer and scarcer as the summer progresses. If I counted on dealers, I know that it would be my luck to have the last worm or minnow disappear just when I needed bait most.

Fortunately, I'm situated so that I can keep my own bait on hand. But I can sympathize with the dealers. Collecting and keeping bait for one's personal use poses problems enough. For the dealer, the same problems are magnified many times.

Nightcrawlers can be picked up almost nightly during the spring and early summer. The job is always backbreaking, but the big worms are very much in evidence during that period of heavy dews and frequent rains, on lawns and golf courses and even between the rows of vegetables in home gardens. Small earthworms are equally abundant during the same period, although they must be dug up with a spading fork or shovel.

Later, when the weather becomes hotter and drier, the nightcrawlers no longer emerge nightly and the small worms retreat to depths beyond the reach of spade or shovel. Obviously, the way around the problem is to lay in supplies which will last all season during the time of abundance and availability. The only lump in the gravy is the difficulty of keeping the supply alive after they have been collected.

There are but few tricks involved in picking nightcrawlers or in digging small worms. You need a flashlight and a can in the first case, and a spading fork and a can in the second. Collecting the small worms is merely a matter of turning over the ground to expose them and then picking them up. Gathering nightcrawlers is not quite that cut-and-dried, for they do have some means of escaping.

Nightcrawlers are keenly sensitive to ground vibrations, so the worm picker should walk slowly and as softly as possible. The worms have no eyes, but they are somewhat sensitive to light. This degree of sensitivity seems to vary with temperature and humidity, and, of course, with the strength or intensity of the beam of the flashlight which is used to spot them. Their reaction to both vibrations and detected light is to duck underground with surprising speed.

On nights when they are extra-sensitive to light, it helps to search for them with only the outer fringe of the flashlight's "spot." If this continues to alert them, tape a piece of red or orange cellophane over the lens.

One more 'crawler-picking tip deserves mention. Grasp them only tightly enough so that they cannot escape, and exercise patience in pulling them from their burrows; simply hold them taut until they release their grip on the earth. This slows down the rate of production a bit, but the increased survival rate will more than make up for the difference. Those which are squeezed hard and yanked from their burrows usually suffer injuries from which they soon die.

There *are* special ways of persuading 'crawlers to emerge during unfavorable conditions. The simplest and best, wherever it is possible, is to soak the ground with a garden hose at sundown. Nightcrawlers of the soaked area will come topside soon after dark. Drive a stake into the ground and then "saw" a rough board across the top. The vibrations will drive 'crawlers to the surface. The mild electric shock from the kind of hand-cranked generators which used to be a part of every telephone will also bring them up. The stronger shock from a house-current outlet will do the same, but there is always the risk that in bringing the worms aboveground it may put the operator underground—permanently. A solution of water and mustard poured over the ground will drive 'crawlers to the surface to escape the irritation which the solution causes. The worms gathered by this method should be rinsed in clean water before storage.

I have tried all the foregoing emergency methods with varying degrees of success. All are somewhat uncertain and, of course, are most likely to fail just when the need is most critical. It is much more satisfactory to lay in large supplies when the picking is easy, and then take steps to keep the worms alive over the entire season.

One of the critical factors in worm storage is maintaining the proper temperature. If you are lucky enough to have an old refrigerator which you can use for the purpose, your troubles in that respect are virtually solved. Most of us find it expensive enough to keep one refrigerator running, to say nothing of a second, so artificial refrigeration is out for the majority. Fortunately, there are alternatives which involve no cost.

Obviously, the ideal temperature is that of the earth itself. Consequently, any container of substantial depth—a couple of feet or more—will provide worms with the proper temperature if it is set in the ground to the full limit of its depth. I have two such worm holders, neither of which cost me anything. One is an old porcelain bathtub; I lowered it into a hole dug to fit it and then tamped the earth solidly around it. A screen over the outlet provides drainage without allowing the worms to escape. The other container is a freezer from a dairy delivery truck which was junked after it went on the blink. This is about two feet square and three feet deep. It has no drainage outlet, but it has a cover which prevents flooding from rain.

Mike and I plan to put about a thousand 'crawlers in each container in April or May. Losses occur, but the net result is a supply of bait that lasts all season.

The sink-in-the-ground principle can be used on a smaller scale. A ten- or twelve-quart pail, for example, will keep a hundred or so 'crawlers alive for a surprisingly long time if it is sunk flush with the top of the ground in a shady spot. Holes should be punched in the bottom to provide drainage.

Another critical matter is the material in which the worms are kept. Earth from areas in which the worms abound suggests itself, but it is not suitable for keeping large quantities of worms in concentration. Special materials can be bought, and these do an adequate job. My favorite material, mainly because it costs nothing while serving well, is the leaves which I rake from my lawn each spring. Most of these are from maple trees.

Originally, I tried rotted leaves. This rich mulch struck me as being exactly the material that I would prefer were I a nightcrawler. The nightcrawlers didn't agree, and registered their protest by expiring. Then I had the good fortune to visit a dealer who kept his worms in *dry* leaves, or leaves that were dry when first put in the worm containers. From then on, the dealer said, he gave the leaves only a very light sprinkling of water daily.

This proved to be the tip I needed. I keep the leaves in the covered freezer slightly moist by sprinkling. The combination of rain and drainage seems to keep the leaves in the bathtub at the proper moisture level.

In any event, moisture control is the third vital factor, with the big danger being on the side of too much moisture, rather than too little. It is best to start with very light sprinklings, with the aim of keeping the material damp but never saturated.

Proper temperature, suitable material, and the right degree of moisture; the three should have added up to perfection, and for a while they seemed to. The first year Mike and I installed our bathtub wormery, we gloried in what promised to be a steady supply of 'crawlers that would meet our need until fall. Then one morning we discovered that our beautiful supply of fat and healthy 'crawlers had all but disappeared. About all that the fork turned up were the remnants of recently mangled worms. More forking finally revealed the villain: a star-nosed mole which had moved in and had been living in the lap of luxury ever since. He paid dearly for his invasion, but we knew that others would soon follow. We hastened to fashion the screened cover which we should have provided in the first place.

Now, with our two covered containers, and other factors under control, we have nightcrawlers and small worms available when many other fishermen are forced to do without. Incidentally, the small worms which we use for trout and panfish do equally well in the same containers.

But as the feller once said, there's no such thing as a free lunch. If you want to have a constant supply of worms you've got to work to maintain it. I've revealed how I go about it. But I'm all ears if others have found easier and better ways.

If the problem of keeping a supply of worms is a tough one, that of obtaining and keeping live minnows is even tougher, especially if you use minnows summer and winter as Mike and I do. However, as with 'crawlers, large quantities of minnows can be obtained at the proper time, although the process is more complicated than worm picking, and involves much harder work.

Here in the Champlain Valley, the time of plenty occurs in October and November when several species of minnows ascend Lake Champlain tributaries to spawn. These spawning runs take place in small creeks, brooks, and even in streamlets that are little more than mere trickles. If you're on the scene with a seine at just the right time, it is possible to take minnows in enormous quantities.

Last winter, Mike and I compared notes with a bait dealer from whom we had just purchased a power ice auger.

"How many minnows did you ever seine in one day?" I asked.

The dealer reached behind him and took a log book from a shelf. He ran a forefinger down a column of figures.

"Twelve hundred quarts," he said finally. "On October sixteenth."

I knew that the guy was speaking of solid quarts—all minnows and no water—which was one helluva lot of minnows.

"How did you *know* that you caught that many quarts?" I asked.

"I damn *well* knew," he replied feelingly, "because we carried them to the truck in twelve-quart pails jammed chock-a-block full. A hundred pailfuls, and we like to broke our backs totin' 'em!"

I decided against further cross-questioning. The purchase of a hundred-and-fifty dollar auger will go only so far in warding off a punch in the nose.

It is interesting to note that the same minnows which die easily in warm weather can be handled safely, as the dealer described, in the near-freezing weather of fall. The dealer's salvation was a truck equipped with aerated tanks.

The going winter price for walleye bait hereabouts is three bucks a quart. It is also interesting to contemplate the day's pay the dealer made, even after making allowances for subsequent losses.

Needless to say, our minnow-seining operations, while somewhat similar, are on a considerably smaller scale. Our aim is to lay in between five and ten gallons, which, if a good share live, will last us and a few friends through the winter and the following spring and summer. Our "truck" is Mike's VW bus, and our "tanks" consist of four or five large garbage cans. Usually, because we go when time permits and seldom hit the run at its peak, we have to make two or three trips to complete our supply, especially if a can tips over on the return trip, as has been known to happen.

Mike and fellow fisherman George Ladabouche drag seine in small Lake Champlain tributary.

Silly though it may seem, we and our friends get almost as much fun from seining our bait as we do from catching walleyes and other fish with it later. Pulling our twenty-foot seine (dealers use much longer ones) is hard work, and results are always uncertain. A snag can upset the net near the end of a long drag, allowing all the bait to escape. There are other difficulties, such as navigating through knee-deep mud and stepping into holes that are deeper than our waders. But when a drag comes off well, and the final lift shows several quarts of shimmering minnows in the net, the sense of gratification is almost as great as that which results from sliding a five-pound walleye atop the ice or leading one the same size into the landing net.

Unfortunately, the acquisition of a year's supply of minnows is the smallest part of the problem. The major part, of course, is keeping the minnows alive indefinitely. My solution was to have a pond dug expressly for the purpose. Obviously, not all fishermen are so situated that a pond is possible, but for those who are a pond is a major blessing.

My home is on a five-acre lot, with a deep ravine on one side and a much shallower gully on the other. A tiny brook flows through the ravine and suggests possibilities. Unfortunately, the trickle becomes a raging torrent when a flood occurs, and any dam within my means would be carried away. There is no brook in the shallow gully, but it is mucky and drains a considerable area. I gambled that the drainage would be enough to fill a small pond and keep it filled.

A local contractor used bulldozer and backhoe to throw up an embankment and to dig a hole which, together, provided for a circular pond about forty feet in diameter, and about eight feet deep in the center when it is full. Although the pond was dug in August, during the driest part of the summer, water began seeping in immediately. By the next morning there appeared to be about two bathtubs full of water in the center of the crater. Close inspection revealed that a squatter had taken up residence: a frog which had materialized overnight from I know not where.

The hole filled slowly during a particularly dry fall, but by minnow-seining time the water at the center was five feet deep, enough to float the wood-and-wire minnow car I had built in the meantime. The car is a screened box with a hinged wooden cover, four by four by four feet. We collected our supply of minnows and dumped them in the cage, and they did splendidly, keeping us in bait all winter and on into the following summer.

The pond filled rapidly in April when melting snow and spring rains added to the drainage. The four-inch plastic pipe which I had installed near the top of the embankment kept the water from flowing over the top; but the embankment itself, still only raw soil, became a soft pudding as the frost came out of it. Leaks developed which I was hard put to keep plugged with sod, and for a spell I feared that the project was going to be a washout in the full sense of the word.

Fortunately, the embankment held, largely because I reinforced the entire face of it with freshly cut sod. As a long-range precaution, I jabbed fresh willow cuttings into the face of the embankment as well, and these took root and are providing steadily increasing reinforcement.

The pond shrinks in midsummer, but never yet to the point where it will not support minnows. Fall rains refill it, and the loss from seepage grows less as the embankment settles and the root structure becomes more lush and matted. I have strong hope that eventually the pond will remain level full, but in the meantime it serves the purpose for which it was constructed. Since it was dug, there have been no times when Mike and I haven't had minnows immediately available.

Those for whom a pond is an impossibility are still far ahead of the game if they have a means of catching minnows when dealers are sold out. Years ago I depended solely on the traditional cylin-

A seine full of minnows. They will be carried home in garbage cans and stored in bait pond. Low temperature (November) assures survival during transportation.

drical traps made of wire mesh. While these are better than nothing, they are never dependable. Usually they must be baited and left overnight, with no guarantee that they will contain any minnows the next morning. Nothing is more demoralizing than to pull up an empty trap when you have your heart set on a day's fishing which requires a supply of minnows for any real hope of success.

A seine is much more productive and reliable. It need not be long; with merely an eight-footer you and a partner can usually scrounge up enough minnows for a day's fishing from some small stream or other, or even along the shoreline of a pond or lake. One of the chief failings of the minnow trap is that it gives the minnows a choice, and many are just too smart to enter the thing. A good drag with a seine provides no such option; all the bait fleeing before it will be caught when it is finally hauled ashore. Accordingly, results are often surprisingly gratifying when chances seem slim, especially when only a few dozen minnows are needed. Drag

From the live box in our minnow pond Mike dips minnows for a day's fishing. Pond makes minnows available on a year-round basis.

through a stretch where nary a minnow can be seen, and a half-dozen or so are likely to show up in the net.

One word of advice about seines. Avoid the cheap seines made of cotton. They are attractively inexpensive, but they tear easily and rot quickly, and most soon develop the same kind of runs that occurs in women's hosiery. Nylon seines cost more, but are much cheaper in the long run. The netting is almost tear-proof, no runs develop, and nylon doesn't rot, even with long use.

When minnows are seined the day before, the fisherman is faced with the problem of overnight storage. This is easily solved by the use of a large minnow pail of the type made from semiporous material. I'm not sure how these pails work, but I assume that they effect cooling by permitting a certain amount of evaporation and that they also allow the water to absorb oxygen through the sides. At any rate, I know from experience that they will keep several dozen minnows alive overnight, and even longer, without any change of water.

Temporary storage of larger numbers of minnows can be accomplished with the help of one of the little vibrator pumps used to aerate aquariums. If one is used, be sure to cover the pail. Minnows don't seem to relish the pulsations of the contraption, and will jump out unless prevented.

Most of the bait that Mike and I seine we use for walleyes, smallmouths, calicoes, perch, and a few other species. These minnows run from two to four inches long for the most part. The larger baitfish that we use for pike, pickerel, largemouths, bowfins, etc. are usually in water that is too deep for easy seining. We pick up a few in the fall seining, of course—suckers, chubs, and horned dace—but for the most part we rely on chubs, which we catch on No. 14 hooks baited with dabs of worms. Very few die from the hooking, and since we keep only a few dozen on hand in a special cage, this rather slow method of collecting is adequate. Bait dealers must rely on seining and trapping to gather the larger quantities which they need. Large bait is always difficult to acquire in quantity lots, and this both explains and justifies the high price of big bait, a price which is rising toward a quarter apiece around here.

Worms and minnows which have been kept alive in storage will serve no purpose if they die on the way to the fishing grounds, or in the boat during the day. In the matter of keeping nightcrawlers

MINNOWS WITH APPROPRIATE HOOKS
Use largest size for northerns, pickerel, and largemouths. Hook size: No. 1/0.
Use next largest for smallmouths. (Will take the above species as well, but larger size is better.) Hook size: No. 2.
Use third for walleyes. Hook size: No. 4.
Use smallest for perch and calicoes. Hook size: No. 8.

and small worms fresh and lively on even the hottest days, Styrofoam comes to the rescue. Mike and I have adapted a container made of this material in which some long-forgotten object was shipped. A counterpart can be improvised from one of the buckets of the same material which are used to keep ice available in fishing camps, motel rooms, etc. All that's needed in addition to the container is a plastic bottle which, with a can of worms, will fit in the Styrofoam container with the cover on. Fill the plastic bottle with water to within two inches of the top and freeze solid. Place both worms and frozen bottle in the container when you set out fishing. If the cover is kept on the container religiously, the worms will stay cold, fresh, and lively throughout the day. Any surplus can go back into storage without suffering any ill effects.

Keeping minnows alive in transport, and while fishing, is a harder problem, especially on hot days. The removable liners of small minnow buckets offer a solution, once the fishing grounds are reached. They can be secured with a rope and dropped overboard, where they will stay afloat with the fresh water keeping the bait alive. However, if a large supply is crowded into a small bucket, the minnows are likely to die before you have a chance to use them. (It's just as demoralizing to arrive at the launching site with a bucket of dead bait as it is to find that none is available at the outset.)

The best answer to this problem that I've been able to find is the large porous bucket which I recommended for the short-term storage of a day's supply of minnows. I use the same bucket in the boat while fishing, preferring the small chore of changing water occasionally over the nuisance of lifting dripping bucket liners aboard each time I change location.

Incidentally, the hardboard cover of the "breather" bucket should be firmly in place while running from one spot to another. Although the vibrations of an outboard motor apparently do minnows no damage, they seem to drive them nuts. If the cover is left off, the bottom of the boat will soon be aflop with minnows that have leaped from the open bucket. With the cover on, they can be heard thumping against it in leaps of desperation, a circumstance which always gives me further reason to rejoice that I wasn't born a minnow.

Worms and minnows probably account for at least ninety percent of the bait by sport fishermen. The remainder—crayfish, hellgrammites, grasshoppers, crickets, etc.—are usually collected in small quantities as the need arises, with little attempt at storage, or they are bought from bait dealers when available. There seems little to justify an "in depth" treatment of their acquisition, although a few simple tips may be helpful.

In riffles—shallow stretches of fast water—both crayfish and hellgrammites can be caught with a seine. First, anchor the seine across the riffle by placing rocks along the lower edge. With the seine in position, turn over the rocks on the bottom for a considerable distance upstream of the seine. (A hoe or rake is a big help.) Dislodged crayfish and hellgrammites will be swept into the seine by the current.

Hellgrammites are almost always found in riffles, but crayfish also live under rocks along the edges of lakes and ponds. Overturn the rocks as gently as possible in an effort to expose the crayfish without putting them to flight. They can be collected by hand, although their capture requires deftness. The hand should approach from the rear, by the way, for crayfish swim backward.

The job is greatly simplified by the use of a large tin can from which both top and bottom have been removed. When a crayfish has been spotted at rest, simply drop the can over it. The trapped bait will scuttle around the inside of the cylinder, but lacks the wits to escape from the open top. It can be grabbed easily while it bounces around inside the can.

Finally, crayfish are scavengers. They can be trapped in wire-mesh minnow traps that have been baited with fish or meat. Traps should be left set overnight, for crayfish are nocturnal of habit.

As for gathering grasshoppers, crickets, grubs, and other natural baits, you're strictly on your own as far as I'm concerned. However, don't overlook freezing as a means of keeping these baits indefinitely. Their year-round availability can sometimes turn failure into success. Given a choice, I like all bait alive and kicking. Nevertheless, I can vouch for the efficacy of frozen bait items, an effectiveness which persists indefinitely after the time of freezing.

An entire book could be written about the capture and storing of natural baits. Such a book *should* be written, in fact, although certainly by somebody who knows far more about the subject than I do. The bulk of my efforts has always been aimed at catching fish. But there are days when I don't think that I've made too much progress in that direction either.

14

THE MYSTERY OF SCENT

ONE MEMORABLE MORNING, Mike and I had the good luck to find ourselves among largemouths when they were really hitting, and we kept after them without pause. By lunchtime our legs were badly cramped, so we ran the canoe ashore in order to stretch our muscles and restore circulation while we ate our sandwiches.

I hadn't then kicked the nicotine habit, and my after-lunch cigarette was dragged down to the last inch when I spotted an enormous bullfrog, stolidly perched atop a raft of lily pads and other vegetation.

"I wonder what the hell he's *doing,*" I remarked to Mike, after bringing the jumbo frog to his attention. "Is he just sitting there, or is he *looking* for something?"

It was an idle question, of course. Mike's empathy with respect to frogs was as lacking as mine, and it was obvious that the squatting frog wasn't about to volunteer an answer.

My thwarted curiosity prompted me to reflect on the inscrutability of wildlife in general, and on that of the sphinxlike frog in particular. In a mild fit of frustration I took dead aim at the enigmatic critter and flipped my cigarette butt at it. Whereupon my question was answered with electrifying speed and clarity.

When the butt splatted down within a foot of the frog's nose, the big amphibian pounced on it with the speed and ferocity of a lurking tiger. It swallowed the butt with a single gulp, returned to its vantage point, and calmly awaited the appearance of more "prey." Mike and I delayed our resumption of fishing to see if the frog would show signs of inner distress, but none materialized. Apparently, all is grist that comes to the digestive mill of a frog!

For once, my curiosity concerning a wild creature's inner feelings of the moment had been fully satisfied. Behind its enigmatic façade of passivity, that frog was as predatorily minded as a starving wolf! Yet it should be noted that I discovered this truth solely by accident. I was powerless to arrive at it by deduction.

For the most part, human observers can do little more than guess about the subjective identity of other creatures. We and they share an awareness of surroundings which makes living things distinguishable from inanimate objects, but the phenomenon of sensibility is ever unique to the creature in which it reposes. It differs in scope and in acuity, and it differs enormously in the ways in which its messages are interpreted.

Human beings exceed all other forms of life in the degree to which they extract meaning from the messages delivered by their sensibilities. Yet herein lies a paradox, for the acuity of human perception ranks far below that of creatures of much less intelligence. Birds see with a clarity which puts human vision to shame; deer hear clearly those sounds which no human ear can detect; bears can smell for long distances those substances which are odorless to humans at point-blank range; comparable differences exist along a front of almost infinite length.

Furthermore, with a disparity approaching perversity, humans are denied utterly many sensitivities which are bestowed upon creatures of supposedly lower orders. The bat, for instance, has its own built-in radar system. Many wild creatures have a sense of direction which has no counterpart in man. Mass surges of activity among wildlife populations clearly suggest a sensitivity to cosmic impulses to which humans are quite oblivious. The list could be expanded indefinitely, for almost every form of wildlife has one or more means of assessing its surroundings that lies beyond the pale of human capability.

I make this point because it is largely ignored by many who enjoy the outdoors, and by fishermen in particular. Most anglers are interested in fish as the objects of their search. They find them considerably less fascinating than the preoccupying skills and techniques employed in reducing them to possession.

A more deeply reflective minority enhance their sport by adopting a broader viewpoint. They concentrate upon their angling efforts no less intently, but they also ponder the true nature of the fish they seek. These individuals are relatively rare. This is unfortunate, for the pleasures of fishing derive not only from the challenge of achieving success, but also from the extent to which the fish themselves take on sufficient identity to inspire wonder and speculation.

For example, it is commonly known among worm fishermen that a sudden rise of water will set the trout of a stream to feeding like crazy. The fisherman who can contrive to descend on a stream with a supply of nightcrawlers when the water is beginning to rise will have fantastic fishing until the trout finally become gorged with washed-in food.

Yet such sudden flooding creates a heavy, brown roil, an opacity which quickly reduces visibility to zero. Nevertheless, trout move to the likeliest feeding stations, spots either in or adjacent to food-carrying currents. There they snap up items that are swept within range, obviously unhampered by what must amount to total blindness. Yet although this circumstance clearly poses a mystery, I have never heard a fisherman marvel at the fact that trout can feed so successfully while temporarily bereft of vision.

Much the same condition prevails in some of the sections of Lake Champlain where Mike and I fish. The water is heavily clouded by a suspension of fine clay. Dive under, and you cannot see your hand if you bring it to within only a few inches of your eyes. The many species of fish common to these murky sections must live out their entire lives with but little help from their eyes!

Yet this circumstance doesn't seem to register as an oddity with most of those who fish the lake. They proceed exactly as though they expect the fish to see despite the prohibitive conditions, and the fish oblige by behaving precisely as expected!

Mysteries of this sort always gnaw at me. Is it possible that fish *can* see in opaque water, much as animals can see on the darkest nights? Maybe. Yet I doubt it, for artificial lures quickly lose their effectiveness in heavily roiled water. Lures which set up a turbulence may continue to draw a sharply curtailed number of strikes, but it seems likely that the striking fish home in on the sound waves created. Roily water is anathema to fly fisherman, not because the roil kills all interest in flies, I would guess, but simply because the inanimate imitations can no longer be detected.

What then? How can a waiting brown trout unerringly detect a tumbling nightcrawler in a swift current which is only a few shades lighter than molasses? I cannot claim to *know,* but I certainly suspect that it is by sense of smell.

I have just checked a prestigious fishing encyclopedia. The fish's sense of smell is not even accorded a heading. Yet it is quite possible that scent plays as vital a role in sport fishing as it does in deer hunting. Most fishermen ignore the possibility that it may be an important factor, but there are some who treat it much more seriously.

One of the benefits of outdoor writing is the letters it draws from other fishermen. Some are critical, which is their right, and a few are pompously boring, but most write as kindred souls who have something interesting to say in a spirit of friendliness.

Several years ago, in a magazine article, I described a scent-oriented trick which I had tried. On the possibility that the scent of my hands was keeping walleyes away from my nightcrawlers, I rendered the fat which often encases walleye intestines and applied the oil to my hands before baiting. I began catching more walleyes, and so reported; but I added the admission that the increase in strikes could have been coincidental.

The article drew the usual number of letters, predominantly from walleye fishermen, of course. However, there was one notable exception. This came from a fisherman to whom my reference to scent was of special interest.

This letter came from Allen Smoger, of Lemont, Illinois. It led to an exchange of correspondence which is now in its third year. I value it greatly, for Allen Smoger is a fisherman after my own heart. In all things pertaining to fishing, he "reads" from left to right while most are busily "reading" from right to left.

To put it less cryptically, the majority of fishermen concern themselves primarily with the alternatives of methodology, seeking to discover those which "work" best and then to achieve success by their exclusive use. Allen Smoger comes at it from the opposite end. He looks first to the fish, sifting among their sensitivities for the reasons for angling success and, particularly, for the reasons for failure.

To the best of my ability, I have written on worm and bait fishing from precisely this standpoint. Unfortunately, I have been forced to neglect the matter of scent, simply because I don't know much about it. Yet scent may well be one of the major determinants of success and failure in sport fishing.

Allen Smoger's observations, experiences, and experiments have convinced him that the foregoing is indeed true. Following the "right-to-left" route, he feels that he has identified the scents which fish like and those which they find offensive. He believes that he has deduced formulae for the scents which fish find attractive, and also formulae for preparations which will eradicate the offensive scents from hands, bait, lures, etc.

Mr. Smoger is no huckster. His original experiments with scent were conducted to improve his own fishing. When his efforts began to bear fruit, he invited his friends to try his preparations. He tells of one incident which will ring a bell with most fishermen.

Allen and a friend were fishing from the same boat. Allen was catching fish regularly, while his friend couldn't get so much as a bite. They swapped seats at Allen's suggestion, but things continued as before. Finally, Allen proffered the bottle of scent which he had been using secretly. As soon as his friend applied the scent to his hands and his bait, he began catching his share of fish.

I have seen the same puzzling circumstance unfold on more than one occasion, and I'm sure that other fishermen have, too. Partners sit maybe eight feet apart in a boat. One catches fish regularly and the other catches nothing. They swap places, but the lopsidedness persists. What the hell *is* the reason? There must be one, and it seems logical to entertain the possibility that it could be the matter of scent.

It has long been known that fish possess a sense of smell. In some cases its acuity approaches the incredible. It is alleged to have been proved that it is by scent that salmon return to spawn, often from thousands of miles, in precisely the tributaries in which they were hatched. It is also alleged that the immersion of a human hand in the water of a fishway will halt the ascent of salmon intent on reaching their spawning grounds. It has been proved that other species are able to detect scent in almost unbelievable extremes of dilution, one part in billions being sufficient to prompt detection.

With fish possessing olfactory powers of such acuity, it certainly seems reasonable to assume that they can be attracted by appealing scents and repelled by those which to them are repugnant or suggestive of danger. Working on this assumption, Allen Smoger has improved his own fishing chances, he believes, and he has won a following of fishermen who agree.

As a result, Mr. Smoger, aided by his wife and the oldest two of their four daughters, operates a small, unique home business under the rather quaint name of "Mossback." It is devoted to the preparation and sale of the scents at which Allen has arrived by experimentation, and to the production of soft plastic lures in which his formulae are incorporated. Because we share common interests, he has provided me with samples of his products for testing, and he has promised more that are now in the developmental stage.

Results have been impressive, but my testing has been too limited to date to warrant endorsement. Yet I feel impelled to write of Allen Smoger because I believe that he is an honest pioneer in an important field of angling that has been largely neglected.

Of course, there is nothing new about fish-calling scents. I remember ads I read in childhood describing "magic" concoctions and guaranteeing equally magical results from their use. The claims were so extravagant that I didn't take them seriously, even at that tender age.

Allen Smoger makes no such claims. He merely believes that he is on the trail of something important, and he is sticking to it. He has been at it for ten years, and along the way he has enlisted the aid of chemists, food processors, and everyday fishermen. He proceeded slowly, and he began marketing Mossback products on a modest scale only when fishermen and certain sporting-goods stores began demanding them.

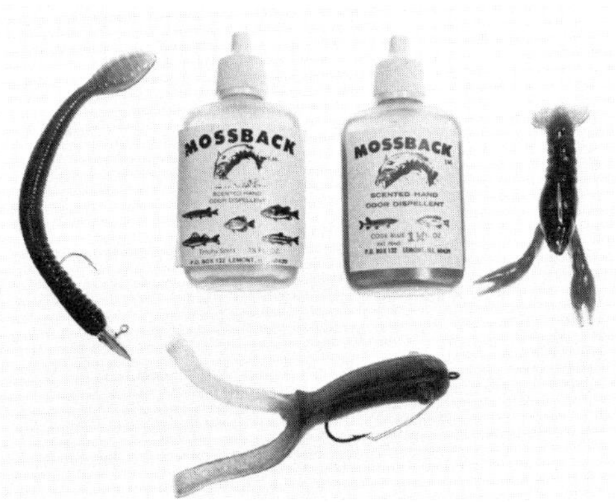

Allen Smoger's preparations and scent-impregnated lures.

Although Mossback preparations are designed to appeal to a fish's sense of smell, their main intent is to counteract the odors which Allen Smoger holds responsible for much fishing failure. This rings a bell with me, for I have long since made clear my feelings that it is more important to study the reasons why fish refuse to bite than to try to deduce their reasons *for* biting. For instance:

Do fish "learn" from the fatal mistakes made by other fish? This question has long had me stumped, for if they don't learn they certainly show every sign of it! I have happened on concentrations of fish so great that the first few casts brought a half-dozen charging at the lure. After a few had been caught, others continued to dash at the lure each time it landed, but only to turn aside. Had they been able to deduce the lure's deadly potential by observation? I have never been able to credit fish with that much reasoning power. But I was at a loss for any other answer until Allen Smoger inadvertently suggested one.

In the course of our correspondence he voiced the conviction that fish were not only alerted by human scent, but that when they are hooked, and struggling for their lives, they exude a special scent which serves as a danger signal to all nearby fish. He believes that this scent clings to a lure after a fish has been caught, and discourages additional strikes until the smell has washed off. It is also his belief that his Mossback preparations eliminate this scent.

Continuing this line of reasoning, he pointed out what he believes to be the mistake made by placing live fish on a stringer. He is convinced that they continue to emit a distress scent which will dissuade other fish from biting.

He supplied me with copies of correspondence from other fishermen who not only agreed but went even one step farther. They claimed that fish tend to expel the contents of their stomachs when hooked, and that the dissemination of the resulting odor serves as an even more powerful warning to all other fish in the vicinity.

As I have already implied, it is because of such unconventional viewpoints that I write of Allen Smoger and Mossback, rather than with any real promotional intent. The guy is just plumb *interesting,* which, I fear, is a helluva lot more than can be said for this particular fishing writer!

It is easy to find apparent refutation of the "distress scent" theory from among my personal experiences. Like all other fishermen, I have caught fish with successive casts of the same lure, and I have enjoyed fast fishing while a rapidly filling stringer dangled alongside. Trout certainly don't make a point of expelling their stomach contents when hooked, if indeed they ever do, for those caught during a heavy hatch have stomachs still crammed with insects. Finally, I have even caught other fish on food items removed from the gullets of those already caught.

Yet, are these refutations complete or only partial? As already reported, I have seen hungry and eager fish turn aside from a fly after it has caught only two or three of their associates. I have caught a bass or pike with almost the first cast, only to draw a blank thereafter with each of a hundred casts. I have started off with a bang more than once, stringing two or three fish in swift succession, only to have my mounting expectations killed by complete inactivity thereafter. While fish certainly don't invariably vomit upon hooking, I have seen many a landlocked salmon disgorge partially digested smelt while being brought to the net. Also, it would be unfair not to point out the high ratio of empty stomachs among the bass, northerns, pickerel, and walleyes that I catch. Who am I to say that they *don't* upchuck whatever is in their stomachs when they are first hooked and well outside the range of my vision?

Continuing to draw upon personal experience, I can find much evidence to support the theory that fish can be attracted by scent. An old and effective trick employed by guides, who must produce fish or else, is to "dress" artificial lures with a dab of worm, a minnow tail, or a sliver of fish skin. Many Maine guides like to add a tiny chub to streamers that are trolled for landlocked salmon, and I have taken many landlocks by trolling this combination.

In each of the foregoing instances, the addition is kept minuscule so as not to affect the lure's action, and because of this restraint the tiny embellishment can hardly contribute to the lure's visual appeal. Consequently it seems logical to conclude that the added appeal must be the result of the scent which the organic particle emits.

In an early chapter I reported my lack of success with Labrador brookies until I hung a slice of trout belly from the streamer I was using. The fleshy sliver certainly didn't make my carefully tied streamer look more fishlike. If anything, it had the opposite effect. Yet it turned trout indifference to eagerness almost magically. I can credit the change to no other factor than attractive scent.

The big question, of course, is whether Allen Smoger has hit on formulae which eliminate objectionable odors and supplant them with those which attract fish as he honestly believes he has done. As I have already confessed, my testing of Mossback preparations and scented lures has been too limited to be conclusive. But I can report that bass and pike have hit the scent-impregnated lures with a regularity which certainly suggests special appeal. I can add further that I have experienced spells of especially fast bait fishing after using Mossback preparations as Allen recommends.

Apparently, the favorable reputation of Mossback is growing among fishermen of the Midwest. Allen reports that first-time users usually become repeat customers, and he observes correctly that this is the real test of proficiency. A number of sporting-goods stores carry his preparations and lures, and Mossback has won editorial support from at least one Midwestern publication devoted to fishing.

Major stirs in the fishing world have been created by the rhetorical elevation of molehills to mountains. Therefore, I offer no apology for calling attention to one humble, but highly empathetic, fisherman's by-the-bootstrap efforts to get at what he believes to be a fishing truth of major importance. I submit that his endeavors are worthy of the interest of those who, like myself, find fascination in the existent mysteries of fishing.

For all who may wish to give Allen Smoger's products a try, here is his address:

Mr. Allen Smoger
MOSSBACK
Box 132
Lemont, Illinois 60439

Readers will be quick to deduce the fact that Allen Smoger and I are in cahoots, and that by drawing attention to him and his products I'm grinding an ax of my own. This is indeed the case. Allen has promised me no less than a dozen scent-impregnated plastic nightcrawlers for the first million dollars he makes from the promotional effect of this chapter!

15

NEW TOOLS OF THE TRADE

THE FRENCH have a saying to the effect that the more things change, the more they stay the same. I suppose that in a profoundly philosophical sense this paradox is true, and that it applies to fishing as it does to all else. The charm of this favorite of all outdoor sports calls to fishermen and fisherwomen of today in exactly the same voice in which it called to anglers long before the day of Ike Walton.

When viewed from another angle, the outward characteristics of sport fishing have changed enormously, even though the basic reasons for its popularity have long remained constant. I am tempted to cite the changes which I have witnessed over the past half-century, but will resist the urge to indulge in nostalgia.

More to the point, innovations are appearing so rapidly that it is difficult, if not downright impossible, to keep up with all of them. In the recent past, such terms as "graphite," "electronic depth finder," "downrigger," "fluorescent line," and others have been added to fishing nomenclature. All are having revolutionary effects on sport fishing.

If I am correct, each new development, and the claims made for it, arouse the curiosity of every fisherman; but expense and other factors stand in the way of equally instant and widespread familiarity. Anglers of ordinary means are understandably hesitant to invest considerable sums of money in items about which they may be curious but about whose real worth they may be uncertain.

Technology gallops by me in the same way, and for the same reasons. But because outdoor writing has helped put grub on my table for some thirty years, I try to keep in touch with new developments to the best of my ability. I cannot do the task justice; but for whatever my comments may be worth to the curious I submit my evaluations of a few of the most important recent innovations. I do so in an attempt to be of service, even though I cannot deliver opinions that are based on substantial experience to date.

Certainly, one of the most talked-of events in recent years has been the introduction of the graphite rod. It seems equally certain that the high cost of these rods has deterred the majority of fishermen from rushing out and buying one or more.

I was with the majority, curious but lacking first-hand enlightenment, until the Shakespeare Company generously furnished one of their Graflite rods for testing. The rod arrived after the fishing season had closed, so I cannot report from true field experience. On the other hand, I have put the rod through its paces on the back lawn again and again, with different line weights and at varying distances. Thus, while I have yet to use the rod on a stream, I have become well acquainted with its remarkable capabilities.

Before attempting an appraisal, I would like to point out that in participating in the introduction of graphite rods, the Shakespeare Company is reliving a pioneering role. Less than three decades ago the same company set the fishing world to buzzing with the introduction of fiberglass rods—evidence, perhaps, that the French are indeed correct!

The unprecedented appearance of the fiberglass rod also aroused great curiosity. Was it all that was claimed for it? Its subsequent popularity and wholesale adoption show clearly that it has lived up to its initial billing, and then some! Only one controversy remains, and this arises only among congenital nit-pickers: Are the best glass rods equal to the best rods of bamboo? The very fact that the issue is debated is testimony to the excellence that has been achieved in glass-rod making. (My preference is for bamboo, but I cannot sift through my sentiments objectively enough to determine whether they are prompted by a lifelong love of fine bamboo rods, or by real differences which I am able to detect rather than to imagine.)

The rod which I took to the back lawn for testing is the Shakespeare GF II FY, an eight-foot fly rod which weighs a mere two-and-a-half ounces. Line recommendation was for a 6-weight line, but company representative Ed Sutton had told me that it would also handle a 7-weight line. I rigged it with a 6-weight for the first try.

I knew from what I had read that graphite's remarkable tensile strength permitted rods of smaller-than-usual diameters, but I couldn't escape the impression of prohibitive frailty as I joined the two sections. But despite the fact that the rod seemed almost knitting-needle thin, it was immediately apparent that it didn't lack guts. I began with short casts, and gradually worked up to my cut-off point—a length of line which threatens no records, but the one with which I'm forced to live. I was most favorably impressed by the rod's evenness of delivery over the entire range.

I changed to a 7-weight line, and no compromise became manifest. My footage gained substantially with the use of the heavier line, but there was not the slightest feel of rod overload. To me, this expanded range of line-weight capacity was revolutionary and of major importance.

In the past, matching a rod with just the right line weight had been a critical problem, and sometimes it was one which defied a completely satisfactory solution. To be more specific, a rod which required a relatively heavy line to bring out its action was likely to perform unpleasantly when used to make short casts. In the same vein, my favorite small-stream rods usually showed signs of complaint if I stepped up line weight a notch, or even when I tried for maximum distance with the lighter line. The graphite rod handled not only one line weight smoothly, from short casts to long, but also the next weight with equal ease over the same range. The one rod was doing easily what only a pair of my rods could do combined.

A fly rod with an innovative "feel" usually takes some getting used to, but this wasn't the case with the graphite rod. The "feel" was unique, no question about that, but it posed no problem associated with timing. In fact, its extra sensitivity (more about this characteristic later) seemed to suggest proper timing, rather than to require any special concession in the achievement of the latter.

I became even more acutely aware of this virtue when Mike tried the rod. Mike has never acquired my love of fly rods and fly fishing, mainly because he is among those who find the timing, so essential to easy fly casting, an exasperatingly elusive goal. His affection is for the spinning outfit, which in his hands becomes a tool of precision. Nevertheless, he was atypically enthusiastic about the graphite rod when it did for his timing, and consequently for his casting, what no other rod had ever done.

His evaluation verbatim: *"Man! That rod is really something!"*

Despite my limited testing of the graphite rod, I agree with Mike. There is something in human nature which prompts a to-the-death defense of the status quo, in this case the axiomatic belief that no other rod material can equal bamboo. I'm convinced that not only has it been equaled, but that it has been surpassed.

I have studied quite an amount of technical data which seems to support this viewpoint. These data relate to fiber strength, weight, methods of construction, recovery rate, vibrations, and other technological characteristics about which most fishermen couldn't care less. They, like me, are interested in the end product —performance. On that basis, from what I've been able to determine to date, graphite outperforms bamboo, just as it outperforms fiberglass.

Fly-rod evaluation may not seem to belong in a book on bait fishing, but this book is devoted not only to bait fishermen but to those who are both fly *and* bait fishermen. Also, there is a unique characteristic of graphite rods which is of special interest to those who fish only with bait. This is the extra sensitivity which is automatically incorporated in a graphite rod, a capacity for transmitting impulses received at the tip over the entire rod with minimal loss. This is an advantage which has application along a broad front: extra touches in bait manipulation; more discriminating lines of communication between fisherman and finicky, bait-stealing biters; increased ability to feel out the contours of the bottom; improved control over hooked fish.

Graphite rods are relatively rare as this is being written. I'm sure that they will be much more in evidence by the time it reaches print. I'm equally certain that graphite will crowd glass out of the picture eventually, precisely as glass has all but replaced bamboo. Maybe fishing stays the same, but technology marches on.

Nylon monofilament has become so abundant and commonplace that carelessly discarded snarls of the material have become a menace to waterfowl and other forms of wildlife, which sometimes become hopelessly entangled in it. It is hard to believe that virtually none was available no more than thirty years ago. I bought my first spinning outfit shortly after the end of World War II, one of the first on the market, and at that time the only spinning lines available were of braided silk. It is quite probable that the eventual combination of spinning outfit and monofilament line changed the outward face of sport fishing more than anything else has done over the sport's entire history.

But both are now old-hat, and to marvel about their joint effect is pointless. I do believe, however, that I have something of interest to report concerning recent developments in monofilament lines.

When I began investigating the possibilities of ultralight spinning with natural baits, the matter of controlling a fine line of only two-pound test posed a serious problem. Since the bait is usually drifted on a relatively slack line, the wispy mono can scarcely be felt by a fingertip as it can in conventional spinning when tension on the line is maintained during retrieves. Sight, rather than touch, must be employed, and most two-pound monofilament is virtually invisible against a background of broken water. The search for line of maximum visibility led to Stren, a DuPont product which fluoresces under the ultraviolet rays which are contained in daylight. This makes even the finest line highly visible to the fisherman, the characteristic I was looking for. Because water filters out the ultraviolet rays, the portion of the line that is below the surface *does not* fluoresce, thus denying fish the advantage which the fisherman enjoys.

The fact that Stren solved my problem led to correspondence and exchanges of information with Bob Roberts and Ed Keller. Bob is in charge of public relations in DuPont's line division, and Ed is Stren's inventor. It turned out that they also had a problem.

This problem centered around Golden Stren, a line developed expressly for its high visibility, as the name implies. Golden Stren is fluorescent, but its color and opacity make it highly visible underwater as well as above. Skeptics were charging that while a highly visible line can be a great help in certain circumstances, the fact that it was also highly visible to the fish would be a deterrent to strikes and bites. Both Bob and Ed doubted the validity of the charges, but they lacked evidence on which to base a refutation.

It occurred to me that Mike's and my extensive ice fishing would make an interesting testing ground. Each year we set thirty tilts in permanent position over Lake Champlain walleye grounds, and then fish them throughout the winter. I proposed to rig alternate tilts with clear and Golden Stren respectively, and then tally all bites according to the color of the line on which they occurred.

While we fish primarily for walleyes, we also catch many yellow perch, numerous saugers, a fair number of northerns, and a scattering of chain pickerel, and last winter we even caught a dozen or more whopping big catfish. In deciding to count bites, rather than fish caught, I reasoned that a bite would be a positive indication of line acceptance. To count only fish that were actually landed would reflect factors quite apart from the point in question.

Our records covered thirty-one days of ice fishing, spread over a two-year period. During that time our spread of tilts registered a total of 1,603 bites. Of these, 744 were on the clear and relatively invisible Stren, and the remainder, 829, were on the opaque Golden Stren.

We carried our experimentation through spring and summer fishing to the best of our ability. Testing could not be carried out with the mathematical nicety that was possible during ice fishing, but results continued to show that fish were insensitive to line visibility. During the spring walleye season we trolled the two colors simultaneously, and as nearly as we could determine, the walleyes hit as willingly on one color as they did on the other.

My notes include the results of a day's fishing in a Champlain inlet on July 7, 1975. On that day we caught a total of ninety-eight fish: perch, bass, calicoes, northerns, sheepsheads, and bowfins. Again the Golden Stren came out ahead, accounting for fifty-four fish while forty-four were caught on the clear Stren.

I carried the testing to smelt fishing, jigging a Golden line with one hand and a clear line with the other. Here it is impossible to count bites, for the small fish bite constantly throughout any good day. Catches run into the hundreds on such days, so an accounting of fish caught would have been a taxing enterprise. However, it was very evident that the smelt bit as readily on one line as they did on the other. And I do remember one rather interesting incident: During one interlude I caught thirty-one smelt on the Golden line while never getting a bite on the clear line that I was fishing with the other hand. This was just chance, of course, but also more clear evidence that the smelt weren't turned off by the more visible line.

Late in the summer I trolled for rainbow and brook trout in a nearby lake. Although I fished alone, I alternated rods rigged with the two colors. I couldn't detect any adverse effect from use of the opaque line.

Finally, Bob Roberts and Ed Keller sent me some experimental tapered leaders made of Golden Stren. I tried these on my favorite stretch of stream, where I have come to know every stump and boulder, and about what to expect under normal conditions. The usual number of trout rose to my dry flies despite the high visibility of the unconventional leader.

Results of the testing have not surprised me. To the contrary, they have supported my long-standing conviction that it is the *behavior* of baits and lures which determines fishing success. Leaders and lines are determinants mainly to the degree to which they hamper or permit natural behavior of natural baits and their imitations. By itself, line visibility seems to be of little or no importance as far as the fish are concerned.

Assuming this to be true, important advantages accrue to the use of highly visible line in certain circumstances. In ice fishing, for example, it is of great benefit to use a line like Golden Stren which stands out clearly against a snowy background. The same visibility is a great help in deep trolling, where bottom-snagging is an occupational hazard. To free lures from snags it is almost always necessary to reverse course until the boat moves to beyond the snag. On windy days this becomes difficult if ordinary monofilament is used, for it is often impossible to keep the line in sight against the broken surface. Quite often the prop chops off the line during what amounts to blind maneuvering. The opaque line can be followed back to the snag much more easily, saving much tackle over the long run, to say nothing of valuable fishing time.

It has been taken for granted for so long that line visibility has a direct bearing on fishing success that to suggest otherwise almost amounts to heresy. Nevertheless, on the basis of much testing, I don't hesitate to advise fishermen to use a highly visible line wherever they find such use to their advantage. Contrary to popular belief, the fish won't give a damn!

I'm certain that as much, or even more, unsatisfied curiosity exists concerning electronic fish and depth finders, and the use of downriggers, as exists concerning graphite rods. Both deep-trolling devices have been on the scene longer than graphite, but the matter of expense has stood in the way of widespread acceptance and use. Like the many who are as yet hesitant to invest in a graphite rod, most fishermen are equally reluctant to shell out for devices without first knowing that they will "work" as advertised.

Here, again, I can report from experience, but experience of only small dimensions as yet. Nevertheless, as in the case of the graphite rod, my experience to date with depth finders and downriggers has been sufficient to inspire favorable convictions.

I have two depth finders. One is the Fish Hawk 600 and the other the Fish Hawk 202A. The first is a hand-held instrument which reads depths up to eighty feet. The second is also a portable model but one of greater sensitivity which will measure depths up to two hundred feet. Both are made by the Waller Corporation, of Crystal Lake, Illinois.

I have used my two depth finders enough to come to two broad conclusions. First, their capabilities are impressive. Second, the fisherman must learn how to take advantage of these capabilities, just as he must learn how to cast before he can capitalize on the potential of a fine fly rod. I'm still learning how to "read" my instruments, but with every confidence that they will become indispensable to my deep trolling and to my hot-weather bait fishing.

My downrigger is a Riviera Model 300RH, manufactured by Riviera Manufacturing, Inc., of Grand Rapids, Michigan. As with the depth finders, I haven't yet learned how to make the most of it, but I hope to eventually. To date, I have progressed sufficiently to feel certain that the combination of depth finder and downrigger represents a giant stride toward solving the perplexing problems of deep trolling.

When fish move into deep water, the fisherman who trolls for them is faced with three difficult questions. How deep is the water under his boat? How deep are the fish? How can he hold his lure at the depth which holds the fish?

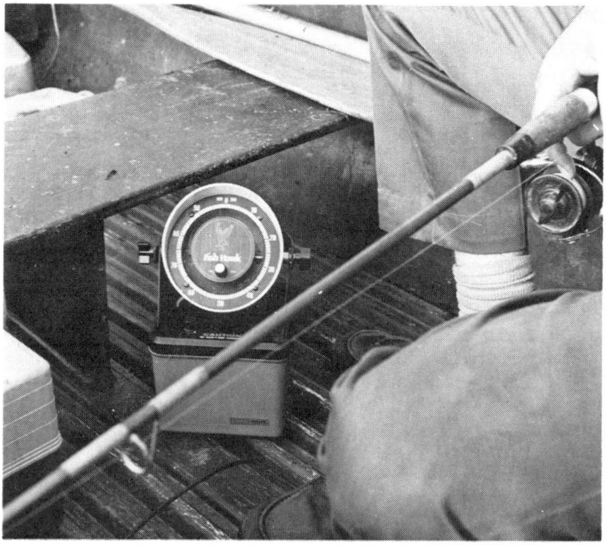

A flashing band on the depth finder's dial shows contours of the bottom. The downrigger can be adjusted to keep lure near bottom and in the strike zone.

Hand-held depth finder is less sensitive, but adequate for moderate depths. It is especially valuable in locating reefs which attract walleyes and smallmouths.

The depth finder provides a continuous answer to the first question. Its flashes register on a depth scale, shifting in accord with bottom irregularities. This last is of great importance, for as already pointed out, fish which retreat to a certain depth prefer those spots where the bottom rises into this depth zone. In addition, depending on the operator's "reading" skill, the instrument will pick up fish and indicate the depth at which they are spotted. These two capabilities do much to introduce certainty into what, at best, has always been a very foggy area.

The matter of holding a lure at a specific depth has been even more uncertain. A fisherman could do no more than take a stab at it. He could fish a certain number of colors of lead-core line or a certain number of feet of wire line, or he could use sinkers of different weights. He might hit fish by trolling five colors or two hundred and fifty feet of wire or by using a six-ounce sinker, but he never knew how deep his lure was running.

Last summer, for example, I caught landlocked salmon by stripping seventy-five "pulls" of stainless-steel wire from my fly reel. By trial and error I finally lucked into the fact that that number of pulls would take my wobbler down to the depth zone which the salmon were favoring. My guide, Jack McKelvey, and I speculated as to how deep the lure was running, but there were no clues to the truth. We knew that we were taking salmon, and that's all we did know. The fine wire may have dragged the lure down a dozen feet, or it could have pulled it down three times that distance. There simply was no way of telling.

The downrigger eliminates all such guesswork. For any who may not know what the device is, it is essentially a windlass designed to lower a streamlined weight on a steel cable to any desired depth. A meter records each foot of cable that is payed out. A line holder is attached to the weight. This holds the fishing line or leader under a pressure that can be adjusted to permit the line to slip free when a fish strikes and is hooked.

The weight furnished with my downrigger weighs seven and a half pounds. When it is let down on the thin wire cable, the latter remains almost perpendicular at trolling speed. Due to this slight angle, the lure runs at a depth that is only slightly less than the length of cable that has been out.

Thus, once the fish-holding level has been determined, the downrigger makes it possible to troll at precisely that level. This comes as close to a guarantee of success as can be achieved in one of the most difficult and challenging phases of sport fishing.

Exactitude of depth is not the downrigger's only virtue. Most fishermen take a dim view of depth dredging because of the heavy tackle which previously has been necessary. Heavily weighted lines require stiff rods. The weighted lines take much of the fun out of playing fish, and the stiff, insensitive rods take a big hunk of what's left. The downrigger, despite its heavy weight, exacts no compromise at all. It permits the use of the lightest tackle at any desired depth. It is possible, for example, to take salmon with fly rod and streamer at the fifty-foot level, with hooked fish snapping free to display all their fighting qualities against the light, sensitive rod.

Mike tests tension of line release. When fish strikes and is hooked, line will snap free of seven-pound weight.

Such latitude is made possible by the fact that although the downrigger's weight is substantial, it is supported entirely by the steel cable and places no strain whatsoever on the rod. The pressure release can be set to free lines of small diameter and low test. Consequently, once a fish is hooked, the fireworks which follow are the same as though the fish had been hooked at the surface.

This feature is rapidly winning the enthusiasm of light-tackle users. One fisherman told me of taking four-pound rainbows on fly rod and streamer from a small lake where the presence of such fish was largely unsuspected.

"Once I found that they were at the twenty-five-foot level, I had it made," he told me. "The downrigger held the streamer at exactly that depth, and the line release worked perfectly. And those four-pound rainbows were really something on a fly rod!"

But nothing is perfect. The depth-finder/downrigger combination is best suited for use with large boats. More sensitive depth finders can be operated off the boat's twelve-volt system. And electrically operated downriggers can also be installed by those who can afford them.

My boat is an old fourteen-footer, with no electric system. I'm an old six-footer with a system that also leaves much to be desired. Consequently, my depth finder is battery-operated, and my downrigger is the manual type. The downrigger is mounted on the boat's transom. I'm cramped for room, and am getting creaky in the joints, and getting a lure down to the desired level is not easy.

The lure should run fifteen or more feet behind the weight, and must be attached to the line release accordingly. Trailing line and lure must go overboard first, with the boat running at trolling speed or a bit faster. Then comes the matter of easing the weight into the water until it hangs directly from the winch. This is never as simple as it sounds. The weight cannot be dropped *kerplunk,* and care must be taken to see that the cable doesn't kink. Anybody who has fished with wire does not need to be reminded of its inherent cussedness, and the downrigger cable is no exception. It will do its damndest to kink and foul things up while you're readying it for descent. But now for the good news: Once it hangs directly from the arm of the downrigger, it works like a charm from then on.

To lower the weight properly, the cable must slip through your hand until it fetches up against the downrigger arm and its pulley. I have learned, via the hard way, to wear a leather glove during this operation to prevent a cut hand. From then on, attaining the desired depth is nothing more than a matter of watching the meter as the cable is lowered by the crank.

While depth finder and downrigger have opened another door for the sport fisherman, deep trolling is still no bed of ease. You

Line has been attached to release so as to trail about fifteen feet behind downrigger weight. Weight will be lowered to desired depth when boat is under way. Note depth finder transducer which is mounted by suction cups at right of transom. Cable leads to finder, which records variations in depth.

still have to work for the fish you take, or at least I do, hard enough to earn all that you catch. The important thing, if my convictions are correct, is that the combination provides substantial assurance that your efforts will be rewarded, an assurance that has always been lacking in the hit-or-miss deep trolling of the past.

The items described in this chapter should all work to the advantage of the fisherman. In the meantime, however, you can bet that the fish are working overtime to develop defenses against these new weapons, and you can be equally sure that they are making notable progress.

16

FROM STRINGER TO TABLE

MOST FISHERMEN would much rather catch fish than eat them, and I'm one of that group. While a minority simply don't like the taste of fish, most like to eat them, even though they prefer the catching to the eating. I fall in that category, too. In fact, I'm particularly fond of fish, everything from eels to salmon, and I count this as a major blessing, for it does much to enhance the fun I get from fishing. Yet there is even more. It's the solid gratification of returning home with a good catch which will be put to use as food, a sense of accomplishment which rounds out the pleasures of a successful day.

I know a short stretch of river where rainbow and brown trout become sleek two-pounders in the short space of three years. It is such a difficult stretch to wade that only a few fishermen fish it regularly. All of us release virtually all the trout we catch.

The aquatic insect life of the short stretch is exceptionally bountiful, and this undoubtedly accounts for the rapid growth and splendid proportions of the trout. Yet the devotees of the spot share the belief that our practice of returning fish has also helped significantly in maintaining a trout population which has not fluctuated perceptibly in the past dozen or more years.

The current is fast and the flow heavy, and the jumbled stream bed makes wading both difficult and hazardous. The trout, when water temperatures bring them to the peak of physical fitness, become living projectiles when hooked on light tackle. They are tough babies to land, not only because of the difficulties posed by the stream, but also because they refuse to come to the net until they have exhausted themselves almost to the point of death. Quite often it is necessary to hold them upright in the current for a considerable length of time before they can regain sufficient strength to swim wearily away.

I would be an out-and-out liar if I pretended that it went any way but against my natural inclinations to go to great pains to raise, hook, and land a sleek eighteen-inch rainbow, only to nurse it back to strength and finally turn it loose. In all honesty, I must admit that my genuine impulse is to rap the fish over the head as a final, satisfying step in reducing it to possession.

If I were guided by sentiment rather than reason, I would tote my prize home and splat it down grandly in the kitchen sink, for all to gaze upon while I indulged the right to do a bit of bragging. Finally, my sense of triumph and achievement would culminate in the gustatory treat which results when a fat two-pound trout is split down the middle and the two halves broiled to a turn.

Although my regard for conservation prevents me from doing what comes naturally, I am instinctively disturbed by the patent absurdity of going to the considerable trouble, to say nothing of the expense, of catching trout which I have no intentions of keeping. Consequently, I do not release the trout I catch in a fine spirit of benevolence. Instead, I release them grudgingly and reluctantly, only because, to paraphrase, I realize that I can't have my trout and eat them too.

Trout fishermen sometimes like to preach what they practice even more than they enjoy practicing what they preach, and the matter of turning back trout is no exception. Among the growing number who do put back trout, with much credit due them, it has become quite the thing to profess that the catching of trout is everything, and that their possession, once caught, is nothing. I very much question that these assertions arise from genuine and unqualified sentiments. As long as human vanity persists, no man likes to seem the fool in the eyes of his peers, and in what way could he contrive to appear more foolish than by expending lavish efforts in the pursuit of that which he has no intention of retaining?

What I'm trying to say, and I fear I'm making a poor job of it, is that while conservation-minded fishermen are willing to forgo the killing and keeping of fish whenever this seems necessary, fishing at any level, whether it be for panfish or trout, is at its very best only when it is complete. This, in my opinion, is when purpose is incorporated in the sport, when the fisherman enjoys not only the catching of fish, but can also enjoy with clear conscience the retention of his catch and the final pleasure of eating it.

Unfortunately, trout and salmon can be endangered by overkill, and the fisherman who stuffs his freezer with salmonids is acting against his own best interests. In virtually all other instances the "completeness" to which I have referred can be enjoyed without apology or fear of adverse effect on fish populations. It is to this aspect of fishing—the utilization of fish as food as a part of the enjoyment of fishing—that this chapter is devoted.

All fish have somewhat different flavors, but I can truthfully say that I know of no freshwater species whose flesh is not palatable to me. The only line I draw is that of intolerable boniness. A few species have not only the usual skeletal structure consisting of backbone and ribs, but flesh that is permeated with small forked bones which are not attached to the skeleton and which cannot be removed by ordinary cleaning methods if, indeed, they can be removed at all. Among those which I hold to be too bony to bother with are suckers, fallfish, and northern pike and pickerel which weigh less than three pounds. I do not rule out larger specimens of the last two species. The forked bones can be removed from between the flakes of flesh after cooking, simply because they are large enough to be easily visible. The flesh quality of both pike and pickerel is excellent.

Other species are sometimes saddled with undeserved reputations of boniness. Every summer, vast numbers of "punkinseeds" and other panfish are tossed back on the grounds that they are too bony to clean. Yellow perch are frequently regarded in the same light, and I've even heard bass described as bony. Not all the fish rejected as bony are put back to go on living; many are carried home only to wind up in garbage pails.

Actually, the above species are no more bony than are trout and salmon, and all are of excellent quality and flavor when properly cleaned and cooked. Their flesh contains none of the forked bones which are present in the flesh of the few freshwater species that are truly prohibitively bony. So, to resolve first things first, don't hesitate to save most of the fish you catch for the table, regardless of their reputation. All but the exceptions I have named are good as far as I'm concerned; the only differences among them are degrees of goodness.

Nobody can truly save money by eating the fish he catches. When the time spent in catching them, plus all the attending costs of travel, equipment, etc., have been taken into consideration, it would be much cheaper to patronize the fish markets. On the other hand, the expense of fishing is reduced by the dollar value of the fish eaten, and this can be a significant amount in the present era of high prices.

There is another aspect of the utilization of fish which seems to me to be of greater importance. Food production threatens to fall short of the needs of a constantly increasing population. Every meal of sport-caught fish that is eaten frees a corresponding amount of commercially produced protein for public consumption. To keep fish and then fail to clean or eat them is a lamentable waste. To keep fish and eat them, when the practice is not contrary to sound conservation principles, cannot but ease a problem of steadily growing acuity.

If fish are to be utilized with maximum enjoyment, they must be brought home in good condition. The flesh of fish is considerably more delicate than that of warm-blooded animals. To ensure an enjoyable meal of fish, the first step is to prevent serious cellular deterioration between the time of catching and the introduction to frying pan, oven, freezer, or smoker.

One of the commonest mistakes is that of trying to keep fish alive on a stringer, especially in warm water. Although the stringer may appear to keep the fish alive, it more truly kills them by inches. Cell structure breaks down during the dying process, and this can only have an adverse effect on the quality of the flesh.

Much better, and far more humane, is to kill fish as soon as they are caught and immediately place them on ice. I know from experience that fish which have been killed and chilled are much better on the table than those which have languished on a stringer.

Some recommend that fish be cleaned as soon as they are caught, but I haven't found this to be necessary. Cleaning messes up the boat and is a serious inconvenience when fish are biting well, and it serves no real purpose. The intestines have no effect on the flesh unless they break down sufficiently to release their contents into the body cavity, and this won't happen if the catch is kept cold.

Keeping fish iced can be a hard project or an easy one. The method Mike and I use is easy. We go equipped with one of the large-capacity Styrofoam coolers which cost little but afford almost perfect insulation. We maintain a supply of ice by freezing half-gallon plastic jugs of water in the family freezer. (Leave a few inches of space for expansion.) When we start out for a day's fishing we put three of the jugs in the cooler. Our lunches go in also, plus beverages. Finally, we tuck in one of the large plastic bags that are used to line garbage pails.

Once on location, fish are rapped on the head as they are caught and dropped into the plastic bag, and there they chill quickly. Our sandwiches, beer, and soda stay cold and clean. No water accumulates in the cooler, and it too remains clean and dry. Equally important, it picks up no fishy smell. Our catch stays cold throughout the day, during the trip home, and right up to the time when it is removed from the cooler for cleaning. As an added benefit, the jugs provide a source of clean ice water, which is always especially welcome on particularly hot days.

Keeping fish cool while stream fishing is a different matter. Most stream fishing is for trout, so keeping the catch chilled is especially important, as the flesh of trout is particularly delicate. Since it is not practical for the stream fisherman to carry a cooler equipped with ice, his best bet is to take advantage of the cooling effect of evaporation. The latter is surprisingly efficient when properly utilized and is usually adequate on even the hottest days.

To my mind, nothing else does the job as well as the old-fashioned wicker creel. Not only does it permit good air circulation to hasten evaporation, but its rigidity and spaciousness prevent the fish from jamming together like sardines in a can as they tend to do in creels which may be handier to carry but are collapsible. To prevent creeled fish from drying out, and to assure constant evaporation and cooling, I carry a clean sponge in my creel and dip it in the stream when I creel my first trout. Occasional redippings thereafter will help greatly in keeping the trout in good condition. Again, I don't find it necessary to clean the fish as I catch them.

Although keeping fish in prime condition is very important, it is a problem which is easily solved. If it were the only problem involved in bringing fish to the table, far more would be eaten. Unfortunately, fish must be cleaned, and the combination of ineptness and dislike for the task deters utilization and results in the waste of untold quantities of potentially fine food.

Fish cleaning is an exasperating and distasteful chore when it is tackled in the absence of knowhow. Honesty impels me to add that merely *knowing* what should be done is insufficient by itself. It must be accompanied by the ability to *do* what needs doing, and the knack can be acquired only through practice.

If learning to clean fish proves to be difficult, it is almost always because a knife is a tool with which the learner is basically unfamiliar. I have fished, hunted, and roamed the woods since I was a kid, and as a result the use of a knife has become second nature. Like all other outdoorsmen of similar experience, I have come to be what Vermonters would describe as "handy" with knives.

I have tried to show many how to clean fish in "one easy lesson," but among those who lack experience with knives the results of their first tries are inevitably disappointing. They watch carefully as I demonstrate each step, but they make a mess of their first attempt and often manage to cut themselves in the bargain.

In this chapter I'm going to explain with words and pictures how to clean various species of fish. I shall try to make the directions clear, but I urge inexperienced knife wielders not to aspire to instant expertise. On the other hand, I vouch for the soundness of the individual cleaning steps, and for the fact that they can be learned with practice.

It is important, of course, to use the type of knife that is best suited for the cleaning job at hand. But before making specific recommendations I can't resist the temptation to comment on a rather quaint circumstance.

There seems to be a steadily growing interest in knives among those who put them to the least use! Almost every mail-order catalog of sporting goods has a section devoted to elegant hunting knives whose prices penetrate the stratosphere. The utilitarian value of these expensive knives cuts off far below the asking price, for a knife can do so much and no more. Yet the knives apparently are in great demand by the many who derive romantic gratification from entering the woods with resplendent sheath knives on their belts.

The plain truth is that the so-called "hunting" knife, apart from effecting a swashbuckling aura, is more nuisance than necessity. It appeals to the spirit of adventure which lies dormant in masculine hearts by suggesting a preparedness to engage in close combat with enraged bears, spitting catamounts, and scalp-minded savages. Yet, aside from its highly unlikely use as a weapon, it has little to recommend it for the average hunter and fisherman. A good pocket knife is all that's needed to gut out a deer or bear, and it is greatly superior to a hunting knife when it comes to cleaning fish, peeling potatoes, whittling shavings for a fire, and almost all other outdoor jobs. It is much easier to carry, is easier to keep sharp, and lacks the ostentation which makes the prominently displayed sheath knife the badge of the tenderfoot.

I believe in giving credit where I believe it is due, and with respect to knives I can vouch for the fine quality of those manufactured by Case & Sons of Bradford, Pennsylvania. Case knives have served me well for more than thirty years, and they are acclaimed by virtually all of the guides I know and have known.

Two distinct types of knives are needed for fish cleaning. For cleaning trout, salmon, panfish, bullheads, etc., choose one with a narrow, pointed blade about three inches long. An altogether different tool is needed for filleting. Again, the blade should be narrow and pointed, but it also should be at least six inches long and easily flexible. (Flexibility is a must during the final step: separating the skin from the fillet by cutting and pressing downward against the filleting board at the same time.)

Knives are advertised as leaving the factories with "razor sharp" edges, but this simply isn't true. Instead, they are given blunt, wedgelike edges that must be ground to a gradual taper before they will cut with authority. It is also alleged that they will hold a "razor edge" indefinitely. This isn't true, either.

The truth is that knives need frequent resharpening, and the ease with which they can be restored to sharpness is much more important than the length of time they will hold a cutting edge. The ability of stainless steel to hold an edge is often advanced as a virtue, but as far as I'm concerned this special toughness is reason for avoidance. I want a blade that will respond to a few licks on the sharpening stone in the middle of cleaning jobs, and Case blades of chrome vanadium steel meet this requirement. A stainless-steel blade "fights" the stone, and restoring a sharp edge on one which has become dull is a long and tedious process.

Finally, sharpening stones, and the ability to use them properly, are as important as the knives themselves. A fast-cutting stone is needed to prepare an edge for finishing. A stone of fine grit should then be used to achieve "razor" sharpness.

It should be kept in mind that a knife with a keen edge will not cut well if the bevel is abrupt rather than gradual. Hold the blade at a low level while grinding to avoid the development of thickness near the cutting edge. The gentler the slope toward the edge, the better the knife will cut.

Fish are vertebrates. Accordingly, they have backbones to which ribs are attached. They have fins which are supported by bones which are not connected to the backbone. They all have skins, most of which are covered with scales. In general, the complexity of their cleaning depends on the degree to which bones, skin, and scales must be removed.

To begin at the simplest level, neither bones nor skin is removed from trout. Cleaning consists merely of cutting off the head, slitting the belly, and removing the entrails. There is no reason to do more. Trout flesh is of such delicate texture that when cooked the backbone and ribs can be lifted free of the meat, and the fins and their bones can be plucked out as easily. The skin can be eaten, or it, too, can be separated from the meat with no trouble.

Perhaps it should be mentioned here that in all fish a dark strip lies under the backbone and stands clearly revealed when the intestines have been removed. Most fish-cleaning directions refer to this as a "bloody strip" which should be scraped out. Actually, this dark strip is the kidney, and its removal is optional. Some who like the taste of kidney leave it in to be enjoyed as a special tidbit.

Now let's move to more difficult areas. Yellow perch are judged by many to be the best-tasting freshwater fish. My wife, for one, prefers them above all other fish, including trout and salmon. They are eaten with relish by virtually all who have acquired the knack of cleaning them properly, and by a certain fortunate minority who have friends who will clean them. But delicious as perch are, they usually are shunned or wasted by the many who haven't learned how to clean them.

To clean a perch so that it can be enjoyed without fear of bones it is necessary to remove the head, the fins and their supporting bones, the skin, and finally the ribs. Only the backbone is left in, and this falls free when the fried fish is forked in half laterally.

Note from the pictures that the proper tool for perch cleaning is a knife with a short, narrow blade, a sharp point, and a razor-sharp edge. This is no job for a fillet knife, nor for any other with a large and cumbersome blade.

Each step is pictured in sequence and accompanied by directions which are as explicit as I can phrase them. As I have warned, execution of the various steps will require practice on the part of a beginner. But once they can be followed they will transform a catch of perch into the makings of a delicious meal, one that can be enjoyed without trouble from bones.

CLEANING PERCH

The following steps make yellow perch easy to cook and a delight to eat. A cutting board can be used, but is not necessary. In the photos, hands and fish have been positioned to provide the clearest views of the respective steps. More comfortable positions will suggest themselves during actual cleaning.

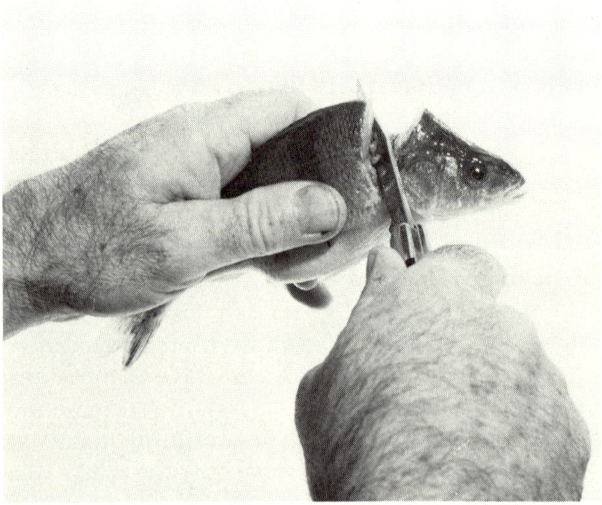

Cut down through the backbone, but do not sever the head.

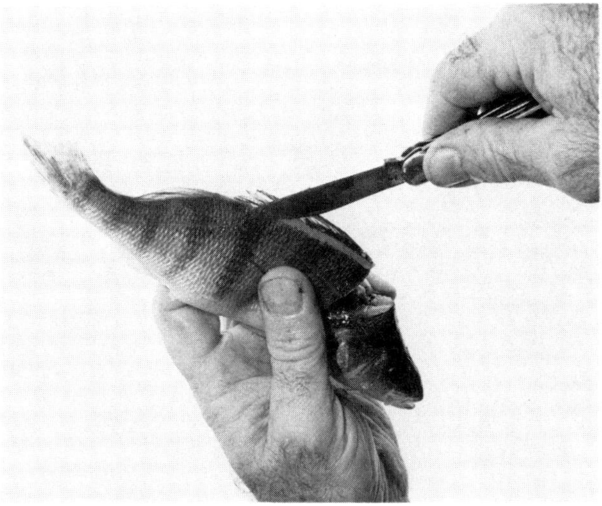

Rip the skin along each side of the dorsal fin. Make cut as shallow as possible.

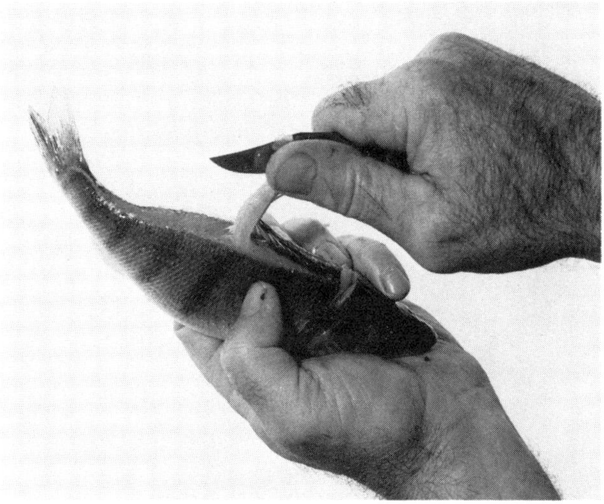

Grasp the end of the fin between the thumb and the flat of the blade and pull toward the tail. All supporting bones will lift free.

Turn fish over and cut under the anal fin until knife comes against the long bone which supports the fin. Do not cut through the bone.

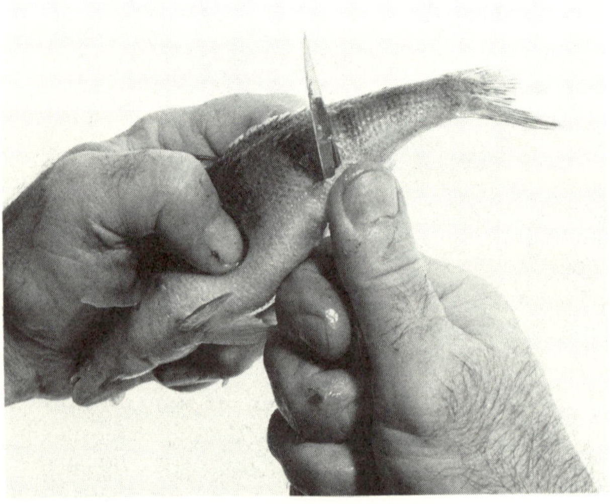

Grasp the anal fin between thumb and blade and twist the fin free. The long supporting bone will come away with the fin.

Rip section of skin between cut and tail as shown.

Return the fish to an upright position and catch the corner of skin at the "shoulder" between thumb and knife as shown.

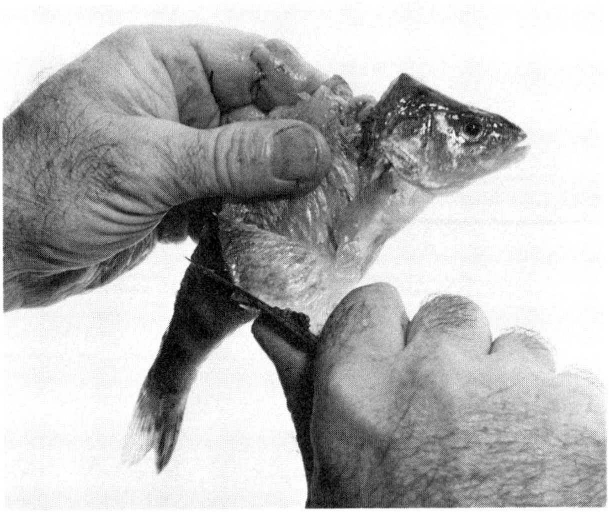

Peel the skin from the flesh to the extent shown. Turn the fish over and do the same on the other side.

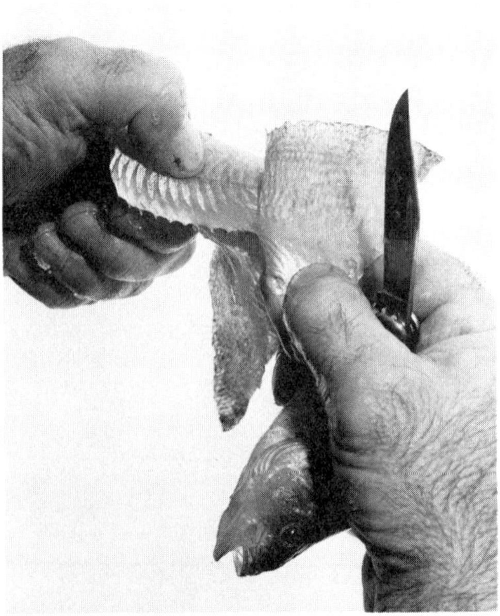

Hold the partially skinned section in the left hand. Grasp the head and skin in the right hand and strip toward the tail. Head, skin, viscera, and remaining fins will come free of the flesh in one piece.

Photo shows waste all but stripped clear of the flesh. The operation cannot be performed by pulling on head of perch alone; skin must also be grasped. Picture merely illustrates how all waste comes away at once.

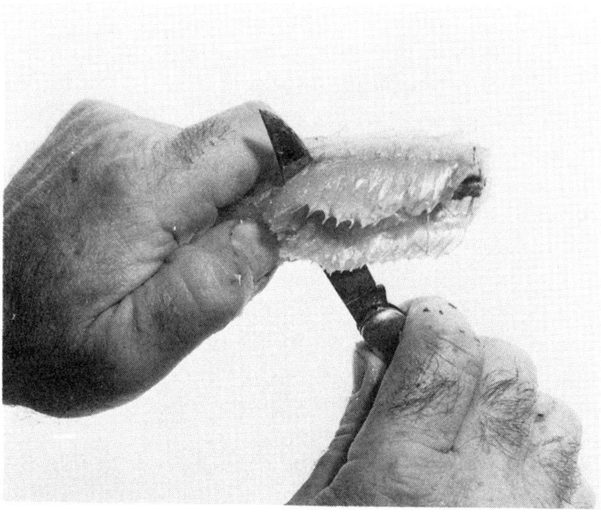

Hold the skinned fish in the left hand, belly up. Start the knife behind the first ribs and shave off the rib cage flush with the backbone.

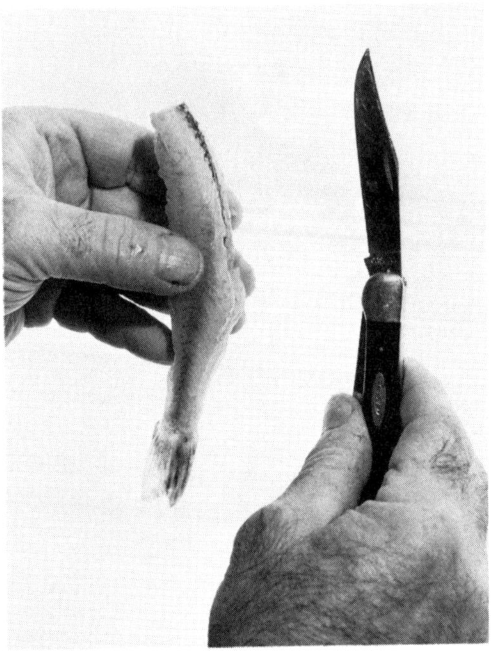

Picture shows perch ready for cooking, freezing, or smoking. When cooked, the flesh can be parted easily from the backbone with fork or fingers.

I must admit that I have never learned to love perch cleaning to any appreciable extent. I can clean them at the rate of one a minute, so cleaning a dozen or so for a meal is no great chore. My dislike for the job applies only to instances when I clean fifty or more for the freezer or smoker. They are so darned spiny—fins and gill covers—that the accumulation of pricks and jabs during a large-scale operation usually leaves me with mildly sore hands. This is but a minor consideration, however, when the high quality of the end product is taken into account.

I have already stated my preference for the humble bullhead over all other freshwater fish. I know of many others who share this view. I'm sure that many more would be equally appreciative if only they could cope more easily with the handling and skinning of these uniquely difficult fish.

Stabs from bullhead spines cannot be shrugged off as can the lesser pricks from the fins of perch, bass, walleyes, and sunfish. They are often deep punctures which are really painful and tend to be long in healing. The job of cleaning without knowledge of how to go about it can be as perplexing as the stab wounds are painful.

Fortunately, both problems can be resolved by employing the proper moves. Safe handling and easy cleaning are explained and illustrated by the photos and accompanying instructions in Chapter 3, pp. 29–34.

To handle bullheads without getting finned, study the illustrated grip and then be sure to apply it boldly and firmly. Grasping a bullhead gingerly is almost certain to result in a stabbed finger or palm.

Successful execution of the illustrated cleaning steps will make it possible to whip through a big catch of bullheads in a surprisingly short time; but again, the doing takes practice. In my own case, after being shown how by an expert, it was an exasperatingly long time before I acquired the knack and became able to pull off the job quickly and easily. Now, I can say truthfully that I look forward to cleaning a mess of bullheads, because of both the ease and speed with which I can finish the job, and the especially fine eating which results.

Incidentally, there is no bone problem in eating bullheads cleaned as pictured. The tender meat can be forked away from the backbone cleanly and easily. The ribs are short but substantial, and can be separated from the flesh with equal ease.

In most angling literature having to do with fish cleaning, the terms "fillet" and "filleting" occur frequently. They are usually used loosely, with "filleting" applied to fish cleaning in general. Actually, filleting does not embrace all fish-cleaning methods. On the contrary, it denotes the special process which reduces fish to boneless and skinless halves. It is a process which can be learned quite easily, for it involves no special knack. Its chief virtues are the admirable way in which it prepares fish for broiling or frying and its elimination of bones from the flesh.

Unfortunately, only a few species of freshwater fish lend themselves handily to true filleting. Of the many species I save and clean, I fillet only walleyes, smallmouths, largemouths, and northerns. The resulting walleye and bass fillets are boneless slabs of meat, but it should be noted that northern pike fillets will still contain the forked bones to which I have already referred. Consequently, I fillet only sizable northerns and then cut the fillets in chunks or strips for smoking. The forked bones of the larger specimens are easily detected in the smoked portions and can be removed before the parts are eaten. Incidentally, well-smoked northern pike are especially tasty in my opinion.

The pictures that follow show the filleting of a walleye. The steps apply identically to the filleting of smallmouths, largemouths, and northerns. Note that the job calls for a flat board or counter, and a filleting knife. The latter should have a thin, narrow blade at least six inches long. It should be flexible and razor-sharp and have a pointed tip. The knife used for cleaning panfish, bullheads, and trout is worthless as a filleting tool.

It should be noted that the pictured operations were performed with the walleye lying on a sheet of translucent plexiglass. This was to allow back-lighting for maximum photographic clarity. Despite the resulting illusion of suspension, the fish was actually lying flat on the plexiglass during each step, exactly as it would lie on a conventional cutting board under normal circumstances.

THE ART OF FILLETING

With fish flat on board, make the first cut behind head and fins as shown. Cut until knife is stopped by the backbone, but do not cut through it.

Start point of knife at upper limit of first cut and slice toward tail. Knife should follow dorsal fin as closely as possible. Cut can be as deep as top of rib cage, but knife should not cut through ribs. Continue cut until opposite vent.

Shove point of knife straight through fish. Tip should emerge at vent, just beyond termination of rib cage. Flat of blade should be as close to backbone as possible.

Continue cut until knife emerges at base of tail. Blade should follow backbone to minimize loss of flesh.

Cut flesh from rib cage. Cut around latter, but do not cut through ribs.

When fillet has been cut free of ribs, separate it from remainder of fish by slicing along belly line. Turn fish over and remove fillet from other side in the same way.

When both sides have been processed, parts consist of two fillets, with skin still attached, plus a one-piece waste item which includes head, bones, fins and viscera.

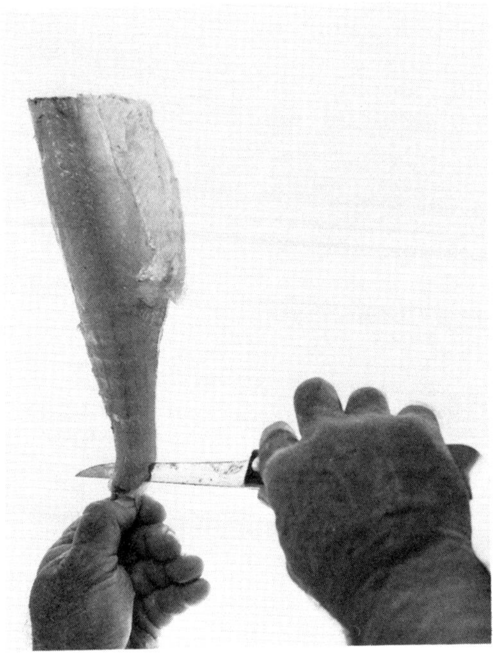

To remove skin, lay fillet flat on board with skin side down. Grasp tip of fillet with left hand and start cut as shown. Knife should cut to skin but not through it.

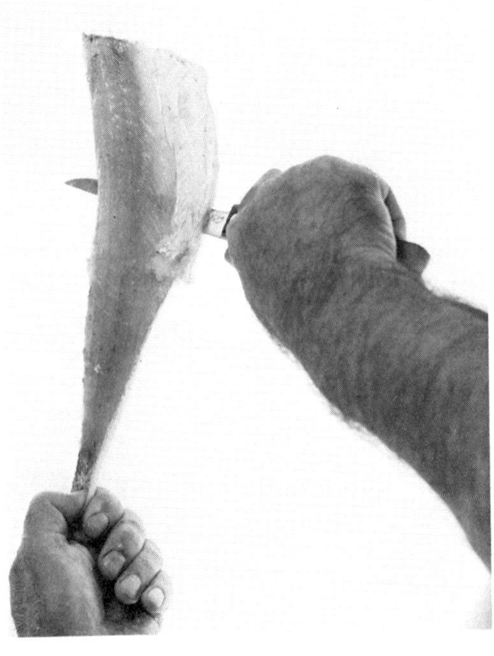

Hold tip of skin firmly with left hand. Pull with left hand while sliding knife forward, between flesh and skin, with right hand. Both downward and forward pressure must be applied to knife, and flat of blade must be held at a very slight angle. Continue until knife emerges at broad end of fillet.

Skin has been removed with almost no loss of flesh. Remove skin from the other fillet and the twin slabs of boneless flesh are ready for broiling, frying, smoking, or freezing. With practice, the entire job can be completed in two minutes, or even less.

What about salmon and large trout? The flesh is much too delicate for true filleting, and much unnecessary waste results from the attempt. Besides, there is no need. The flesh is so tender that both bones and skin fairly fall away from the meat after the fish is cooked.

To prepare a salmon or big trout for broiling I cut off the head, slit the belly, and remove the entrails. Following that, I hold it belly up on the cleaning board and split it lengthwise. This results in two slabs, one containing only half the ribs and the other the backbone and remaining ribs. The slabs lend themselves to broiling as do true fillets, but bones and skin must be removed after cooking. This is often referred to as "filleting," but it is actually nothing more than splitting.

Because the number of photos is limited by cost, I'll do my best to describe the cleaning of the various sunfishes by word alone. My favorite sunfish is the calico or black crappie, because of both its flavor and the comparative ease with which it is cleaned.

My first step is to remove the scales by scraping against the grain with knife or scaler. Unlike the scales of many fish, those of the calico come off very easily. After the scales have been removed, I cut off the head and slit the belly to remove the entrails. The next step consists of slitting the skin along both sides of the dorsal fin from front to rear. I then grasp the fin spine closest to the tail between my thumb and the flat of the knife blade and pull forward. (If you're afraid of cutting yourself, you probably will; so use pliers instead.) The entire fin will pull free, accompanied by the sharp bones which support it. Work the same deal on the anal fin, and the job is finished.

Other kinds of sunfish do not scale so easily. To clean them, I omit the scaling but follow each of the other steps. When head, viscera, and fins have been removed, grasp the skin of one side where it comes to a point at the "shoulder" and strip it from the flesh by pulling toward the tail. (For grasping, use thumb and knife blade, or pliers if you prefer.) Do the same on the other side. Finally, I cut off the rib sections exactly as I do with perch.

I'm especially fond of baked fish: walleyes, bass, and larger northerns. To prepare them for baking I scale them, even though they are by no means as easy to scale as are calicoes. After scaling, I cut off the heads and remove entrails and fins in the same way that I remove them from sunfish. Fish for baking should weigh at least three pounds, in my opinion. Smaller ones tend to dry out, and their smaller bones are often difficult to find and remove.

If you scale fish indoors, flying scales are a nuisance. To prevent scales from flying all over the kitchen, I fill the kitchen sink and hold the fish under water while I use the scaler. Not only does this prevent the scales from becoming airborne, but the water seems to make the scales easier to loosen.

Surplus fish keep well in the family freezer, losing little or none of their original flavor. Some recommend freezing them in solid blocks of ice to prevent drying, but I have never found this to be necessary. My wife wraps our fish in freezer paper, seals the packages with tape, and that's it. Eating is sometimes postponed for as long as six months, with no apparent loss of quality.

Much more important is to wrap fish so that it's possible to remove large or small quantities for eating as the need varies. My wife freezes packages that are meal-size for our family of three, but she also freezes individual fish and single fillets. She wraps these in plastic film and puts them in the freezer spread out on trays. When frozen, she transfers the individually wrapped pieces to large plastic bags and seals the tops. From then on she can take as many, or as few, fillets from the bag as she needs at a given time.

Three years ago I hinted that an electric fish smoker would be a welcome present. Exactly as I hoped, there it was under the tree come Christmas morning, a "Little Chief" that is made and sold by Luhr Jensen & Sons, Inc., Hood River, Oregon.

The little smoker has seen continuous service ever since as a source of delectable appetizers. All necessary directions came with it. It is simple to use and virtually foolproof. About all that can be said against it is that to smoke a batch of fish is a long-drawn-out process: up to six hours of brining, an hour for drying and glazing, and then six or more hours of actual smoking. There's not much work involved; it's just that you have to stick around for a long period.

After cleaning the fish, the first step in smoking is to soak the fish in brine. The booklet of directions recommends six hours, but I put my fish to soak when I go to bed and leave them overnight. If the extended brining has any effect, it is only to make the end product taste even better.

My favorite brining solution consists of a quart of water in which are dissolved a half-cup of table salt and a half-cup of sugar and to which a tablespoonful of Worcestershire sauce has been added. While this quantity seems rather small, it will cover just about all the fillets or pieces that the rig will hold. (My only complaint is its small size; I would love to have a similar smoker of twice the capacity.)

The next step after brining is to rinse the fish thoroughly in cold water and then lay them out to dry on clean towels. After patting them dry with another towel, I rub each fish piece with brown sugar. After a half-hour, I turn the fish over and apply brown sugar to the other sides. Individual tastes vary, of course, but all who have sampled my output agree with me that the brown sugar achieves a crowning touch.

At the end of the second half-hour of drying, I arrange the fish on the three trays of the smoker, placing them as close together as possible without any overlapping. It's a good policy to put the larger pieces on the bottom tray where they will be closest to the heat. From then on it's merely a matter of refilling the smoker-material pan as needed, usually once an hour for about six hours, or over a shorter period for smelt or other very small fish.

Hickory sawdust is a good smoking material, and can be bought in packages. I do a lot of gardening and also some wood turning, and have found that corncobs and lathe chips from butternut turnings are also excellent.

A single batch from the smoker will remain fresh and tasty in the refrigerator for longer than it takes me to polish it off. When I make successive smokings I store all but the first batch in the freezer, where the fish stay fresh indefinitely.

During the past three years I have smoked the following: smelt, sunfish, perch, bass, bullheads, walleyes, eels, trout, sheepsheads, and northern pike. I rank bullheads and smelt at the top of the list. Northern pike are almost as tasty, and walleyes rank third. Trout, surprisingly enough, were a disappointment, and I have smoked none since my first try. Eels were good, but excessively oily, and I have struck them from the list, too. What few I bring home go directly into the frying pan.

I'm enthusiastic about the little smoker because it has brought me one step closer to my goal of deriving maximum enjoyment from my fishing. Not only does it produce some delicious eating, but it adds purpose to my sport. When I set out to catch a batch of fish for smoking, I enjoy not only the catching of fish but also the satisfaction of fishing with a specific objective in mind. I recommend it highly to all whose philosophy of fishing agrees with mine.

If maximum utilization of the catch contributes to maximum fishing enjoyment, as I fully believe it does, I should pass along another form of fish processing about which I learned just during the past year. This consists of marinating fillets or fish strips in lime juice, to which can be added whatever best tickles the palate of the consumer. The juice of fresh limes can be used, but it is not necessary. Bottles of "reconstituted" lime juice can be bought in grocery stores, and this will serve as well. Here's the recipe which I have arrived at by trial and error.

To eight ounces of juice add the following: a teaspoonful of salt, a tablespoonful of Worcestershire sauce, a dash of Tabasco, a sprinkling of garlic flakes, and a heaping tablespoonful of brown sugar. Pour the mixture into a Pyrex loaf pan—nine by five by three inches—and add enough fillets, or strips of fillets, to fill the dish about two-thirds full. (The eight ounces of juice will cover this amount of fish.) Place the dish in the refrigerator. The fish will be ready to eat in twenty-four hours, and will keep for a week or more under refrigeration.

My first sampling was mildly disappointing. It almost made the grade but a certain something seemed to be missing. I have since discovered what it was: a liberal application of soy sauce after the fish have been taken from the lime juice. This transformed the pieces of marinated fish into appetizers which I relish on a par with those which come from my smoker.

So far, I have confined my marinating to walleye fillets, not only because they predominate in my freezer but also because they are so tasty that I haven't yet been tempted to try other kinds of fish.

One of my oldest and closest friends claims that my appetite ranges to extremes that would make a cannibal retch, and he is particularly repulsed by the prospect of eating what he looks on as a raw fish. I'm sure that others will agree with him, but to those of more daring I recommend at least a try of marinated fillets. In my opinion, they have it all over "dips" and most other conventional appetizers.

There are elaborate ways of preparing fish, but in this household most reach the table after broiling or pan frying. My wife broils the fillets of walleyes, smallmouths, and largemouths, and does the same with the split halves of salmon and any large trout I'm lucky enough to catch and which I elect to kill. Smaller trout, smelt, perch, calicoes, bullheads, etc. are rolled in cornmeal and fried in plenty of fat. Simplicity is the keynote, allowing the true flavor of the fish to come through, undisguised by special sauces or seasonings.

As I have already noted, I'm fond of baked fish, but the other members of the family can take it or leave it. Consequently, I sit down to a baked and stuffed walleye or northern pike only on those occasions when my plea for personal indulgence has been heard and granted.

Those who have plodded through this chapter deserve a special reward, and here it is: my dear wife's recipe for fish chowder, which, by itself, should win her admission to cooking's hall of fame.

Edna B's Fabulous Fish Chowder

1 lb. boneless fillets (walleyes or bass)
2 cups cubed potatoes
1 cup chopped onion
1 small can evaporated milk
2 tablespoonfuls bacon fat
1 tablespoonful butter

Make a fish stock by cooking fillets in a quart of boiling salted water until they can be broken into chunks with a fork. Do not overcook. Remove fish from water and set aside.

Fry chopped onions in bacon fat until soft. Set aside.

Add potatoes to stock and boil for ten minutes.

Add fish and onions. Boil until potatoes are cooked.

Add can of evaporated milk and tablespoonful of butter.

Salt and pepper to taste.

Talk about good to the last drop! This chowder gets steadily *better* with each spoonful, and the last is so good that no man of sound health and mind can do else but holler for more!

This chapter was started with the conviction that too little has been written about the utilization of the fish which fishermen catch. Now, perhaps too much has been written! Nevertheless, I offer no apology. While the keeping and eating of fish has never been the primary motive behind my fishing, the practice has added important dimensions to a sport which has been a lifelong passion. I hope that what has added to my pleasure will do the same for others.

17

IN GRATITUDE

IT IS ALWAYS HARD for me to write instructively about fishing, and this book has been no exception. I'm always uncomfortably aware of my presumption in posing as a know-it-all concerning a subject about which I know all too little.

This will be my fourth fishing book, and I've long since lost count of the magazine articles I have written on the subject. Inherent in their publication has been the implication that I'm an expert, one well qualified to advise, and the disparity between this impression and the truth is so great that it makes me squirm.

Here in Vermont we have a stock question we put to smart alecks: "If you're so *smart,* why'n hell ain't you *rich?*" I often ask myself the paraphrased equivalent: "If you're such a helluva fisherman, why don't you catch more fish?"

The ironic truth is that the more I presume to tell others how to catch fish, the fewer I seem to catch myself. I suppose that it's the penalty I pay for getting too big for my britches. Yet if the fish conspire to take me down the peg I deserve, I bear them no grudge. Fishing has helped make my life worth living for more than half a century. I owe it much, and I hope that readers will indulge my wish to offer thanks in this last chapter.

I'm a man of few means, who has long since relinquished all dreams of attaining riches. Yet my favorite stretch of Furnace

Brook lies less than half a mile from my door; and this, in my eyes, makes me a man of considerable wealth.

The Furnace rises high in the nearby mountains, a convergence of cold, sparkling trickles which issue from a multitude of springs. It gains volume steadily as it absorbs a succession of other spring-fed streamlets. The deep shade of the forested mountainside helps retain much of the icy temperature of its waters, and the lack of bordering habitation preserves their purity. The frothy, bouncing descent of the gathering stream induces a steady infusion of life-sustaining oxygen. This pristine flow gains maturity in the almost complete absence of contamination, and is thus an anachronistic marvel.

At the beginning of its last mile, Furnace Brook plunges dramatically down a steep and narrow gorge to the outer edge of the Otter Creek Valley. The tiny village in which I have lived for thirty years owes its presence to this precipitous drop, for it was settled more than two centuries ago by enterprising pioneers who capitalized on the gorge's water-power potential.

The series of wooden dams which once constituted a watery stairway have long since crumbled and yielded to spring floods, and the mills whose wheels were turned by the harnessed flow have also disappeared. Only fragmentary traces of their stone foundations remain to serve notice of their onetime presence.

A scattering of rusting relics, alternately exposed and buried by freshets, furnish partial insight to the varied activities which once were the lifeblood of the community. At the very bottom of the gorge, ponderous millstones of imperishable granite tell not only of ancient grist mills, but testify to the awesome power of past floods which swept the heavy stones down the gorge as though they were but mere pebbles.

Although the mills have come and gone, creations of progress and then its victims, Furnace Brook itself has undergone but little change. Its water still runs cold, clear, and pure, and the output of its supporting springs continues to provide a constant flow which is proof against the severest drought and the highest of summer temperatures.

Although the stream is no longer valued for its water power, its worth has in no way diminished. Indeed, there are those who would insist that its value has increased, for this remarkable stream is a recreational asset which could not be duplicated by the most lavish expenditure of money or by the most prodigious human effort.

The brook trout which once made up its only trout population are now rare in all but its upper reaches, but they have been replaced by an equally populous mixture of naturally propagated browns and rainbows. Fortunately, or so I choose to regard the circumstance, the stream is a bit too small, and too few of its trout grow to trophy size, to win widespread recognition and prominence. It is, therefore, a stream made to order for the small community which it serves, a handily available source of enjoyment, but of too modest dimensions to evoke the mass inroads which would be its undoing.

From a personal standpoint, Furnace Brook fits me as perfectly as the sleek pelt of a red fox fits the musculature of its owner. In counting my blessings, I rank Furnace Brook beneath only my beloved wife and son, and my exquisitely talented little Brittany spaniel.

The close proximity of Furnace Brook would be enough to make me a man of exceptionally good fortune, yet I have much more to be thankful for. Otter Creek, no more than a mile distant, is not only the home of large and savage northern pike, but its twisting route is a delight to one who loves canoes as I do. I can be on it in a matter of minutes, utilizing its smooth and gentle flow to bring me within casting distance of an unending succession of deep and mysterious lairs in which I know that big northerns are lurking.

Finally, I am less than an hour's drive from Lake Champlain, a hundred-mile-long body of water which was once an arm of the sea. This distinction sets it apart from all glacial lakes of the northeast, and is manifested by its unusually wide variety of fishlife. The bass, pickerel, perch, and sunfish which are common to the glacial lakes are there, of course, but they coexist with other species not to be found in other New England waters: gar, catfish, sheepsheads, bowfins, saugers, and others. Sturgeon were once numerous, and it is possible that a few still exist.

Lake Champlain is by far the greatest walleye fishery of the Northeast, and it probably deserves the same ranking as a northern pike fishery. The southern end of the lake provides the most varied fishing, and it is here that Mike and I fish frequently. We troll for walleyes in season, and sometimes we set our sights specifically on bass or pike. But the days we enjoy most are those when we fish for all that will come to the hook, reaching into a grab bag which can produce a ten-inch perch and then follow with a fifteen-pound catfish, a burly bowfin, or some other contender for the tackle-busting crown.

Our favorite time of year for this grab-bag fishing is late September, and our favorite location is a reed-bordered creek which twists through several miles of marshland before joining the lake. Other fishermen are seldom in evidence at this time of year, but it is then that the marsh teems with wildlife that is spurred to peak activity by the imminence of fall.

Florida gallinules cackle from within the bordering forest of reeds, and patter in and out of view. Grackles and starlings gather to feed on the ripening seeds of the equatic grasses in flocks so vast that the roar of their mass shiftings can be heard for a quarter of a mile. Black ducks and mallards come and go, usually high overhead, restively torn by the first stirrings of migratory intent. By contrast, hedge-hopping squadrons of teal buzz our boat, the explosive suddenness of their arrival blending indistinguishably with the dazzling speed of their departure. Solitary great blue herons beat their way laboriously to new positions, encumbered in flight by the stiltlike legs which serve them so well while stalking frogs and fish. Cruising gulls inspect us periodically, swooping down to gobble any dead minnows we may have discarded.

We relish all with the affection reserved for seasonal joys: the first robin of spring; the taste of the year's first sweet corn; the all-day rain that puts an end to an extended drought.

But we are intent on more. We know that if we have hit it right the fish will be equally active, and we have come prepared. A hundred fat nightcrawlers repose in the bait cooler, and our minnow bucket holds dozens of minnows and chubs of all sizes.

We round a sharp bend and idle toward a favorite spot. Position is critical, so I jockey carefully while Mike stands ready to drop anchor. We figure the wind direction and the probable result of its effect and that of the anchor rope. Mike finally drops the anchor and I cut the motor. The boat swings slowly. Finally it lies with its bow to the breeze.

"Out too far, aren't we?" Mike's words are more statement than question.

"Looks that way to me," I agree. "Haul up, and we'll try again."

I swing the boat through an arc and then make a fresh approach. Mike takes the error of his first calculations into account, and this time the boat comes to rest where we want it to be. When its position has stabilized I drop a small stern anchor to prevent further shifting.

When Mike and I fish as we are fishing now, we both usually fish a nightcrawler on a fly rod and a minnow on a spinning outfit. Although Mike has never acquired the love of a fly rod as a casting tool, he shares my liking for it in bait fishing. So his first move is to bait his fly rod with a fat nightcrawler.

"I'm not bothering with small stuff," I say, and dip a five-inch chub from the minnow bucket. Soon it's towing a bobber around.

Mike's 'crawler draws an immediate bite, and he brings in an average-size perch. But the freezer is well stocked, and we aren't out to keep a lot of fish.

"Let's just keep enough for a meal," I say. "Nothing but real big ones."

Mike releases the perch. He's into another as soon as he relowers his 'crawler, now a bit worse for wear.

In the meantime, my chub has towed the bobber close to the edge of the reeds and suddenly the little red-and-white float is yanked under.

"This will teach you to waste time on perch," I tell Mike. I let line pay from the spool of my spinning reel. As always, the thrill of anticipation becomes increasingly delectable. The conviction that the unseen fish is a monster is inescapable.

The bobber reappears, yards from its original spot. Has the fish dropped the chub? I close the bail of the reel and retrieve line very gently. It tightens against solid resistance; the lunker is still on! I slack off immediately and reopen the reel bail. Down goes the bobber again, and, out flows more line. I close the bail, and just before the line comes taut I set the hook as though gaffing a tuna.

I know instantly that I have been victimized by the extravagance of my expectations, an oft-repeated occurrence. My "monster" turns out to be a pike that will be a ten-pounder only after it puts on another nine pounds or so.

The perch slack off momentarily, and Mike reaches for the minnow bucket.

"I guess I'll have to take over the big fish department," he says as he stabs with the dip net for an especially big chub.

I'm trying to think of a suitable reply when the tip of his propped fly rod is yanked underwater and his single-action reel screeches a mechanical protest that is hair-raising to hear. Mike grabs the rod and snubs hard, and the line becomes wire-tight against what appears to be an immovable object. But only for a second. Suddenly, the taut line lifts so rapidly that it creates a fine trail of spray as it cuts the surface. Then an indignant fish bursts into the sunlight, a sleek, bronze, rattle-gill improbability.

"Smallmouth!" Mike and I yell in unison and with delight.

It is, indeed, and a real smallmouth at that. Three and a half pounds, the De Liar reads, but only after a fray almost too violent for family viewing.

The day progresses, giving up exactly that to which we have looked forward: sights and sounds that are as balm to us who love the outdoors and the wild things which inhabit it; fishing that is both low-key but exciting, unpredictable and thus replete with surprises.

The breeze dies. We hear a mighty slosh from somewhere in the reeds, and we yield to the temptation to switch to casting. I hold the boat to its slowest crawl while Mike casts weedless lures to pockets of open water in the midst of the vegetation. Just to keep my chances alive, I troll a big spoon on a short line.

Fish swirl at Mike's lures with fair regularity. The weedless lures, as usual, engage all too infrequently and Mike complains bitterly.

"Trouble with weedless lures," he grumbles, "is that they're also fishless."

But on almost the next cast he hooks up on a two-pound largemouth. This goes into the cooler to join the smallmouth and the few jumbo perch we have saved.

My spoon finally takes a hard rap, undoubtedly from a pike, but the boat is moving too slowly for the big hooks to drive home.

We tire of the routine after a half-hour or so, mainly because we know that our artificials will account only for bass and pike. We resume bait fishing and anticipation of the unexpected.

We drop anchor in a spot attractive to calicoes, one in which we have made fine catches over the summer. We lower small minnows, and jig them enticingly. Sure enough, king-sizers swirl up to take them. I'm particularly fond of calicoes, but our freezer is well stocked. We release all we catch. Most are lightly hooked by the thin, seemingly bloodless tissue which makes up their large mouths, and we relish the knowledge that we have done them no significant harm.

Mike pauses long enough to place a big chub on the hook of his spinning rig. He lowers it close to the bordering reeds.

"That's not for one of your pint-size pike," he says pointedly. "That's strictly for bowfins."

The calico business continues to boom, but while I'm unhooking one of the willing biters I notice a movement of Mike's spinning rod and call it to his attention. Something has the big chub and is carrying it back into the reeds.

"A bowfin for sure," Mike exults, letting line pay out from his reel.

I agree mentally. Bowfins leave their cover only long enough to grab a bait, and then retreat into hiding to swallow it. I'm happy for Mike, for he loves to wrestle with the ugly, bulldoggish bruisers. I only hope that he can get the fish back into open water without busting his line.

Mike sets the hook, then whoops at the commotion which immediately develops amid the tangled vegetation. The tall reeds bend and quiver, but fortunately the hooked bowfin bulls its way toward open water, rather than in the opposite direction.

A long struggle ensues, marked by powerful rushes and Mike's exclamations of delight. Finally, the brutish critter gives up and Mike nets it unassisted.

"How I love to tangle with those babies," he gloats redundantly.

The sun goes down like an anchor, a sobering reminder of the rapidly shortening days and the near end of another fishing season. Ducks begin homing in on their nighttime resting places, and I note that it will be dark by the time we have the boat on the trailer. But before giving the word to haul anchor, I delay to reflect on the blessings of such a day.

Mike owns and operates his own dairy-delivery business. He enjoys the independence of being his own boss, but he works long hours, in all kinds of weather, and copes with an ever shifting multitude of problems and frustrations. His is a hard way of making a buck, and sometimes, when his morale is low, he threatens to give it up.

As for me, I'm getting old, and the knowledge that my string is running out is often worrisome.

But in this day we have found a haven from all cares. For an entire day we have basked in an atmosphere completely devoid of irritants. We have shared our love of fishing and the affection we have for each other.

We have fished the same creek together since before Mike reached his teens and before I felt more than casual concern for the inexorability of aging. Yet the joys of the day have been identical to those of days long past, and I marvel at the miracle.

It is perhaps in this light that fishing is most properly regarded, as an avenue to rebirth and restoration, truly a worker of miracles.

Yet the day could not have attained perfection in the absence of success, for success is a major ingredient of fulfillment. Thus, in closing, I reassert my premise that the purpose of fishing is to catch fish. My dull prose will perhaps be justified if it proves to be of some small help to others in achieving this end, for it is my hope that it will contribute, even though no more than proportionately, to the sum total of human happiness.

Mike triumphantly nets a bowfin which gave him the tussle he was looking for.

INDEX

Page numbers in italics denote illustrations.